"Original and groundbreaking, this book by Togashi and Kottler constitutes the most important contribution to self psychology's theory in many years, and thus expands also the range of relational psychoanalysis. Their focus on experience of otherness in yearning for connection, for the sense of being human among humans, will make this a classic. A great gift for every clinician."
Donna Orange, Institute for the Psychoanalytic Study of Subjectivity, New York, USA

"In a work of superb scholarship, Togashi and Kottler offer an expansion and refinement of Kohut's concept of twinship (which originated in his studies of narcissism) entailing a delicate balance of sameness and difference that constitutes a sense of what I prefer to call existential kinship, of being a human among humans. They show with rich and convincing clinical examples how twinship/existential kinship experiences in the therapeutic relationship can be enormously beneficial for those who suffer from profound feelings of alienation, estrangement, meaninglessness, and existential anguish—feelings that are a ubiquitous legacy of emotional trauma."
Robert D. Stolorow, Ph.D., author, *World, Affectivity, Trauma: Heidegger and post-Cartesian psychoanalysis*

"This is an important book. Too often psychoanalysis is perceived as a universalizing theory that neglects the cultures and contexts of psychological experience. The authors, one from Japan, the other from South Africa, bring their unique perspectives to bear on the question of human relating. They suggest that while the human need to relate is present across cultures, it is shaped by the specific cultural practices in which each person develops. Chapters on the role of cultural difference and gendered discourses illustrate the veracity of their perspective. The authors convincingly demonstrate the evolving nature of contemporary self-psychology and its intersection with relational psychoanalysis. Above all this is a study of what it means to be human and how to think about the fundamental issues raised by our relational existence."
Roger Frie, Ph.D., Psy.D., R. Psych, Professor, Simon Fraser University and University of British Columbia, Canada

"Arguably Heinz Kohut's most central, phenomenologically based concept, the twinship selfobject experience ultimately has its roots in what it means to be human among humans, and to feel at home. Togashi and Kottler masterfully elaborate and expand these fundamental themes in highly original and creative directions—a testament to how cutting edge contemporary psychoanalysis and psychotherapy continue to be. Reflecting a true advance in our field, and with exceptional scholarship, these authors bring into striking relief the dialectical role of sameness and difference, and the role of traumatic dehumanization as the darker side of what it means to be human: that we are relentlessly vulnerable. This seminal work is a must-read for all clinicians wanting to deepen their immersion in and understanding of their patient's humanness, sense of belonging, and the embedded vulnerability inherent in bein
William J. Co   or,
Emeritus, *International Jour*   gy

"Awakening us to the profound importance of twinship through their penetrating exploration of this complex phenomenon, Togashi and Kottler not only deepen our understanding of what it means to be human but, perhaps even more importantly, show us what it means to suffer the devastating loss of a sense of being human. They provide new ways of understanding the ethnic, cultural and societal contexts of the human condition through their introduction of such evocative concepts as 'the mutual finding of oneself and not oneself in the other,' and 'self-place experience.' Richly detailed clinical vignettes that bring their theoretical innovations into clear focus make this a must-read for clinicians of every persuasion."

Doris Brothers, Ph.D., co-founder and faculty member, Training and Research in Intersubjective Self Psychology Foundation (TRISP), author, *Toward a Psychology of Uncertainty: Trauma-centered psychoanalysis*

"Koichi Togashi and Amanda Kottler joined forces to rescue the twinship experience from its too often neglected place as a bit player on the psychoanalytic stage. In so doing they have given the practicing clinician an enormous gift. These two seasoned therapists, familiar with their own cultures (Japanese and South African) and experienced in western psychotherapy practice have conceptualized detailed and accessible clinical work that bridges the longing for twinship experiences with what it means to be human, in the context of the analyst's intimate participation in the therapeutic process. Their detailed and compelling clinical vignettes and case histories illustrate the widely sought-after twinship experience, the feeling 'I am like you and you are like me' as it appears in carried guises and simultaneously embodies basic human needs. This book will sensitize western clinicians to these subtle but urgent longings. The cultural diversity at the core of this book will be of benefit to all analyst–patient dyads since the twinship experience calls for a joint humanity that is at the heart of psychoanalytic treatment."

Frank M. Lachmann, Ph.D., Founding Faculty, Institute for the Psychoanalytic Study of Subjectivity, New York, USA

Kohut's Twinship Across Cultures

Kohut's Twinship Across Cultures: The Psychology of Being Human chronicles a ten-year voyage in which the authors struggled, initially independently, to make sense of Kohut's intentions when he radically redefined the twinship experience to one of being "a human being among other human beings."

Commencing with an exploration of Kohut's work on twinship and an illustration of the value of what he left for elaboration, Togashi and Kottler proceed to introduce a new and very different sensitivity to understanding particular psychoanalytic relational processes and ideas about human existential anguish, trauma, and the meaning of life. Together they tackle the twinship concept, which has often been misunderstood and about which little has been written. Uniquely, the book expands and elaborates upon Kohut's final definition: being "a human being among other human beings." It problematizes this apparently simple concept with a wide range of clinical material, demonstrating the complexity of the statement and the intricacies involved in recognizing and working with traumatized patients who have never experienced this feeling. It asks how a sense of being human, as opposed to being described as human, can be generated and how this might help clinicians to better understand and work with trauma.

Written for psychoanalysts and psychoanalytic psychotherapists interested in self-psychological, intersubjective, and relational theories, *Kohut's Twinship Across Cultures* will also be invaluable to clinicians working in the broader areas of psychoanalysis, psychotherapy, social work, psychiatry, and education. It will enrich their sensitivity and capacity to understand and treat traumatized patients and the alienation they feel among other human beings.

Koichi Togashi, Ph.D., L.P. is a Professor at Konan University, Kobe, Japan, and a Faculty and Training and Supervising Analyst at TRISP, New York, USA. He works in private practice in Kobe and Hiroshima, Japan.

Amanda Kottler, M.A. (Clinical Psychology) was a Senior Lecturer at the University of Cape Town for a number of years. She works in private practice in Cape Town, South Africa.

PSYCHOANALYTIC INQUIRY BOOK SERIES
JOSEPH D. LICHTENBERG
SERIES EDITOR

Like its counterpart, *Psychoanalytic Inquiry: A Topical Journal for Mental Health Professionals*, the Psychoanalytic Inquiry Book Series presents a diversity of subjects within a diversity of approaches to those subjects. Under the editorship of Joseph Lichtenberg, in collaboration with Melvin Bornstein and the editorial board of *Psychoanalytic Inquiry*, the volumes in this series strike a balance between research, theory, and clinical application. We are honored to have published the works of various innovators in psychoanalysis, such as Frank Lachmann, James Fosshage, Robert Stolorow, Donna Orange, Louis Sander, Léon Wurmser, James Grotstein, Joseph Jones, Doris Brothers, Fredric Busch, and Joseph Lichtenberg, among others.

The series includes books and monographs on mainline psychoanalytic topics, such as sexuality, narcissism, trauma, homosexuality, jealousy, envy, and varied aspects of analytic process and technique. In our efforts to broaden the field of analytic interest, the series has incorporated and embraced innovative discoveries in infant research, self psychology, intersubjectivity, motivational systems, affects as process, responses to cancer, borderline states, contextualism, postmodernism, attachment research and theory, medication, and mentalization. As further investigations in psychoanalysis come to fruition, we seek to present them in readable, easily comprehensible writing.

After 25 years, the core vision of this series remains the investigation, analysis and discussion of developments on the cutting edge of the psychoanalytic field, inspired by a boundless spirit of inquiry.

PSYCHOANALYTIC INQUIRY BOOK SERIES
JOSEPH D. LICHTENBERG
SERIES EDITOR

Vol. 2
Psychoanalysis and Infant Research
Joseph D. Lichtenberg

Vol. 8
*Psychoanalytic Treatment:
An Intersubjective Approach*
Robert D. Stolorow, Bernard Brandchaft,
& George E. Atwood

Vol. 10
Psychoanalysis and Motivation
Joseph D. Lichtenberg

Vol. 12
*Contexts of Being:
The Intersubjective Foundations
of Psychological Life*
Robert D. Stolorow & George E. Atwood

Vol. 13
*Self and Motivational Systems:
Toward a Theory of Psychoanalytic
Technique*
Joseph D. Lichtenberg,
Frank M. Lachmann, &
James L. Fosshage

Vol. 14
*Affects as Process:
An Inquiry into the Centrality
of Affect in Psychological Life*
Joseph M. Jones

Vol. 16
*The Clinical Exchange:
Techniques Derived from
Self and Motivational Systems*
Joseph D. Lichtenberg, Frank M.
Lachmann, & James L. Fosshage

Vol. 17
*Working Intersubjectively:
Contextualism in Psychoanalytic Practice*
Donna M. Orange, George E. Atwood,
& Robert D. Stolorow

Vol. 18
*Kohut, Loewald, and the Postmoderns:
A Comparative Study of Self and
Relationship*
Judith Guss Teicholz

Vol. 19
*A Spirit of Inquiry:
Communication in Psychoanalysis*
Joseph D. Lichtenberg,
Frank M. Lachmann, &
James L. Fosshage

Vol. 20
*Craft and Spirit:
A Guide to Exploratory
Psychotherapies*
Joseph D. Lichtenberg

Vol. 21
Attachment and Sexuality
Diana Diamond, Sidney J. Blatt,
& Joseph D. Lichtenberg (eds.)

Vol. 22
*Psychotherapy and Medication:
The Challenge of Integration*
Fredric N. Busch & Larry S. Sandberg

Vol. 23
*Trauma and Human Existence:
Autobiographical, Psychoanalytic,
and Philosophical Reflections*
Robert D. Stolorow

Vol. 24
*Jealousy and Envy:
New Views about Two Powerful
Feelings*
Léon Wurmser & Heidrun Jarass
(eds.)

Vol. 25
*Sensuality and Sexuality
across the Divide of Shame*
Joseph D. Lichtenberg

Vol. 26
Living Systems, Evolving Consciousness, and the Emerging Person: A Selection of Papers from the Life Work of Louis Sander
Gherardo Amadei & Ilaria Bianchi (eds.)

Vol. 27
Toward a Psychology of Uncertainty: Trauma-Centered Psychoanalysis
Doris Brothers

Vol. 28
Transforming Narcissism: Reflections on Empathy, Humor, and Expectations
Frank M. Lachmann

Vol. 29
Mentalization: Theoretical Considerations, Research Findings, and Clinical Implications
Fredric N. Busch (ed.)

Vol. 30
From Psychoanalytic Narrative to Empirical Single Case Research: Implications for Psychoanalytic Practice
Horst Kächele, Joseph Schachter, Helmut Thomä & the Ulm Psychoanalytic Process Research Study Group

Vol. 31
Toward an Emancipatory Psychoanalysis: Brandchaft's Intersubjective Vision
Bernard Brandchaft, Shelley Doctors, & Dorienne Sorter

Vol. 32
Persons in Context: The Challenge of Individuality in Theory and Practice
Roger Frie & William J. Coburn (eds.)

Vol. 33
Psychoanalysis and Motivational Systems: A New Look
Joseph D. Lichtenberg, Frank M. Lachmann, & James L. Fosshage

Vol. 34
Change in Psychoanalysis: An Analyst's Reflections on the Therapeutic Relationship
Chris Jaenicke

Vol. 35
World, Affectivity, Trauma: Heidegger and Post-Cartesian Psychoanalysis
Robert D. Stolorow

Vol. 36
Manual of Panic Focused Psychodynamic Psychotherapy – eXtended Range
Fredric N. Busch, Barbara L. Milrod, Meriamne B. Singer, & Andrew C. Aronson

Vol. 37
The Abyss of Madness
George E. Atwood

Vol. 38
Self Experiences in Group, Revisited: Affective Attachments, Intersubjective Regulations, and Human Understanding
Irene Harwood, Walter Stone, & Malcolm Pines (eds.)

Vol. 39
Nothing Good Is Allowed to Stand: An Integrative View of the Negative Therapeutic Reaction
Léon Wurmser & Heidrun Jarass (eds.)

Vol. 40
Growth and Turbulence in the Container/Contained: Bion's Continuing Legacy
Howard B. Levine & Lawrence J. Brown (eds.)

Vol. 41
Metaphor and Fields: Common Ground, Common Language and the Future of Psychoanalysis
S. Montana Katz (ed)

Vol. 42
Psychoanalytic Complexity: Clinical Attitudes for Therapeutic Change
William J. Coburn

Vol. 43
*Structures of Subjectivity:
Explorations in Psychoanalytic
Phenomenology and Contextualism,
2nd Edition*
George E. Atwood and Robert D. Stolorow

Vol. 44
*The Search for a Relational Home:
An Intersubjective View of
Therapeutic Action*
Chris Jaenicke

Vol. 45
*Creative Analysis: Art, Creativity
and Clinical Process*
George Hagman

Vol. 46
*A Rumor of Empathy: Resistance,
Narrative and Recovery in
Psychoanalysis and
Psychotherapy*
Lou Agosta

Vol. 47
*Enlivening the Self: The First Year,
Clinical Enrichment,
and The Wandering Mind*
Joseph D. Lichtenberg, James L. Fosshage
& Frank M. Lachmann

Vol. 48
*Kohut's Twinship Across Cultures:
The Psychology of Being Human*
Koichi Togashi and Amanda Kottler

Vol. 49
*Psychoanalytic Theory, Research
and Clinical Practice:
Reading Joseph D. Lichtenberg*
Linda Gunsberg & Sandra G. Hershberg

Out of Print titles in the PI Series

Vol. 1
Reflections on Self Psychology
Joseph D. Lichtenberg & Samuel Kaplan (eds.)

Vol. 3
Empathy, Volumes I & II
Joseph D. Lichtenberg, Melvin Bornstein,
& Donald Silver (eds.)

Vol. 4
*Structures of Subjectivity:
Explorations in Psychoanalytic
Phenomenology*
George E. Atwood & Robert D. Stolorow

Vol. 5
*Toward a Comprehensive Model for
Schizophrenic Disorders:
Psychoanalytic Essays
in Memory of Ping-Nie Pao*
David B. Feinsilver

Vol. 6
*The Borderline Patient:
Emerging Concepts in Diagnosis,
Psychodynamics, and Treatment, Vol. 1*
James S. Grotstein, Marion F. Solomon,
& Joan A. Lang (eds.)

Vol. 7
*The Borderline Patient:
Emerging Concepts in Diagnosis,
Psychodynamics, and Treatment, Vol. 2*
James S. Grotstein, Marion F. Solomon,
& Joan A. Lang (eds.)

Vol. 9
*Female Homosexuality:
Choice without Volition*
Elaine V. Siegel

Vol. 11
Cancer Stories: Creativity and Self-Repair
Esther Dreifuss-Kattan

Vol. 15
*Understanding Therapeutic Action:
Psychodynamic Concepts of Cure*
Lawrence E. Lifson (ed.)

Kohut's Twinship Across Cultures

The Psychology of Being Human

Koichi Togashi and
Amanda Kottler

LONDON AND NEW YORK

First published 2015
by Routledge
27 Church Road, Hove, East Sussex, BN3 2FA

and by Routledge
711 Third Avenue, New York, NY 10017

Routledge is an imprint of the Taylor & Francis Group, an informa business

© 2015 Koichi Togashi and Amanda Kottler

The right of Koichi Togashi and Amanda Kottler to be identified as authors of this work has been asserted by them in accordance with sections 77 and 78 of the Copyright, Designs and Patents Act 1988.

All rights reserved. No part of this book may be reprinted or reproduced or utilized in any form or by any electronic, mechanical, or other means, now known or hereafter invented, including photocopying and recording, or in any information storage or retrieval system, without permission in writing from the publishers.

Trademark notice: Product or corporate names may be trademarks or registered trademarks, and are used only for identification and explanation without intent to infringe.

British Library Cataloguing in Publication Data
A catalogue record for this book is available from the British Library

Library of Congress Cataloging in Publication Data
Togashi, Koichi (Psychoanalyst)
Kohut's twinship across cultures : the psychology of being human / Koichi Togashi and Amanda Kottler.
pages cm
Includes bibliographical references.
1. Self psychology. 2. Narcissism. 3. Psychoanalysis. 4. Cultural psychiatry. 5. Kohut, Heinz. I. Kottler, Amanda. II. Title.
RC489.S43T64 2016
616.89'17--dc23
2015012645

ISBN: 978-1-138-81916-0 (hbk)
ISBN: 978-1-138-81917-7 (pbk)
ISBN: 978-1-315-73999-1 (ebk)

Typeset in Times
by Saxon Graphics Ltd, Derby

Printed and bound in the United States of America by Publishers Graphics, LLC on sustainably sourced paper.

Koichi Togashi dedicates this book to his dear twins, Tomomi and Satomi Togashi.

Amanda Kottler dedicates this book to her mother and late father, Naomi and Norman Kottler.

Contents

Preface by Joseph D. Lichtenberg, M.D.	xv
Acknowledgments	xxi
Introduction	1
1 The many faces of twinship: from the psychology of the self to the psychology of being human	7
2 A new dimension of twinship selfobject experience and transference	25
3 Twinship and "otherness": a self-psychological, intersubjective approach to "difference"	41
4 Mutual finding of oneself and not-oneself in the other as a twinship experience	59
5 Trauma, recovery, and humanization: from fantasy to transitional selfobject, through a twinship tie	73
6 Contemporary self psychology and cultural issues: "self-place experience" in an Asian culture	95
7 Placeness in the twinship experience	107
8 "I am afraid of seeing your face": trauma and the dread of engaging in a twinship tie	119

9 Is it a problem for us to say, "It is a coincidence that the patient does well"? 137

10 Being human and not being human: the evolution of a twinship experience 157

Epilogue: what is "being human"? 169

References 173
Index 183

Preface

Joseph D. Lichtenberg, M.D.

Reading *Kohut's Twinship Across Cultures: The Psychology of Being Human* is a multiple treat. First, Koichi Togashi and Amanda Kottler provide a scholarly rendering of Heinz Kohut's evolving accounts of a twinship experience/transference. Second, they present numerous clinical examples of the application of their own evolving accounts of the therapeutic usefulness, or, I would add, necessity of recognizing twinship yearnings in their patients. These two contributions would be sufficient to make the book valuable, but, indeed they are only the beginning. The scholarly and the clinical expand into the philosophical and the book becomes essentially an essay to explore existence—the essence of being a human among humans. Finally, there is the unique perspectives of the authors—one, a Japanese man growing up immersed in an Asian culture and the other, a white woman growing up first as an ex-patriot in Uganda and then in South Africa during its struggle with apartheid.

Science advises: be clear and appeal to human reason; the humanities advise: appreciate the metaphoric and appeal to human sensibility. Kohut, like Freud and most psychoanalytic theoreticians, may have espoused the science perspective but inevitably ended up employing both (Lichtenberg, 1985). The authors delineate Kohut's struggles to achieve conceptual clarity about twinship as evidenced by the seven "faces" they identify. Kohut's struggle to conceptualize twinship is parallel to his attempt to stay close to ego psychology. Reluctantly, he recognized the incompatibility between a multipartite mind based on drive theory and his main thrust about human needs for mirroring, sameness, and idealization to ensure a cohesive self. Once sameness—being a human among humans—is regarded as an important, even necessary, contributor to connectedness, questions emerge. Sameness in regard to what—thoughts? Feelings? Appearance?

Fantasies? Gender? Sexual orientation? Attitudes? Beliefs? Locale? Culture? All? A high point of the book is that in one clinical description or another, each aspect of sameness becomes a critical factor for the particular patient and therapist. But now a seminal contribution enters the twinship discussion: a sense of similarity or sameness is vitalizing only if the complexity of similarity *and* difference is appreciated. This offers the reader a wonderful conundrum to play with—the dialectic tension between an appreciation of sameness and difference—we (my therapist and me, my patient and me, my parent and me, my child and me, my husband and me, my wife and me, my same sex partner and me, my business partner and me) are similar in this way and that is good or bad for our connection, and we are different in this way and that is good or bad for our connection. The authors' discourse on similarity *and* difference invites an analyst to wonder: does a particular analysand find himself in his analyst and also find not-himself in his analyst? And the same question applies to the analyst finding himself and not-himself in a particular patient. This dialectic adds to self psychology's appreciation of therapeutic disruptions that emerge when a balance between similarity and difference is lost, and analyst or analysand or both only find him or herself or not-self in the other.

I believe I have made my point that the reader will richly appreciate the subtleties of connection that emerge from expanding the twinship concept clinically—I certainly did. But the book broadens still more to what they refer to as the psychology of being human. Experiencing one's self as a human among humans is not a sensing that simply descends on one as a given. Experiencing twinship is about forming a connection to another or others as an act of agency—a *doing* in an active sense of seeking and finding fellowship, and a *doing* in the passive sense of opening and exposing oneself to the seeking of another or others. Seeking, accepting, being sought, and being accepted is the essential ingredient for best friends, brothers and/or sisters under the skin, and kindred spirits. The authors note that the active yearning for human connectedness can be observed in a patient's striving toward establishing a twinship tie in an environment in which he or she is aware that his, or her, or the other's subjectivities are formed differently. The seeking for twinship connectedness can be observed in children who create imaginary playmates and in adult patients who create fantasies of others who accept them. The authors see these fantasy others as facilitating transformation to actual ties.

The striving to belong, to connect, to experience similarities along with differences, and to be accepted all too often fails. On the clinical side is the impact of trauma detailed in the book. For example, the authors illustrate a twinship failure in a traumatized patient who rejected all commonality. The patient insisted that his suffering was unique and his alienation total. He had become a subject-without-others. Dehumanization is the perfect description for the impact of rape, physical and sexual abuse of children, the assaults of war, and severe accidents. Less dramatic but nonetheless very painful is the dehumanization experience that comes with being marginalized—being an "other"—by virtue of race, gender, sexual preference, skin color, religion, appearance, manners, accent, education and socioeconomic level, and country—or even section—of country of origin. Clinically, this was dramatically illustrated to me by my first analytic patient. Looking back from the expanded view of twinship striving, I now recognize how my patient—having been marginalized as her mother's less desired twin (actual)—was trying desperately to overcome her fear of rejection by me. We had struggled along through lengthy periods of silence when she felt free to describe to me golden moments in which her mother had held her tight—"close to her heart," she stated in Yiddish. Moved, I tried by repeating what she had said in her own words to indicate my appreciation of these moments in which she had felt deeply accepted and close to her mother. She erupted in a rage—my attempt to render Yiddish, which I had not learned as a child—had come across to her as proof that I was a German Jew—one of the "other" who looked down on Eastern European Jews. The exposure of this difference, this dissimilarity, opened a link to a negative transference that had remained hidden. As a background prejudice, it had been an influential impediment to our establishing trust as a "pair" who belonged together.

The authors illustrate the inevitable intersection of the personal and the political in everyday lived reality as it presents in the clinical field. The reader will, I believe, be drawn to reflect on that intersection as it presents in the powerful sociological polarization of feeling a human among humans vs dehumanized and alienated. Holding on to the sense of being a human among humans is a challenge groups and individuals often fail to meet. The dehumanizing of schizophrenic patients led Sullivan to state that we are all more human than otherwise. To southern whites, blacks were monkeys fresh from the trees. To the British in the Napoleonic years, the French were frogs. To Americans in the First World War, the Germans were Huns who raped Belgium; and in the Second World War, the "Japs" were the yellow peril. Kafka portrayed his defeated hero as having metamorphosed into a cockroach.

Sadly, dehumanizing comes all too easily to individuals and societies. Dehumanization is shockingly evident in current news about the frequency and general acceptance of rape in India, the mistreatment and devaluing of women in many cultures—such as in the Nigerian kidnapping and the carnage in Iraq—the almost continuous tribal and religious wars in many areas in the world. These tragic aspects of the uncertainty and anguish in human existence give weight to the significance of Koichi and Amanda's effort to present a dynamic account of the human ability to negotiate differences and retain a sense of sameness. Psychoanalytic theorizing often has avoided the more broadly philosophic existential issues, thus the great value of the authors' contribution. They state: "It is our belief that the twinship concept has to do with an essential element of all human emotional connections between people. We believe that without a twinship experience there is a deep sense of alienation, emptiness, and worthlessness, or a profound feeling of being 'non-human.' This creates the fundamental anguish about being in the human world."

As a developmentalist I ask: what are the origins of a sense of sameness, of being a human among humans? The authors cite a child's yearning for a sense that her caregivers can and do find themselves in her. For a mother of a girl, this might principally be she is like me as a female, like me in a non-gendered aspect of my being and doing, and like me in some sense of my also sometimes being like a man. So a child's sense of belonging to an integrated family would emerge when the child experiences mother and father seeing likeness in the child, and siblings and grandparents are also experienced as seeing some degree of likeness. In each instance, being not like or different plays an important part as well. Here, the authors contribute another principle—the power of *context* to determine whether likeness or difference dominates broadly or in a specific instance. Unfortunately, in some contexts, for parent or child, analyst or patient, seeking sameness or difference can have a negative impact. If seeking sameness in the other becomes a rigid requirement it acts as an entrapment—a demand for a pathological accommodation or the connection breaks. If in seeking sameness in the other, a small difference is magnified into an insurmountable obstacle, alienation will follow. A child reads his caregiver's face, gestures, and body tension to determine if he is like her or him; and if he is like, is he safe with the servant, postperson, or visitor? Clinical examples in the book help to make all these dynamics clear.

The expansion of Kohut's theory, the entry in the philosophic understanding of the existential significance of being a human among humans, and the clinical yield, make this book about twinship a valuable contribution to both self psychology and psychoanalytic theory and practice. But yet there is more. And that is the unusual backgrounds of the authors individually and together and how that illuminates the very substance of their proposal. Koichi is a Japanese man, trained in New York and practicing in Kobe and Hiroshima. Amanda is a white South African woman practicing in Cape Town. "Different" jumps out from the geographic facts alone. Then when you add in their achieving a sense of sameness in each geographic locale within their respective cultures and then also with the broader cultures of the Americas and Europe, the reader can appreciate that these authors are positioned by their experiences to tell us something about belonging that many of us would not ordinarily think about. Independently, despite the geographic disparity, they shared an interest in a similar career and theoretical constructs. Another variable—their gender difference—inevitably plays a role in the viewpoint each takes to similarity and difference across a spectrum of issues, but I find its subtle effect difficult to discern. That is the sameness and difference in perspective that emerges from being a gendered human among gendered humans, maybe another thread to be sorted out.

In Chapters 6 and 7, written by Koichi, he argues that self psychology has not sufficiently elaborated on the subjectivity of an individual who is embedded in a non-Western or non-North American cultural context. He gives as an example that for someone raised in the Japanese culture commonality and likeness between two individuals depends on feelings that both have been in the same place in the past, are currently in the same place, or, in fantasy will be in the same *place* in the future. This leads Koichi and his Japanese patient to explore another philosophic issue of twinship—what I would call a "destiny dialectic"—does the individual experience herself primarily as an independent center of initiative (Kohut's definition of self) and/or subject to or a "play toy" of fate? And of course fate has two faces—the serendipitous opportunity and the traumatic disruption. Koichi and Amanda illustrate the serendipitous. For ten years each independently had been intrigued with twinship—possibly influenced by their own geography. They then discovered each other at a meeting in Chicago and recognized their commonality. Opportunity called (good fate) and they grabbed it (each of their own center of initiative).

The authors examine the broad question of the meaning of life by citing the dialectic between lived events being experienced as contingent or random or, stated differently, both contingent and necessary. They conclude that a twinship tie refers to how two people came to meet each other and how they have been together rather than the substance of what connects them. Life's meaning for some patient and analyst dyads derives from their having met coincidentally and the uniqueness of their being together, both being irreplaceable. In the exploration by the authors, twinship expands from what is familiar to us about being a human among humans toward the edge of the knowable, toward the ineffable meaning of life. All in all, readers will find it a valuable experience to join Koichi and Amanda on their conceptual journey from twinship as simply sensing of sameness and commonality to the dialectic challenges that lead them, and us, to postulate about the meaning of life.

Acknowledgments

This book is an account of a ten-year journey in which both of us were trying to make sense of Heinz Kohut's thoughts when he changed his definition of the "twinship" experience to one in which there is a "feeling that one is a human being among other human beings" (Kohut, 1984, p. 200). In an uncanny similarity to twins separated at birth, for over a decade, from linguistic and geographically distinct countries; one in the Far East in the Northern Hemisphere, and the other in the center of the Southern Hemisphere, we were both researching the twinship concept. We first met in Chicago in 2006, when Togashi presented what has become Chapter 2 in this book. A rich and exciting series of coincidences and experiences followed. Together and separately, we shared the ideas that have culminated in many of the papers that form part of this book.

Apart from Chapter 5, written by Kottler and Togashi, all chapters have been presented at international conferences, published as journal articles, or as book chapters authored by one or both of us. Chapter 1 was drawn from Togashi and Kottler (2012b); Chapter 2 from Togashi (2009a); Chapter 3 from Kottler (2007); Chapter 4 from Togashi (2012a); Chapter 6 from Togashi (2011c); Chapter 7 from Togashi (2012b); Chapter 8 from Togashi and Kottler (2012a); Chapter 9 from Togashi (2014a); and finally, Chapter 10 from Togashi and Kottler (2013).

We would like to jointly, and separately, acknowledge those who have been significant to us throughout the process of writing. We are both grateful, first, to our patients who have given us the opportunity and the privilege of sharing their lives with them. Each one has directly and indirectly contributed profoundly to our discovery and the depth of our understanding of the concepts developed in this book. Secondly, we both thank the psychoanalytic communities who have influenced our thoughts and minds in various ways:

The International Association for Psychoanalytic Self Psychology, The Training and Research in intersubjective Self Psychology, The Taiwan Self Psychology Group, The Japanese Forum for Psychoanalytic Self Psychology, The Cape Town Psychoanalytic Self Psychology Group, and the International Association of Relational Psychoanalytic Psychotherapy. Each of these communities has, to greater and lesser extents encouraged our fascination with the issue of "being human" and provided us with a place to discuss and present our ideas.

We have shared some history and from this communal place would both like to thank Doris Brothers, Ph.D., William J. Coburn, Ph.D., Joseph D. Lichtenberg, M.D., Donna M. Orange, Ph.D., and Robert D. Stolorow, Ph.D., for the interest they have shown in our work, the support they have offered us and their contribution towards providing us with an opportunity to publish this book. We especially thank Joseph D. Lichtenberg for his preface. We both acknowledge the appreciation we also feel towards Arthur A. Gray, Ph.D., Amy Joleson, M.A., and Maxwell Sucharov, M.D. for their careful reading and productive critiques of original articles that have transformed into chapters of this book.

Individually, from Koichi Togashi: I am grateful to Frank M. Lachmann, Ph.D., Peter B. Zimmermann, Ph.D., Roger Frie, Ph.D., Richard B. Ulman, Ph.D., John Riker, Ph.D., and Margy Sperry, Ph.D. in the United States; Soh Agatsuma, M.D., Ph.D., Ken Okano, M.D., Ph.D., Satoshi Fukui, M.D., Koichi Yokoi, M.D., Toshihiko Maruta, M.D., Ph.D., Yutaka Kakuta, Ph.D., Makiko Kasai, Ph.D., Kazunori Nakanishi, M.A., Naoki Yasumura, M.A. in Japan; and Hao-Chung Hsu, M.D. and Ming-Shoung Lin, M.D. in Taiwan, for their actual reading of my works and for the way in which they have encouraged my aspiration for this long-term exploration. I most cordially acknowledge Masako Togashi, M.A., for her support in so many dimensions, and my long-lasting editor and friend, Donald Davidson, for his careful editing of all my works.

From Amanda Kottler: I am separately grateful to Arthur Gray, and Amy Joelson for their friendship, support, and encouragement of all kinds throughout the process of writing this book. I also thank Penny Murdock for sharing this journey with me, Anne Greenwell for her encouragement and generosity always, and Peter Buirski for his part in making me feel so at home in Self Psychology.

Coincidentally, the book that Peter Buirski and I (Kottler) (2007) co-edited was instrumental in our meeting in the first place. This brings us to our penultimate acknowledgment of each other—for a wonderful collaborative journey and a profoundly meaningful experience of being human with another human being—a twinship experience.

Finally, we both thank Routledge and Kate Hawes, Susan Wickenden, Rob Brown, Renee Last, and Hélène Feest for giving us the opportunity of publishing this book and helping out through its production.

We would like to officially acknowledge Taylor & Francis for kindly permitting the reprinting of the following articles in this book:

Koichi Togashi Ph.D., L.P. (2014) Is it a problem for us to say, "It is a coincidence that the patient does well"?, *International journal of psychoanalytic self psychology*, 9:2, 87–100, DOI: 10.1080/15551024.2014.883681.

Koichi Togashi Ph.D., L.P. and Amanda Kottler M.A. (Clin. Psych.) (2012) The many faces of twinship: from the psychology of the self to the psychology of being human, *International journal of psychoanalytic self psychology*, 7:3, 331–351, DOI: 10.1080/15551024.2012.686158.

Koichi Togashi Ph.D., L.P. (2012) Mutual finding of oneself and not-oneself in the other as a twinship experience, *International journal of psychoanalytic self psychology*, 7:3, 352–368, DOI: 10.1080/15551024.2012.686157.

Koichi Togashi Ph.D., L.P. (2009) A new dimension of twinship selfobject experience and transference, *International journal of psychoanalytic self psychology,* 4:1, 21–39, DOI: 10.1080/15551020802337492.

Furthermore, we would like to acknowledge The Rowman & Littlefield Publishing Group for kindly permitting the reprinting of "Twinship and 'Otherness'" as found in *New developments in self psychology practice* edited by Peter Buirski and Amanda Kottler.

Finally, we would like to officially acknowledge Pro-Ed Publishing Company for kindly permitting the reprinting of:

"Contemporary self psychology and cultural issues: 'self-place experience' in an Asian Culture" as found in *Podium of psychoanalysis: self psychology*, Vol. 9 edited by Li-Fei Wang.

"Placeness in the twinship experience in an Asian Culture" as found in *Podium of psychoanalysis: self psychology*, Vol. 10 edited by Li-Fei Wang.

Introduction

Koichi Togashi, Ph.D., L.P.
Amanda Kottler, M.A. (Clin. Psych.)

Twinship, a captivating self-psychological buzzword, has little to do with actual ideas about twins or siblings. Heinz Kohut first introduced the concept in 1968, in his paper entitled "The Psychoanalytic Treatment of Narcissistic Personality Disorders," as a type of narcissistic transference. He believed that this type of transference developed in the psychoanalytic treatment of patients with narcissistic personality disorders. As self psychology developed, Kohut replaced the idea of a "narcissistic transference" with that of a "selfobject transference." Accordingly, by 1971, twinship was considered as a type of selfobject transference, but not one of great import. This had, however, shifted toward the end of Kohut's life, as we will demonstrate in this book (see also, Togashi and Kottler, 2012).

As a concept, twinship has had a complex and unique history in the development of Kohut's self psychology. First, Kohut referred to twinship using two interchangeable but very different terms that he did not sufficiently clarify: "twinship" and "alter-ego" (Kohut, 1968, 1971, 1984), which means "second or other self." Second, Kohut originally considered the concept as a subcategory of the mirror transference (Kohut, 1968, 1971). In this sense, he understood twinship as an archaic version of the mirror transference. However, toward the end of his life, Kohut's ideas had changed radically. He had begun to recognize twinship as an independent selfobject transference, with an elevated status sharing equal standing with idealizing and mirroring selfobject experiences. This significant shift is under-recognized and under-represented in contemporary self psychology. Third, Kohut represented twinship in many, sometimes quite obscure, ways. As described in Chapter 1, Kohut referred to the twinship experience in at least seven different ways. What he had in mind therefore, whenever he referred to the twinship experience, was not always clear. His untimely death prevented him from elaborating on this and from achieving the coherence we believe is missing in contemporary self psychology.

In spite of the lack of clarity, a number of post-Kohutian self psychologists, ourselves included, have underscored Kohut's (1984) idea that twinship is the most prominent and fundamental selfobject experience (Basch, 1992; Martinez, 1993, 2003; Ulman and Paul, 1992; Shapiro, 1998; Gorney, 1998; Kottler, 2007; Togashi, 2009a; Philipson, 2010). We believe the concept has to do with a fundamental element of each and every emotional connection between human beings. Without twinship experiences people feel deeply alienated, empty, and worthless; they experience a profound sense of discomfort in the world—a sense of not being human. This creates an essential anguish about being in the human world, something we believe Kohut attempted to illustrate by making reference to Kafka's *The Metamorphosis*. In other words, an absence of a twinship experience leads to a pervasive sense of uncertainty about being—an existential emptiness (Brothers, 2008; Stolorow, 2009; Togashi, 2014a, 2014c). For this reason, we believe that an understanding and sensitivity to the way in which patients organize twinship experiences in analytic relationships is crucial.

Throughout this book, with reference to the theory and practice of psychoanalytic self psychology and intersubjectivity theories, we discuss different aspects of the history, the shifting definitions, the evolution, and the clinical implications of twinship selfobject experiences. Our examination of twinship from a range of perspectives draws attention to the different ways in which heightened sensitivity to a patient's psychic organization, the intersubjective process in an analytic dyad, and the particular therapeutic processes involved, occur. The book also illustrates that twinship is a relational, dialectic, intersubjective, and existential concept. Using a range of clinical vignettes, we demonstrate how numerous facets of the twinship experience are all related to the existential anguish of living in our contemporary and increasingly uncertain world. These include experiences of longing, development, attachment, mutual recognition, a dialectic between sameness and difference, cultural differences, and the circumstances of birth.

By tracking the way in which Kohut's definition of twinship changed, the book shows how Kohut's "psychology of the self," which began as a "psychology of narcissism," then evolved into the "psychology of the self", and finally toward the end of his life, shifted to the "psychology of being human." From this perspective, the book attempts to understand the environment and the particular processes that are necessary for individuals to experience themselves as "being human." The book also suggests ways in which therapists can help patients who, in the wake of some kind of relational trauma, are unable to experience themselves as "being human."

Historically, psychoanalysis has paid attention to the human anguish involved and organized around a sense of being human (Frie, 2011, 2014; Togashi, 2014c). Freud himself was deeply involved in the consideration of "humanity" in psychoanalysis (Boss, 1963). As a clinician, he attempted to find a way of viewing his patient as a whole human being. However, in Freud's theory, his description of being human is, in a certain sense, simple and mechanistic; it is described as a production of the ego's ability to control primitive, beastly impulses. The recent humanistic trend in psychoanalysis has, however, more directly provided a psychoanalytic perspective from which to access human anguish, trauma, and the meaning of human life (Friedman, 1982; Lichtenberg, 1985; Fromm, 1994; Orange, Atwood and Stolorow, 2002; Stolorow, 2007; Brothers, 2008; Togashi, 2014b, 2014d). Our book is seated within this trend.

In Chapter 1, we introduce the reader to the historical shifts involved, and to Kohut's, by his own admission, incomplete theorizing of the twinship experience. Then, we tease out and describe seven faces of twinship: (1) twinship as something between merger and mirroring; (2) twinship as a process of mutual finding; (3) twinship as a sense of belonging; (4) twinship as a way of passing on talents to the next generation; (5) twinship in silent communication; (6) twinship as a sense of feeling human among other human beings; and (7) twinship in trauma. We conclude that what may have looked like insignificant shifts in Kohut's definition of twinship over time reveals a distinct theoretical transformation from the psychology of the self to the psychology of being human.

In Chapter 2, Togashi proposes an additional dimension of a twinship selfobject need: the patient's yearning for a sense that the analyst can recognize himself or herself in the patient. Through clinical vignettes, Togashi illustrates that this new dimension and Kohut's original definition are related but represent two different kinds of transferences. He discusses whether this new dimension of twinship is the essential source of the selfobject milieu in which an individual experiences him or herself as being human.

In Chapter 3, Kottler illustrates the intersection of the personal and the political in everyday lived reality as it presents in the clinical field. Drawing on postmodern ideas of dominant discourses, she illustrates how particular gendered discourses influence the subjectivity of both therapist and patient in contradictory ways. Contextualized in this way, Kottler's focus on the twinship transference, with its early implication of sameness, reveals the significance of a felt sense of not only similarity but *also* of difference in the clinical encounter.

In Chapter 4, Togashi describes the perceptual-cognitive processes that are going on in twinship relatedness. He presents a case vignette that emphasizes the difference between an analyst and a patient who longs for a twinship tie. He uses this to argue that a twinship experience can be described as one which is organized as a delicate balance between context sensitive mutual findings of oneself and not-oneself in the other, at the explanatory level, at a particular moment in a particular dyad.

In Chapter 5, Kottler and Togashi focus on traumatized patients whose style of relating impedes them from feeling human among other human beings. They suggest that such patients create objects in their fantasies with whom they fantasize an emotional tie. Drawing on the ideas of fantasy selfobject experiences, the chapter demonstrates how such experiences have the capacity to transform themselves along a forward, rather than a trailing edge/repetitive dimension. The chapter draws attention to how a fantasy selfobject can be transformed into a *human* selfobject experience in which patients develop the capacity to negotiate a sense of sameness *and* difference in the dyad.

In Chapter 6, Togashi focuses on cultural issues and self psychology. He presents the concept of a "self-place experience," which is deeply connected to Asian and, especially, Japanese culture. Through case material with a Japanese male patient, he concludes that a patient's working through of a self-place experience leads to a dialectic between committing himself to fate and experiencing himself as an independent center of initiative. Togashi argues that this dialectic is a process in which both patient and analyst are able to recognize first, each of their selves in the "analytic place" and the "place" in each of their selves.

In Chapter 7, Togashi illustrates the importance of "placeness" in a twinship experience. He hypothesizes that a twinship tie relates to a feeling of being in the same place as the other. A particular affective connection in a twinship tie is based on more than a sense of commonality and alikeness between two individuals; it is a feeling that both members of a dyad have been in the same place in the past, that they are currently in the same place, or, in fantasy, that they will be in the same place in the future. Togashi concludes that for analysts, it is often essential to be more sensitive to the concept of "placeness" than to sameness or alikeness.

In Chapter 8, Togashi and Kottler use a case vignette to illustrate the complexity of a traumatized dyadic system, which is organized around a twinship tie. They use this to explore how and why this patient, having sought out others who had suffered similar traumatic experiences to his own, rejected the apparent similarities and insisted that his experiences were different and in fact, "unique." Togashi and Kottler argue that the "uniqueness" to which a traumatized patient clings can be usefully understood as emanating from earlier alienating experiences of being "a subject-without-others."

In Chapter 9, Togashi explores how a patient and analyst experience the therapeutic encounter or success as coincident or contingent. Discussion of a case vignette drawn from a patient who cannot live with the fact that, in this world, events occur without particular reason, Togashi concludes that contingency and necessity are significant ideas through which patient and analyst can make sense of their emotional exeriences together (Orange, 1995). Togashi emphasizes that a traumatized person or a relational organization can easily fall into a dualism between contingency and necessity, and that a traumatized system can be perturbed if an analyst and a patient allow themselves to confront the possibility that any phenomena could be both contingent and necessary.

In the final chapter, Chapter 10, Togashi and Kottler examine the circumstances that engender the loss of a sense of being human, and how this might be transformed in a therapeutic relationship. They suggest that a sense of being "a human being among other human beings" (Kohut, 1984) in a twinship tie is about how two people come to meet each other and how they experience their being together, rather than about the substance of what connects them. They suggest that with this kind of patient, it is essential for the therapist and patient to make sense together of the meaning of their having met coincidentally, and the uniqueness of their experience of being together, both of which are irreplaceable.

It is noteworthy that although some authors have attempted to distinguish the twinship and alterego concepts (Detrick, 1985, 1986; Brothers, 1993, 1994), we use the word "twinship" rather than "alter-ego." The latter term is seldom, if ever, used by contemporary authors in the development of self psychology after Kohut. This is another theme discussed in Chapter 10, i.e. why it is that the word twinship rather than alter-ego, resonates more powerfully with a fundamental sense of feeling securely and emotionally connected to the human world.

Chapter 1

The many faces of twinship
From the psychology of the self to the psychology of being human

Koichi Togashi, Ph.D., L.P.
Amanda Kottler, M.A. (Clin. Psych.)

Twinship has a unique history in the development of Kohut's psychology of the self. Originally considered a subcategory of the mirror transference (Kohut, 1968, 1971), it had little theoretical weight and was referred to using two interchangeable but very different terms ("alter-ego" and "twinship"). However, towards the end of his life, Kohut's ideas had changed radically. He began to recognize twinship as an independent selfobject transference and gave it equal status to the idealizing and mirroring selfobject experiences. In spite of this shift, at the time of his death, in comparison to other selfobject experiences, Kohut had written very little on the concept.

A number of post-Kohutian self psychologists (Basch, 1992; Martinez, 1993, 2003; Ulman and Paul, 1992; Shapiro, 1998; Gorney, 1998; Kottler, 2007; Togashi, 2009a; Philipson, 2010) have developed Kohut's ideas, making reference to the fact that twinship is the most prominent and fundamental selfobject experience. In spite of this, it has still not received any more attention than the other selfobject experiences. Further, it remains the insufficiently developed and understood challenge that Kohut left us at the time of his death.

We take up this challenge by responding to Kohut's (1984) last statement that "much remains to be done" (p. 194) on the twinship selfobject needs. We tease out and clarify the many faces that Kohut introduced us to regarding what we now see as the multifaceted notion of twinship.

Twinship as Kohut left it

Kohut (1984) left us with twinship defined in two significantly different ways; first as a sense of "essential alikeness" and second, as a feeling that one is "a human being among other human beings". He did not comment specifically on the two correlated but very different definitions. This begs the question of what he and other contemporary self psychologists have in mind whenever they refer to the twinship experience.

We describe seven "faces" of Kohut's twinship, each elaborated by contemporary self psychologists. We also show their relevance to Kohut's personal history supporting Atwood and Stolorow's (1979) argument that a theory of psychoanalysis and the theorist's personal life are intricately entwined. We argue that Kohut's change in the way he defined twinship represents a fundamental shift in his theory. We believe the two different definitions of twinship represent a transformation that was taking place for Kohut, both personally and theoretically. We see the transformation as a shift from the *psychology of the self* to what we refer to as the *psychology of being human*. At the same time we see a transformation from the psychology of the disorder of the self to what Brothers (2008) refers to as trauma centered psychoanalysis.

The many faces of twinship

In addition to leaving us with two distinctly different definitions, Kohut represented the twinship transference and experience in many, sometimes quite obscure, ways. While the diversity of his descriptions may have helped to deepen discussion on the concept by his followers, it also created confusion and a range of contradictions. In this section, in an attempt to tease out some of this confusion, we develop and describe seven different "faces" to help us focus on Kohut's multifaceted notion of twinship.

Face 1: Twinship as something between merger and mirroring

When Kohut (1968) introduced twinship, he argued that the mirror transference could be divided into three forms: the merger, the twinship, and the mirror transference, in a much narrower sense. In that paper, he described what he would call "the *alter-ego* or *twinship* transference" (p. 489, italics in original) as "a less archaic form in which the patient assumes that the analyst is like him or that the analyst's psychological makeup is similar to his" (p. 489). Kohut follows this position in his 1971 book, *The Analysis of the Self*, stating that the yearning for twinship is experienced by an individual who seeks a merger with the other, but who to some extent recognizes the other as a psychologically separate existence. He posits that in the twinship transference, "not a primary identity but a likeness (similarity) with the object is established, [which] corresponds to a more mature developmental phase than that from which the merger transference takes its origin" (p. 122). He adds that in the transference, a patient experiences his analyst "as the separate carrier of his own (repressed) perfection" (p. 123).

In this discussion, the essential difference between the three forms of mirror transference is based on the degree to which an individual can see the other as an extension of himself. A patient's claim that his analyst is essentially like him is, in this paradigm, understood as a less archaic form of his longing to merge with his analyst in complete union, but a more archaic form of his longing to be mirrored by his analyst, as a separate person.

Our attempts to understand what Kohut had in mind when he saw twinship in this way have led us to believe that this face of twinship was influenced by, and related to, Kohut's relationship with Ernst Morawetz who entered Kohut's life when Kohut was ten years old. Until then, Kohut's mother was virtually his only companion. Their relationship was intense and unusual. She was "crazy," kept a "tight grip" on him, and was overly intrusive (Strozier, 2001, pp. 22 and 160). She obsessively searched for any blemish on her son's skin every day and squeezed his blackheads when she found them. She was insensitive to how painful it was for her son whose body and skin were, for her, simply an extension of herself. The relationship between Kohut and his mother in his early childhood seems, therefore, to have been organized at the level of a merger, until Kohut's mother took on a lover when he was ten years old. With a largely absent father and the loss of his mother in this way, it was clearly a traumatic time for Kohut (Strozier, 2001). His psychological survival is attributed, at least in part, to the arrival of Ernst Morawetz.

Morawetz was ten years older than Kohut and was expected to provide company and intellectual stimulation for Kohut. He did this and more. As Kohut's first real friend, the companionship and connection that Ernst provided was "psychologically lifesaving" for him (Strozier, 2001, p. 24). They would play creative intellectual games like imagining what would have happened to the architecture of Vienna had Socrates not died, and Kohut learned a huge amount about the world from Ernst.

Kohut (1984) said, "if earlier mirroring responses are badly flawed the child will intensify his search for the structuring presence of a [twinship] selfobject experience ... for the uplifting, self-organizing experience that comes from the availability of a selfobject that is idealizable" (p. 205). Clearly, this was the case with Ernst whose presence sustained him at a time of great stress. What happened between them was a symbolic representation of what else was being experienced: love, intimacy, and deep empathy. From what Kohut says, Ernst certainly provided him with a twinship selfobject experience that, by definition, vitalized him and his potential for learning.

Their relationship was, according to Strozier (2001), so intimate that they became absorbed with each other psychologically and physically, and the relationship was often sexualized. Referring to his relationship with Ernst, Kohut argued that it was not the sexuality, but the empathy and affection that counted. Kohut (1984) emphasized their sharing of interests and said, presumably thinking of their relationship, "the subtlety of love and connection can arise even in deeply unequal relationships" (p. 200). This is quite different to the merger evident in Kohut's relationship with his mother. In other words, we suggest that the basic quality of twinship between Kohut and Ernst is a more archaic form of mirroring, but a less archaic form of merging with others.

Face 2: Twinship as a process of mutual finding

Another question about Kohut's early depiction of twinship is why Kohut originally put twinship and mirroring into the same category. We argue that they provide very different experiences for an individual, but that they are organized as a result of both different and similar psychological processes, which we describe as mutual recognition and mutual findings. In spite of his traditional terminology, Kohut describes the mirroring experience in a bidirectional way. He states that a mirroring need is activated "by looking at the mother and by being looked at by her" (Kohut, 1971, p. 117). We believe he sees the two different psychological processes in this experience. A good example is found in Kohut's discussion of a child's experience in the Oedipus phase:

> If the little boy, for example, feels that his father looks upon him proudly as a *chip off the old block* and allows him to merge with him and with his adult greatness, then his oedipal phase will be a decisive step in self-consolidation and self-pattern-firming.
>
> (Kohut, 1977, p. 234; italics added)

In this statement, Kohut (1977) mainly uses the phrase "chip off the old block" to describe a mirroring experience. However, some seven years later, he uses the same phrase specifically as an example of twinship (Kohut, 1984, p. 199). We believe that in this process a boy finds himself in his father's mind in two ways: first, through the boy's recognition of his father's affective passion and responsiveness to him, namely the "gleam in the father's eye," and second, through his recognition that his father has found a similar aspect of himself and his own subjectivity in the boy.

From a nonlinear dynamic systems view, VanDerHeide (2009) expands Kohut's description stating that mirroring "comprises both reciprocal forms of responsiveness and mutual experiences of being recognized and appreciated" (p. 433). A patient and an analyst both experience being seen, accepted, and understood by one another, and both respond to another's recognizing of being recognized by one another. In the context of mutual mirroring-recognizing processes between VanDerHeide and her patient, she discusses how they share and experience the similarities and differences between themselves. In her response to VanDerHeide's article, Hershberg (2011) discusses and reveals how a twinship selfobject experience is activated in the process of a mutual mirroring process.

In Chapter 4 (see also Togashi, 2010), Togashi posits that a mutual finding process between an analyst and a patient is the essence of a twinship experience. He argues that a twinship experience is organized as a delicate balance between a patient's finding herself and not-herself in her analyst, and an analyst's finding himself and not-himself in his patient. For Togashi, the finding of oneself or not-oneself is not equivalent to recognizing or validating the other's subjectivity. It is a psychological process in which two participants, consciously and nonconsciously, regulate a sense of sameness and difference in their effort to match some aspects of their subjectivity. This, for us, is the key to distinguishing the difference between a mirroring experience and twinship relatedness in an analytic dyad.

Kohut's confusion between mirroring and twinship experiences is evident in his struggle to fit in with American psychoanalysis. Although Kohut recognized the limitations of mainstream psychoanalytic thinking early on, he, for a long while, clung to the organizing selfobject function of "Freudian theory" (Mollon, 2001, p. 107) in an attempt to remain "essentially alike." At the time of writing *The Analysis of the Self* (1971), Kohut was especially struggling to gain their recognition. He was vigilant about the advancement of his career. He played expertly by the rules, and became "Mr. Psychoanalysis" in the United States, ultimately serving as president of the American Psychoanalytic Association (Strozier, 2001). His early theorizing attempted, in his own words, "to pour new wine into old bottles" (Kohut, 1984, p. 193) as he tried to make his ideas appear less radically new and more acceptable to his fellow analysts *and* to himself. We believe that for him initially being recognized (mirrored) by the American ego psychologists and having an experience of twinship with them (essential alikeness) were almost equal.

Face 3: Twinship as a sense of belonging

Towards the end of the 1970s, Kohut's evolving ideas had become unpopular with the mainstream classical fraternity and severely criticized by traditional ego psychologists. They saw him as a maverick, or a misfit. This in spite of the fact that in the process of establishing his own psychology Kohut was pivotal in the paradigm shift of the psychoanalytic field into a relational or two-person psychology (Strozier, 2001; Fosshage, 2009). Coinciding with this painful struggle is a shift in Kohut's definition of twinship. In his book, *How Does Analysis Cure?* published posthumously, Kohut (1984) describes the twinship experience as a sense of belonging. He states:

> The mere presence of people in a child's surroundings—their voices and body odors, the emotions they express, the noises they produce as they engage in human activities, the specific aroma of the foods they prepare and eat—creates a security in the child, *a sense of belonging and participating*, that cannot be explained in terms of a mirroring response or a merger with ideals.
>
> (Kohut, 1984, p. 200, italics added)

Self psychologists in the post-Kohutian era have elaborated on this type of twinship experience from a contemporary perspective. White and Weiner (1986) argue that "the essence of the twinship selfobject relationship is a similarity in interests and talents, along with the sense of being understood by someone like oneself" (p. 103). Basch (1994) redefined a twinship transference as "the need to belong and feel accepted by one's cohort" (p. 4), in which he saw two needs; that is, a need to feel that members of the group are alike and a need to feel that one is experienced by group members as essentially alike.

Wada's (1998) description of his own experience of the disruption of twinship during his stay in the United States for his psychoanalytic training is useful in an attempt to understand this process. He reveals that the "alien-culture" experience profoundly influenced his sense of self. He observes himself being overwhelmed by a paranoid anxiety that others are looking at him with scorn or dislike. He states, "I felt completely defeated when those around me not only used English freely, but also could be spontaneous and relate naturally to each other" (p. 113).

Kohut's conflict over this type of twinship tie could be found in his exile and assimilation to a new culture. In spite of becoming an American citizen five years after arriving in Chicago, Kohut continued to appear conflicted over a sense of belonging. Given the many references Kohut made to the intrapsychic significance of familiar language to illustrate twinship experiences, it is interesting to note that for the rest of his life Kohut was never sure if he dreamed in English or German (Strozier, 2001). Although Jewish, he became a participating member of the Unitarian Church in Chicago where he preached sometimes. He also repeatedly and convincingly claimed to have no personal identification with Judaism. He indicated his ineradicable conflict over being Jewish by denying any knowledge of Jewish customs to the point of making scenes in kosher delis by insisting on having a ham sandwich with a glass of milk (Strozier, 2001).

In the professional field, in spite of his success we believe it is unlikely that Kohut ever felt like he really belonged to, or was accepted by, the mainstream of American psychoanalysis, particularly towards the end of his life. We suspect that feelings of being somewhat marginalized were always present for Kohut. It is understandable therefore that he sought followers with whom he could feel that sense of belonging but also to whom he could hand down his ideas and thoughts. And so, another face is revealed.

Face 4: Twinship as a way of passing on talents and skills to the next generation

Kohut introduced the idea of a bipolar self in 1977, in his book *The Restoration of the Self* where he maintains that there is a "correlated set of talents and skills" (p. 177) between the ambitions and ideals of the nuclear self. Although Kohut did not explicitly address twinship in this model, by 1980 he had ultimately linked twinship with the intermediate area of the bipolar self (Detrick, 1985).

Kohut (1977) discusses talents and skills using the example of Mr M, a writer who is not fully satisfied with his job. Kohut describes that Mr M's talents and skills in the area of language and creative writing are related to "his dictionary-collecting, word-loving, language-wise father" (p. 12), even though the "phase-appropriate, chip-off-the-old-block-type merger with (or twinship relation to) the idealized father" (p. 13) was not fully met. Still, according to Kohut, with regard to Mr M, "in the area of the talents and skills that the self needed in order to express its patterns, the damage [of Mr M's self] seemed to be slight and circumscribed" (p. 48). In the process of the analysis, Mr M decided to establish a writing school, and came to experience "in combination with this specific talents and skills ... a 'constant flow of energy'" (p. 48). For Kohut, the most significant aspect of Mr M's effort to educate students in his school was in the way he created an environment in which "by proxy, the students had to acquire a new skill" (p. 48). In other words, in the writing school, he passed on his skills to the younger students and tried to create himself in them.

We can see another example in the same book (Kohut, 1977), where Kohut discusses an archaic type of twinship tie through Proust and *Remembrance of Things Past*. He argues that Proust's trauma is manifested in the relationship between the narrator in the book and Albertine. He says, "the narrator does not love her, he needs her, he keeps her as his prisoner ... and *he molds her to a likeness of himself by educating her*" (p. 181n, italics added). Another well-known description of twinship is "the little girl doing chores in the kitchen next to her mother or grandmother; the little boy working in the basement next to his father or grandfather"

(Kohut, 1984, p. 204). These descriptions indicate that in this context, Kohut saw twinship also in an individual's effort to look for a successor. For Kohut, an individual's effort to educate others is often based on her yearning for a person who she can experience as essentially alike, and/or for a person in whom she can find herself.

As Togashi notes, using Kohut's example of a child's experience about his caretaker seeing him as a successor in Chapter 2 (see also Togashi, 2009a), the two dimensions of twinship, "Like-to-feel-we-are-alike and Can-you-find-yourself-in-me?" should be differentiated, and an analyst needs to be aware of these two, quite different, selfobject functions. He emphasizes that twinship is fundamentally an interactive process in a dyad, and particularly focuses on a child's yearning for a sense that his caretaker can and does find herself in him. Both case vignettes described in that chapter indicate that the yearning for twinship appears in the area of a patient's feelings that his or her caretaker does not value or consider him or her sufficiently to want to pass on their talents and skills.

This type of twinship experience can be seen in Kohut's effort to organize his own group and followers. In the 1960s, at age 47, increasingly marginalized and feeling painfully like a "misfit" among his classically informed contemporaries, Kohut turned to the younger and brightest students at the Chicago Institute with whom he developed his ideas. Out of these discussions came his first book (1971) and the force of his originality which was still mostly disguised. However, by 1981, (aged 68) the disguise had been dropped. The group (known by some as the Sacred Seven) and others, clearly provided ongoing twinship selfobject experiences for Kohut. He enjoyed sharing the same interests and ideas, and, more importantly, finding and creating himself in them.

For Kohut, one of the valuable aspects of human civilization is its function to pass on intelligence and creativity to the next generation, unlike Freud (1930) who simply sees human civilization as a function to control and repress people's infantile impulses. Kohut (1977) does not believe the Oedipus complex is the pre-wired conflict all boys experience universally in the process of development. He emphasizes that healthy parents are pleased and attracted to the dynamic energy involved in the development of their children. This is evident in Kohut's response to his sister-in-law, who expressed concern about Kohut spending money on his son and his son's wife: "Look, the best guarantee for your old age, or anyone's old age, is the good will of the next generation" (Strozier, 2001, p. 234). Creating and finding oneself in the next generation is, for Kohut, the future of humanity.

Face 5: Twinship in silent communication

In another effort to illustrate a twinship experience, Kohut (1984) describes a female patient who has a fantasy of a genie in a bottle, which is experienced as "someone just like herself" (p. 196). She can talk to and keep company with the genie any time she wants to, and "her self was sustained simply by the presence of someone who she knew was sufficiently like her to understand her and to be understood by her" (p. 196). The unique feature of the relationship between her and the genie is that their twinship tie was organized in silent communication. For her, Kohut states, "being together with the twin in silent communication was often the most satisfactory state" (p. 196).

For Kohut, one of the significant features of a twinship tie in a dyad is that both participants can sense and share the feeling of connection without verbal communication. The participants in the tie, according to him, do not have to see the gleam in the other's eye or to recognize the strength of the twinship tie. Without verbal or cognitive confirmation, they can experience their similarities (and probably differences) and sense they are affectively connected in a special form. Describing this type of experience, Livingston (1998) states, "examples of twinship in later life are also easily found in two concert lovers sitting quietly together and listening" (p. 58).

Kohut (1996) also describes this type of connection beautifully in his lecture in the 1970s:

> In the twinship transference the patient experiences you like himself: his thoughts seem to be present in you also, and what's going on in him he feels is going on in you too. When he feels distant, you are distant from him too. When he is enraged, he feels you are enraged too.
>
> (Kohut, 1996, p. 34)

This type of process can be understood in terms of interactive regulatory processing illustrated by recent infant research (Fosshage, 2004, 2005; Beebe and Lachmann, 2002; Sander, 2002; Stern, 2004; Lachmann, 2008). Lichtenberg's (2003) summary of the findings of infant research helps us to understand the development of communication in infancy. It includes not only an explicit dimension, which is described as symbolic verbal interaction, but also an implicit dimension, i.e. the preverbal behavior-procedural realm such as vocal rhythms, facial expression, gaze, and arousal. Lichtenberg (2003) sees a form of fundamental twinship as mutually seeking commonality in this implicit dimension. This could be described as "I can match my affect with hers making me implicitly aware that I too have identifiable affects" (p. 508). As discussed in Chapter 4 (see also Togashi, 2012a), Togashi also argues that one of the roots of a twinship tie is the infant's and the adult's regulatory process of matching (and not matching) one another in an implicit dimension.

It is difficult to answer the question that comes to mind about who might have provided Kohut with this type of twinship tie. Implicit regulatory processes are not easy to retain for record unless this dimension of communication and information processing is the focus, which, unfortunately, in Kohut's era, was not the case. However, many of the descriptions of twinship given above are so profoundly evocative of what we know of his relationships with Ernst Morawetz, and more particularly Robert Wadsworth, that we feel confident in suggesting that there is a significant link between these relationships and this dimension.

Robert Wadsworth seems to have been Kohut's most significant figure in his adulthood. They met on the day Kohut arrived in Chicago and came to call each other "birthday brothers" because they were born on the same day (Strozier, 2001). Wadsworth was brilliant, musical, and, like Ernst, highly literate. Kohut, who did not suffer fools gladly, felt that Wadsworth was one of the few Americans he knew whose "education, learning, and general culture approached his own" (Strozier, p. 68). Strozier (2001) says "no-one was more significant in Heinz Kohut's adult life" (p. 68) and the two "immersed themselves in each other's lives" (p. 69). We believe their intimate tie went far beyond verbally sharing their interests, thoughts, and mutual understanding. We infer that much of their commonality was specifically found in silent communication, including the implicit dimension.

Face 6: Twinship and feeling human among other human beings

For us, the most significant face of twinship is a "confirmation of the feeling that one is a human being among other human beings" (Kohut, 1984, p. 200). Kohut states:

> Some of the most painful feelings to which man is exposed, unforgettably described by Kafka in *The Metamorphosis* and observable during analyses of many people with severe narcissistic personality disorders, related to the sense of not being human. The awareness of such a central distortion in the personality stems, I believe, from the absence of *human* humans in the environment of the small child.
>
> (Kohut, 1984, p. 200; italics in original)

Here, Kohut's language has become more experience-near and familiar to contemporary self psychologists. His point is clear—an individual wants to be surrounded by humans whom she experiences as essentially human rather than as not-human or as things. If she is unable to experience them as human, she cannot experience herself as human. Instead, she will experience herself as not being human, or as being a thing.

We argue that the most important aspect of this face is that Kohut's description has begun to transcend his metapsychology of the self. It aims and begins to reveal a more fundamental and existential conflict of "being" in the world. What Kohut discusses here is not a psychological process of how an individual experiences himself as whole, vital or cohesive, but in what environment or in what interaction with others individuals can experience themselves as human (or not-human). Towards the end of his life, therefore, it appears as if Kohut's attempts to grapple with the issue of twinship had changed Kohut's psychology from the *psychology of the self* to what we refer to as the *psychology of being human*.

There is evidence to support that Kohut's main concern around 1980 had already shifted to a sense of being human rather than a sense of a cohesive and vital self. Kohut's preoccupation with this is evident in his many attempts to elaborate and describe this idea from a range of different angles. In the discussion of empathy and an emphatic environment, he uses the story of the astronauts whose space capsule lost power in outer space (Kohut, 1981, 1984). He refers to their yearning to return to Earth regardless of the serious risk of being burned to death during atmospheric entry. He describes their yearning as "the expression of their ultimate deepest desire [which is] the wish to be symbolically reunited with Earth: the symbol of human meaning, human warmth, human contact, human experience" (Kohut, 1984, p. 545n). Although there is a theoretical contradiction in this concept because he uses this episode as an example of both an empathic environment and a twinship experience, many contemporary self psychologists argue that a sense of being a human among human beings is a key to understanding the most fundamental and existential conflict of human beings (Basch, 1992; Martinez, 1993, 2003; Ulman and Paul, 1992; Shapiro, 1998; Gorney, 1998; Brothers, 2008; Togashi, 2009a, 2012a; Philipson, 2010).

Taking this idea further, Ulman and Paul (1992), not satisfied with the concept of twinship as a selfobject experience serving the function of acquiring skills and tools, nor as a sense of belonging, argue that a twinship selfobject experience serves the function of "humanization, that is, the developmental process of coming to feel human" (p. 111). They stress that addicts tend to experience both themselves and others as if they were non-human things or activities. For addicts, as a result of an arrested psychological development, "rather than things becoming more human, humans become more thing like" (pp. 116–117).

Their discussion points to the importance of distinguishing between: (1) being used by others as an extension of themselves (Kohut, 1971); and (2) being treated by others as a non-human thing. In Kohut's original discussion, he described how people with narcissistic or self-pathology tend, in relationships, to use others and to experience being used by others as if each is an extension of the other. He states that such an individual "controls and possesses with a self-evident certainty that is akin to the adult's experience of his control over his own body and mind" (1971, p. 90). But he says in this context, that a sense of being human (or experiencing oneself as not human) is a fundamentally different experience. He is suggesting that people cannot experience themselves as even an extension of a human being, if others have treated them as non-human things.

We argue that this face of twinship is connected to two of Kohut's own severely traumatic experiences: the exile from his beloved Vienna in his younger years and his struggle with what he eventually died of, lymphoma.

In Vienna, Kohut graduated with a medical degree in 1938, having been reluctantly allowed to take his final exams because he was a Jew. He and his mother were forcibly removed from their home, by the Nazis, for which they were paid a ridiculously small sum of money. A year later, Kohut fled the Nazis and was in a transit camp for a year in England. At 27 years of age he arrived in Chicago, with only $25 to his name (Strozier, 2001).

This period of his life was clearly traumatic. Many twinship experiences were obviously being disrupted, filling him with the disintegration anxiety and feelings of fragmentation about which he theorized so well. With regard to twinship, it is significant that Kohut strongly identified himself as a Viennese. He loved German culture and history, in which he was able to "find himself." However, suddenly, in spite of the fact that for no apparent reason, Kohut did not identify himself as a Jew, he found himself primarily identified as a Jew for which he was rejected. Other Viennese and Germans no longer regarded him as a member of their culture—they could no longer see themselves in him. In the refugee camp for Jews in England, Kohut could not find himself in the other inmates, all of whom identified and carried with them a Jewish identity. Another key issue of this experience for him is how he was treated and had witnessed others being treated as non-human things by the Nazis. In Nazi Germany, Jews were not considered human—they were things—they might just have been cockroaches that had to be exterminated. And Kohut was seen as one of these.

A second trauma occurred in 1977 when Kohut was diagnosed with cancer, which, for the most part, he kept secret. Again, he had to face an environment in which he experienced himself increasingly as a non-human thing. He could not control his body or the illness despite his obsessive effort to check for vital signs. Basic bodily functions stopped working; he began to experience his body as no longer human—it became an uncontrollable "thing." Given what was happening, his preoccupation with the fate of the astronauts is not surprising. Nor is it surprising that his final words on twinship included the need for further investigations into selfobject needs that "accompany specific life tasks including those shifts to a new cultural milieu that deprive a person of his 'cultural selfobjects,' during his mature years or when he has to deal with a *debilitating illness, or the confrontation with death*" (1984, p. 194, italics added).

Face 7: Twinship in trauma

Discussion of Kohut's psychology of being human, suggests that for Kohut, psychological trauma is not always as a consequence of an individual's experience of being isolated or alienated from others or society, but often in his experiencing himself as a non-human thing. As such, like our case material demonstrates in Chapter 5, the individual does not feel like a human being nor does he feel like a "being" connected to other human beings. Rather, the individual lives in a non-human world, surrounded by nothing or by non-human things.

Contemporary authors have discussed the need for twinship as a reaction to psychological trauma (Stolorow, 2009; Brothers, 2008). Stolorow (2009) regards "longing for twinship or emotional kinship as being reactive to emotional trauma" (p. 49). According to him, a longing for twinship is present when an individual experiences himself as shattered or destroyed by trauma. He states: "When I have been traumatized, my only hope for being deeply understood is to form a connection with a brother or sister who knows the same darkness" (p. 49). In contrast to Kohut, Stolorow (2009) does not always see twinship as an inherent human longing.

Brothers (2008) also discusses how psychological trauma destroys a sense of certainty in an individual. According to her, a traumatized individual no longer experiences the world as familiar, or meaningful, and he often creates dualities or dichotomies in which all people and things are categorized into one side or the other. She argues that an individual cannot tolerate feeling different to others whom he believes are essentially supposed to be in the same position as he is. Equally, he cannot bear any hints of sameness with others whom he identifies as divergent to himself. In this discussion, while Brothers recognizes that a loss of a sense of being a human being among other human beings leads to traumatization, she maintains that an individual's extreme need for a sense of kinship or a sense of sameness is often a secondary reaction to the trauma.

Considering Kohut's description from this perspective suggests that by the end of his life, Kohut's theory had changed from the psychoanalysis of self pathology to the psychoanalysis of pathology as a result of trauma. When individuals are traumatized, they will not experience themselves as being human among other human beings. Extreme attempts to experience a sense of essential alikeness to others will follow. If the effort fails, they are likely to experience themselves and others as non-human things. Such individuals lose "the symbol of human meaning, human warmth, human contact, human experience" (Kohut, 1984, p. 545n). Kohut probably saw the disruption of two faces of twinship here: an individual's strong need to recognize the similarity in others and a fundamental sense of being human among other human beings.

From the psychology of the self to the psychology of being human

Strozier (2001) claims that, in order to understand why Kohut needed to develop his self psychology, we have to understand the historical and social context in which he lived. When Kohut began to work, Strozier says many traditional psychoanalytic concepts—such as the Oedipus complex, repressed libidinal impulses, or guilt-laden psychopathology—had become less relevant because the historical context had changed. Most families, at least in Western developed countries, had become nuclear households. Fears of castration by paternal figures or being smothered by maternal figures had been replaced by feelings of loneliness and isolation or disconnection from other people. In such a society, an essential part of the pathology with which patients present includes a lack of vitality and a sense of feeling like a whole self, which is ideally supposed to be obtained through human contact.

The historical and social changes reflected in the transformation of psychoanalytic theory, and reciprocally, the theoretical changes in psychoanalysis that are reflected in historical and social changes, are evident in the changes we identify in the meaning of twinship in Kohut's theory. In our view, Brothers' (2008) trauma-centred perspective is fundamental to understanding the significance of twinship in our contemporary analytic work. We currently live in a world in which it is commonplace for people to experience themselves as not human and to be treated by others as non-human things. War and genocide are rampant globally. And in our work as analysts, we see that traumatic early experiences of parallel psychological magnitude are equally common.

For example, a female patient, who was sexually abused by her relatives in her childhood, referred to herself as a "toilet bowl." She experienced herself as an object into which someone's sexual impulses were disposed. She finally found a kind and warm man with whom she began to live. Immediately, she became depressed and anxious. To her therapist's query about what might have made her feel depressed, she answered, "because he treats me like a human being," which was not something she had ever experienced before; others had always treated her as a "thing" and she needed time to adjust. Her partner was concerned about how she felt in response to his attempts to, for example, engage her in selecting movies or TV programs to watch together and choosing meals at a restaurant. Such attempts to engage her in ordinary discourse were unfamiliar and made her feel anxious. In this context, what shattered her mind was not the fear of castration by an authority figure, an internalization of a bad object-representation, nor a lack of availability of others through whom she could experience herself as vital or whole; she was shattered by the unexpectedness and fear that came with this treatment. Being treated as a non-human thing by others whom she had come to also experience as non-human entities was the norm for her, and this new face of the other was terrifying—it was a lie.

This example suggests a need to explore how and through what process people come to experience themselves as non-human, surrounded by non-human things, and through what process people—like the patient just described—are paradoxically, afraid of the experience of themselves and others as human. The relationships, therefore, between the many faces of Kohut's twinship do need further elaboration and exploration to help us understand more fully the humanization of the self or the experience of being human in the world.

Chapter 2

A new dimension of twinship selfobject experience and transference

Koichi Togashi, Ph.D., L.P.

Kohut's (1984) original definition of twinship is "a need to experience the presence of essential alikeness" (p. 194). In other words, he addresses the twinship need as a patient's yearning for experiencing himself as like his analyst, or as a patient's yearning for experiencing his analyst as like himself. Although I view this as the essential dimension of twinship, I contend that Kohut's (1984) definition needs to be expanded to include the patient's yearning for a sense that the analyst recognizes herself or himself in the patient. This new dimension of the twinship experience may also be stated as a patient's need to experience that an analyst recognizes the essential element of his or her own subjectivity in a patient.

Knowing myself to be like someone else and experiencing him or her as recognizing himself or herself in me are subjectively very different. I developed this notion through my own training analysis with a self psychologist in the United States, who is himself an immigrant from Europe. In my analysis, twinship was the most important subject as regards my personal background and my acculturation in the wake of my moving from Japan to the United States. My analyst and I found that Kohut's (1984) original definition of twinship did not always capture my subjective experience. In many instances, my sense of twinship was established around my need for my analyst to recognize himself in me, rather than around my need to experience myself in him. In the circumstance where it is obvious to me that my analyst's background is different from mine in many areas, although not all, I sometimes found myself experiencing myself as being like him; but I felt this longing could not be fully met unless I was convinced of my analyst's finding himself in me.

I contend that the two twinship selfobject needs, *Like-to-feel-we-are-alike* and *Can-you-find-yourself-in-me*,[1] should be differentiated in our clinical practice because they require an analyst to look toward the two different selfobject functions, and thus to provide two different interpretations. Although previous self-psychological literature suggests the reciprocity of twinship experiences expressed as Like-to-feel-we-are-alike, the researchers neither address this new dimension as an independent need, nor do they sufficiently pay attention to the reciprocity of this new dimension of twinship needs. The two needs are related and nested, but they represent two different kinds of transference. I provide two clinical examples after reviewing relevant literature.

Historical overview of twinship

Kohut (1971) originally addresses the twinship, or alter-ego, transference as a subcategory or a special form of mirror transference. As Kohut's thinking develops, he (Kohut, 1984) comes to view the twinship need as an independent selfobject need, and gives the twinship transference equal status with mirroring and idealizing transferences.

Kohut (1984) describes a female patient who has a fantasy of a genie in a bottle and who experiences this genie as "someone just like herself" (p. 196). She can talk to and keep company with the genie anytime she wants to, and she can "survive the hours of loneliness when she felt that no one other than her companion in the bottle cared for her" (p. 196). The uniqueness of this patient's experience is that her need is "for a silent presence" (p. 196). She could talk to the genie, but the genie did not have to respond to her. "Being together with the twin in silent communication was often the most satisfactory state" (p. 196). So, what kinds of interaction does she fantasize unconsciously that she and the genie have in this silent state? At the core of her unconscious fantasy, how does she believe the genie experiences her?

If we interpret her subjective experience in the light of my hypothesis, we could say that, in her unconscious fantasy, this patient experiences the interaction of two types of needs—a need to experience the genie as essentially alike and a need to experience that the genie recognizes itself in her. Kohut (1984) writes, "her self was sustained simply by the presence of someone she knew was sufficiently like her to understand her and to be understood by her" (p. 196). In this fantasy, I believe, she knows herself to be like the genie and she fantasizes that the genie recognizes the essential elements of the genie in her.

Kohut (1984) expands the twinship experience to include the most basic sense of existing in human society, and he addresses the twinship experience as a "confirmation of the feeling that one is a human being among other human beings" (p. 200).

The sense of being human among humans cannot be established by an individual unless he or she experiences that other members of a group perceive themselves in him or her. The concept of selfobject in itself includes the notion that there is a reciprocity and mutuality of twinship needs between people in the intersubjective context. However, as far as I can tell, Kohut (1971, 1984) does not make explicit in his definition of twinship this reciprocal, mutual dimension that I propose. Kohut's (1971, 1984) view of twinship merely covers a patient's or an analyst's need to experience the analyst or the patient as alike—that is, the need to identify the other as having a similar or identical subjectivity. He does not sufficiently address how a patient attempts to establish a secure twinship tie with an analyst who the patient feels possesses a differently formed subjectivity.

The same is true of authors in the post-Kohut era, who study the reciprocity of a twinship experience in a human relationship. White and Weiner (1986) argue that "the essence of the twinship selfobject relationship is a similarity in interests and talents, along with the sense of being understood by someone like oneself" (p. 103). Basch (1994) prefers the term "kinship transference" to the twinship transference, and redefines it as "the need to belong and feel accepted by one's cohort" (p. 4). Livingston (1998) states that "examples of twinship in later life are also easily found in two concert lovers sitting quietly together and listening or two writers sharing their thoughts in a mutually stimulating discussion" (p. 58). Although these authors certainly address the usefulness of the mutual interaction of twinship experiences, they do not sufficiently explore the twinship need expressed as Can-you-find-yourself-in-me, nor do they address the importance of distinguishing the two different twinship needs.

The vertical relationship in Japanese culture

Why have these researchers not differentiated the two twinship needs? I believe this is a cultural bias that originates in a perspective provided by North American culture in which a sense of kinship tends to be organized between individuals who belong to the same or similar social rank.

Nakane (1972), a social anthropologist, explores the difference between the structure of kinship relations in Japanese culture and that found in North American culture. Nakane divides the essential relationships into two categories: vertical and horizontal. She asserts that, whereas the horizontal relationship is dominant in North American culture, the vertical relationship predominates in Japan.

In a horizontal culture, individuals who are of the same social rank develop a sense of kinship with each other, and any conflict of interest arises between individuals in different social ranks. For example, a sense of kinship between workers is stronger than that between an employer and a worker. In contrast, in a vertical culture based on a hierarchical social system, the sense of kinship between individuals who belong to different social ranks is stronger than that between individuals of a similar rank, and a conflict of interest tends to arise between individuals who are of a similar social rank, rather than between individuals who are in different ranks. Parent–child, employer–employee, and teacher–student relationships are examples of vertical relationships.

From a self-psychological perspective, this vertical relationship could be theorized as a culturally unique form of a mutual selfobject tie. Although this relationship often contains an aspect of an idealizing or mirroring selfobject tie, the essential aspect of this relationship is a twinship selfobject experience.

For the Japanese, who are always exposed to the differences between people in their ranks or roles in a hierarchical culture, it is crucial to make certain that the other person who is in a higher rank than his recognizes himself or herself in him first. Otherwise, the effort to find himself in the higher-ranking person may be experienced as an act of submission to a superior person.

Taketomo's (1989) study of what he refers to as "teacher transference" includes this type of twinship connection, although he does not argue this from a self-psychological perspective. Taketomo, a Japanese psychiatrist and psychoanalyst who lives in the United States, describes in his article a traumatic experience in his adolescence. Despite his strong motivation to study philosophy at university, his father, a famous Japanese poet, refused to allow him to do so. Instead, his father insisted that he study natural science. In other words, Taketomo was traumatized by his father's failure to allow him to experience that his father recognized himself in his son.

What helped Taketomo to restore his injured self was his conviction that his teachers experienced a special concern for him. In relationships with these teachers, he sensed their caring for him and their trusting him. Through their reassurance, he developed a yearning to be worthy of his teachers' care and trust.

Taketomo (1989) had a similar transference to his analyst: "I wanted to be worthy of his care and trust" (p. 431). He attributes a prototype of these feelings to his relationship with his grandfather, with whom he shares a twinship selfobject fantasy. By his grandfather, who "tried to duplicate his own experience" (p. 443) through him, Taketomo was taught Japanese philosophy, Japanese calligraphy, a few Chinese classics, and Japanese history written in classical Chinese, before he began school. Taketomo's self was sustained by a selfobject fantasy in which the teachers and his grandfather recognized essential elements of their subjectivity in him first.

Amae, which is a unique type of mentality in Japanese culture, illustrated by a Japanese psychoanalyst, Doi (1962, 1981, 1986), also contains a child's yearning for a parent to recognize herself in the child. Amae is the term that the Japanese use to refer to an individual's presumption of a right to another's favors; it originates, according to Doi (1962, 1981), in a need for "passive" love or care. It is "an emotion that takes the other person's love for granted" (1981, p. 168). As Doi (1981) states, despite his classical formulation, "The prototype of amae is the infant's desire to be close to its mother, who, it has come vaguely to realize, is a separate existence from itself, then one may perhaps describe amae as, ultimately, an attempt psychologically to deny the fact of separation from the mother" (p. 75); in amae, an interaction is, in this sense, established within a mutually shared selfobject fantasy.

Here is an orthodox example of a Japanese couple using the term amae. A friend of mine went to a zoo with her five-year-old son. They watched the animals all day. On their way home, she found her son throwing a glance at her face. The boy did not say anything, but she recognized through his eyes that he was very tired and wanted her to carry him on her back. So, she did this without asking if he wanted her to do so. Her husband heard about this later and said, "I think that you should have taught him to express what he wanted. Otherwise, you should not have given him a piggyback ride, because he is no longer a little baby who is allowed to show such amae." Her answer was, "No. He is just five years old, and he needs amae still."

What kind of interaction might this boy experience in this shared fantasy? I suggest that the essential aspect of this relationship is a shared belief that the boy's mother recognizes herself in his need. The boy does not verbalize his need. For this boy, in this relationship, the mother has to do something first. It is the boy who has a need, but in his fantasy he changes its psychological role and needs to believe that the first person to find this need is his mother rather than himself. Through his mother's action, the boy can be convinced of his mother's recognizing herself in his need before he finds himself in the need.

I do not contend here that the new dimension of twinship experience is a uniquely Japanese phenomenon, but I emphasize that my finding of this dimension of twinship is deeply related to my cultural background. In my analysis, the differentiation between my analyst and me was obvious in many senses: age, culture, appearance, language, social standing, and so on. Yet, I found myself experiencing myself as like him in the transference; and then I immediately raised the question with myself, as I usually do in relationships with Japanese people, "What aspect of himself does he see in me?" Unless I confirmed that he had found himself in me, my recognition that I experienced myself as like him would not be confirmed. To establish a sense of twinship with a person who possesses a separate subjectivity, the primal issue with me was whether the person found himself in me rather than whether I could experience him as like myself.

Clinical illustrations

All therapeutic work in the following clinical cases was conducted in Japanese, and the quotations are my English translations of the original Japanese.

Ken

Ken is a handsome and brilliant Japanese male student in his early twenties. I had seen him in the United States for three years on a once-a-week basis. He came to the United States to pursue his undergraduate study in computer science.

He entered therapy because of paranoid tendencies. On a bulletin board he found a piece of paper with a facial caricature of an Asian male and a few derogatory comments about Asians. He became suspicious that someone did it to make fun of him. He went to his mentor to ask him if he could determine who might be responsible for it. He was referred to me for psychotherapy, but he insisted that his interest was only "to find the person who drew the caricature."

Despite his suspicion about the effectiveness of psychotherapy, Ken demonstrated an emotional attachment to me immediately. It is interesting to note that he avoided bringing his own unique experiences and feelings into therapy. Instead, he limited his topics to his daily activities outside of the university, such as drinking with his friends at a bar and joining an amateur baseball club. He preferred to talk about music, movies, or TV shows of my generation rather than of his generation.

Although his interest was in finding some differences between his experience and mine, he was more interested in fantasizing that I found myself in him, through his stories and talking. In Japan, a stereotypically shared image of university students is that they do not study very hard. Rather, it is assumed that they actively engage in group activities instead of studying. The stories Ken brought into his therapy sessions fitted this stereotypical image, perhaps because he thought I could find in them my own similar experiences in college. When I reminisced about my own personal stories as conveyed in a movie and briefly mentioned them to him, he always listened to me with a facial expression of calmness. As long as he felt confident in his belief that I recognized myself in his descriptions, he did not become suspicious about the effectiveness of therapy and kept talking to me enthusiastically.

Then, one day, I learned he was doing well in his university activities, and he was quite successful as a freelance software designer. I found myself very curious about his outstanding performance in these areas, and I was proud of him. I said, "I am very impressed with your good performance. Don't you think that it indicates your unusual talents in computer design?" With a disappointed look, however, he answered laconically, "Maybe."

My further questions about software design frustrated him. He showed his disappointment in me by changing the topic during the session as well as by sudden cancellations of appointments. I recognized this problem was caused by my curiosity about his unique experiences, which

I had never experienced before. If, even by a single misstep, I showed an interest in his original experiences, he wondered whether I might have seen him in a different way than I see myself.

Up to this point, my understanding of the transference had been based on Kohut's (1984) original definition of twinship. I asked Ken if he might feel disappointed in me because he no longer felt that I was similar to him. He denied my suggestion in a definite manner by saying, "It does not make sense to me. I feel similar to you. We are living in the United States, and I am pursuing a professional job just as you do." As we continued to talk, he became increasingly disinterested. Irritated, he said, "Your question is strange, because anytime I want to, I would feel that you are similar to me." This statement indicated that the issue was not *his* willingness, but his feeling about *my* willingness.

After this session, Ken's suspicions about the necessity of psychotherapy were revived. He stopped talking about himself and became suspicious that I was trying to make him someone with the same thoughts as me. He then started to talk about a male friend, who was four years older than he—his *sempai*.

The Japanese word sempai means "senior" or "superior," as in an academic or corporate organization in Japanese society. The counterpart term is *kohai*, meaning "junior" in rank or standing. Japanese students encounter their first sempai in junior or senior high school when they enroll, and they believe this relationship lasts after their graduation. This relationship extends to their personal life as well. Whereas kohai are often expected to obey their sempai at some cost to their personal welfare, sempai assume a corresponding obligation. Once the two establish this relationship, they fantasize that they are bound to it by fate.

One central aspect of this relationship is a culturally systematized social system for disseminating it. Sempai themselves have their own sempai. The sempai–kohai relationship is perpetuated from one generation to the next. If we focus on a kohai's subjective experience, we may say that a kohai expects a sempai to share the kohai's experiences by revealing a sempai's own similar experiences in the past as well as to provide guidance regarding the kohai's formal and personal life. A kohai wishes to have a sense that a sempai is thrilled to have a kohai who has a similar spirit, and is delighted to hand his experiences and skills on to a kohai.

Ken repeatedly told me that his sempai took care of him on many occasions, although the sempai sometimes manipulated him in a sadistic manner. I asked him to describe what might make him feel the sempai was so special to him, and he stated, "The sempai sensed the same odor[2] in me first." He added that he would not have felt secure if the sempai had not showed his willingness to become his sempai to him.

For Ken, it was of primary importance to have a sense that his sempai or his analyst wanted to recognize himself in Ken first, rather than that he should experience his sempai or analyst as his twin. My looking toward his need to experience me as alike without recognizing this need led only to his fear that I was trying to make him my clone. We can see here that Kohut's (1984) original definition of a twinship need was not an experience-near description for him.

One day, Ken began to talk about an episode in his childhood when his father gave his older brother an electric razor as a gift, whereas his father gave him a toy. His father, a software designer who runs a computer system consultation office in Japan, sees the brother as a successor who could manage the father's business. In his earliest memories, Ken said, his father compared him with his brother and kept saying that Ken looked like his mother. Although he realized that his mother was proud of his resemblance to her, he felt sad about his feeling that his father did not recognize any similarity to him.

Ken recognized that his father was delighted at his choosing to major in computer science at the university and proud of his success in freelance software design. However, this recognition was not a delight for him. He knew these successes did not change his father's view that Ken did not have something his father had. His brother was still seen by the father as the person who would take over the business. In these circumstances, even if Ken became successful in this area, Ken's effort to be like his father would be experienced by him only as a submission to his father. His analyst's paying attention to his need to experience his analyst as alike was a retraumatization for him.

Our exploring and sharing his feeling about this story changed our therapeutic interaction dramatically. His story reminded me of a similar experience. In my childhood I had a fantasy that a significant person experienced me as alike. However, as far as I know, he had never seen me in that way. This countertransference made it easy for me to experience and recognize myself in many aspects of Ken's story.

Although I did not reveal my own experiences to Ken—and he did not want to hear about how I perceived him—he indicated that he felt secure in our relationship. One day, in a diffident manner, Ken told me a story about being asked about me by his friends. He had answered them with a prideful feeling: "My therapist is something like a sempai of life. He seems to have had experiences similar to mine." We finally shared the recognition that he would not feel secure *unless* he developed confidence in his belief that I recognize myself in him.

I emphasize that Ken has experienced a type of twinship selfobject *milieu*. His father's profession is in computer science. To become like his father, Ken aims at having a profession in computer science or in a related area. In other words, Ken was the little boy who works next to his father in the basement (Kohut, 1984) and experiences a certain type of twinship connection to his father. However, this little boy's need was not fully met because he lacked a conviction that his father recognized himself in the boy. For Ken to have an assured sense of twinship with me, I had to understand and empathize with his yearning for a sense that I experienced myself in him.

Ryoko

Ryoko is an unmarried Japanese female whom I have seen for eight-and-a-half years on a twice-a-week basis. For the first four-and-a-half years, I practiced in Japan, and she appeared for analysis in person. After my departure from Japan, we continued to work together over the phone between the United States and Japan.

When Ryoko first sought psychotherapy, she was an undergraduate student in her early twenties. She complained that she always felt isolated and alienated from her family. She had no substantial communication with any family members and became conflicted about her mother. For no apparent reason, she became agitated with her mother's talking to her. No matter what her mother said, she responded to her in a blunt or angry manner.

For the first three years of analysis, Ryoko evolved a stable idealizing transference. She completed her undergraduate program in a mental health field and started to work for an organization as an assistant to mental health professionals. In this context, she found it difficult to tell me about the emotional experiences of her daily life. She stopped speaking about herself and started to ask me to say something to relieve her discomfort.

Very often, even at the very beginning of a session, she claimed, "There are a few things I want to tell you today. But I won't tell you. I want you to make me feel more at ease in sessions." I questioned her about how uneasy she was and how this made her feel. She replied, "I feel insecure. That's all. I cannot tell you anything further." When I asked her to describe her feelings to me or to talk about our relationship in that session or in previous sessions, she said, "Please do not try to relate my feelings to you or our relationship." Neither she nor I found a reasonable answer as to where this therapeutic impasse originated. This stalemate lasted for about six months.

One day, she began talking about a colleague who handled psychotic patients mechanically. She was upset by this and asked her boss to arrange a meeting to discuss how different workers treated their patients. She emphasized that she wanted patients to be treated empathically and humanely. In the middle of this discourse, she suddenly stopped talking and asked me, "Do you think what I did was strange?" I asked her to tell me how she felt at that time. She paid no attention to my request, and she insisted that I answer her.

At first, I said, "I think your feelings and behavior are very understandable. I understand your wish to provide empathic treatment for these patients. What you did is not wrong." She quickly disagreed and said, "I did not ask you if I was wrong. I wonder if you feel I am strange." The anger in her voice did not allow me to resist her question: "No, I don't think you are strange." She replied suspiciously, "Are you sure?" I answered, "Yes. I am sure. If I were you, I would experience your colleague in a similar way, and I would deal with the situation in a similar way." It is interesting to note that she immediately became calm—this statement seemed to be the answer that she was waiting for. I finally recognized that the main issue between the two of us was a twinship experience, and she agreed with this.

My leaving Japan for the United States and our use of phone sessions made her anxious. She occasionally expressed her wish to terminate therapy. We frequently discussed her sense of isolation and loneliness, which she believed was caused by our living in different countries.

At this point, a key phrase for both of us in understanding her anxiety was "living in different countries." When she fell into a panicky state, I always used this key phrase to tell her that her anxiety was caused by a rupture of our twinship tie. Ryoko also used this phrase, and never objected to my using it; but she insisted that the term did not fully explain her feelings. I tried to explore the meaning of "not fully," but she was unable to explain it clearly. One day, she brought to me a dream that was full of anxiety. She described it as follows:

> I give birth to a baby. It is strange because my belly is not large with a child. My figure is normal. The baby is low in birth weight and looks weak. My friend also gives birth to a baby. She looks very happy. I am not envious. Rather I feel happy somehow, too. But I feel confused, because she looks at me with a facial expression of feeling sorry for me.

Ryoko told me the friend had always been her twin. Since high school, the friend had been her best friend. She was the only female friend she had who was not married yet. Because Ryoko thought that the friend shared the same psychic position as her, she was afraid the friend would find someone to whom she wanted to get married before Ryoko did. She began crying and said, "My feelings mean nothing if she does not experience me the same way I experience her! I should not have felt anything before I made sure how she saw me!"

This dream provided an answer to the question as to why our key phrase—"living in different countries"—did not fully cover her sense of isolation and loneliness. What was missing in our relationship was not a circumstance that we could share the same experience, but her conviction that I had to be willing to recognize myself in her. She was sure that she experienced herself as like me. Although our key phrase captured the rupture of a twinship experience, it did not appropriately address the type of twinship need she yearned for with me. As I shared this understanding, she replied, "Yes. How could you feel secure in an environment in which people do not find themselves in you?"

Soon afterward, she revealed a secret: she wanted to become a clinical psychologist like me. Although this thought had come to mind many times in our sessions, she had not verbalized it. Why had she not dared to tell me about it? She said, "I knew that you would be happy if I told you I experienced you as similar or wanted to do the same thing as you do. But

I had to see how you experienced me first. I wanted you to experience me as like you before I told you. Otherwise, my feeling similar to you would have made it seem that I was complying with your wishes."

Ryoko's divorced mother teaches traditional Chinese arts. When Ryoko was a child, she learned these art forms from her mother and fantasized about becoming a teacher like her mother. She believed her mother was delighted by her engaging in the same field, and felt they were on the same wavelength in these customs at that time. However, her mother was ambivalent toward Ryoko. She often criticized Ryoko by saying, "You are so different. Whose genes do you have?" Another time, her mother made fun of her by sarcastically saying, "I know you want to be like me." Even if she constantly perceived her mother as essentially alike, her twinship could not become secure *unless* she felt confident that her mother constantly recognized herself in Ryoko.

Discussion and conclusion

I have presented my hypothesis that there is a new and additional dimension of a twinship selfobject need: a patient yearns for a sense that the analyst recognizes himself or herself in the patient; namely, the need for "Can-you-find-yourself-in-me?" My clinical examples confirm the validity of this hypothesis and establish that this dimension of twinship and Kohut's (1984) original definition are related, and that they represent two different dimensions of the twinship transference. They should be strictly differentiated in our clinical practice because we are required to look toward the two different selfobject functions, and thus to provide two different interpretations.

Although previous self-psychological literature has studied the mutuality of twinship selfobject experiences, this notion is not always sufficient for an analyst to capture a patient's unconscious need in a twinship experience. My two case vignettes demonstrate that an analyst is not able to sufficiently understand a patient's experience unless he or she pays attention to a patient's yearning for the analyst's recognizing himself or herself in the patient. The analyst's paying attention to the original twinship need without the knowledge of this new dimension can lead to retraumatization.

Both clinical vignettes illustrate that the new dimension of a twinship experience is developmentally and functionally more primal than the twinship that Kohut (1984) originally described. Both Ken and Ryoko wanted to be sure that the analyst found himself in them before they could allow themselves to experience a twinship transference. In both cases, the rupture of this dimension of twinship led to a sense of alienation and to the loss of a basic sense of security. Lacking a conviction that the other found him or her in them, they were not able to experience themselves as a human being among other human beings.

In the ideal situation, a baby is delivered into an environment in which his or her parents look forward to finding themselves in the baby. The parents are thrilled to discuss an infant's similarities to themselves. They look for the features or traits of a new baby that are similar to their own. Even parents who have adopted a baby enjoy recognizing some elements of their personalities in the child. This dimension of twinship is the essential source of the selfobject milieu where a child feels like a human being among other human beings. In other words, this milieu is a *sine qua non* for an individual's feeling himself or herself as a human being.

This finding is consistent with the understanding among recent self psychologists that twinship is the most basic and primal selfobject phenomenon. Gorney (1998) states, "The full import of twinship derives from a fundamental and inextricable experience of intersubjectivity that underpins the entire human trajectory, from the first breath of birth to the last heartbeat of death" (p. 87). As Ulman and Paul (1992) have stated, "We view humanization, that is, the developmental process of coming to feel human, as a selfobject function of twinship" (p. 111); they regard the twinship selfobject environment as the most primal source of humanization. Wada (1998) describes his experience of moving to the United States from Japan for his psychoanalytic training and reveals that the lack of a twinship experience led to a very painful state of alienation.

Finding yourself in the other and experiencing that the other finds himself in you are the most essential facets of humanization. In any types of discrimination and in many artificial tragedies such as war, genocide, and hate crimes, people refuse to find themselves in others. How is it possible that we should bomb people in whom we find ourselves?

On the issue of recognizing that his own and the other's subjectivities are differently formed, referring to the work of Tonnesvang (2002), in her thoughtful discussion at the Conference on the Psychology of the Self in Chicago, Martinez (2006) posits that this new dimension of twinship is a mature form of selfobject experience on the developmental trajectory of the twinship selfobject. Martinez (2006) states:

> We can posit a continuum of twinship experience that reaches across the level of self, from undifferentiated, unarticulated longing for alikeness to more mature selective, necessarily reciprocated affirmations of alikeness. I would see his yearning for his analyst to find himself in him as emerging from a second-order self, a self that recognizes the separate subjectivity of the other and yearns for the exquisite connection of alikeness with that distinct and separate self.
> (Martinez, 2006, p. 10)

A second-order self is the most mature form of self in Bertelesen's (1996) conceptualization of the three developmental levels of the self: zero, first, and second orders. The zero-order self refers to the newborn infant's basic strivings for connectedness that is not yet differentiated, articulated, and integrated enough to form a cohesive self. The first-order self is the self as adequately differentiated, articulated, and integrated enough to connect with a specific selfobject milieu, but the self lives this connectedness without reflecting on or choosing it. The second order is the higher organizational level, which has a reflective and volitional relationship to its own ambitions; in it an individual can truly choose an adequate selfobject milieu and strive toward and idealize his or her own ambitions and ideals. Tonnesvang (2002), referring to this concept, names the selfobject relationship formed in the second-order self as a *selfsubject* relationship, which "refers to those mature and symmetrical experiences of self-sustaining others that imply the experience of the other as an independent center of initiative and perception" (p. 158).

I agree with the understanding that recognizing the new dimension of twinship experience requires an individual to have a more "sophisticated" level of perception; he or she has to have enough to be aware of his or her own subjectivity and the separate subjectivity of the other. However, I do not necessarily view this new dimension of twinship as emerging from a more developmentally "mature" or "high-order" form of the self on the continuum of its developmental trajectory. The understanding that being aware of his or her own and the other's subjectivity is mature includes in itself a cultural viewpoint that originates in a perspective provided by

North American culture in which people believe that the ideal goal of psychological development is the recognition of the difference between his or her subjectivity and the other's.

My clinical vignettes indicate that the need expressed as Can-you-find-yourself-in-me can come from any level of the self on the developmental trajectory. Both Ken and Ryoko sometimes retreated to an archaic state and yearned for the undifferentiated and unarticulated connectedness. Ryoko's requesting me to immediately relieve her discomfort would be an example of this. Even in that context, she needed to have an environment that provided her with a confirmation that her analyst found himself in her.

Recognizing that his or her subjectivity and the other's are differently formed does not immediately mean that the person's self is mature enough to experience the other as an independent center of initiative. An individual's cognitive capability for recognizing his or her own subjectivity and the other's subjectivity is different from the maturity of the self.

From a relational perspective, discussing the rapprochement phase in female development, Benjamin (1991) illustrates mutual recognition between a child and a father. She states that a child's identification with the father "is not merely an internal structure, it is a relationship in which the subject recognizes herself or himself in the other" (p. 277). Viewing this notion "as an important bridge between classical theory and self-psychological theory with respect to this important stage of development," Kieffer (2004) understands this concept to be a selfobject experience organized under "the notion of self and other, in which each is integrated with the other, and yet autonomous" (p. 79). My discussion of the new dimension of twinship experience could be addressed as the primal and elemental aspect in this mutual recognition.

Note

1 "Can-you-find-yourself-in-me" is owed to Dr. Diane Lawson Martinez, who made this remark in her thoughtful discussion of this article at the 29th International Conference on the Psychology of the Self, in Chicago, October 28, 2006.
2 "Sense the same odor in someone" is a Japanese expression meaning that one experiences himself or herself in someone else. It is the equivalent in English of "having the same spirit." This expression is rarely verbalized between two people who are in this relationship. The Japanese prefer to value this tie in silent communication.

Chapter 3

Twinship and "otherness"

A self-psychological, intersubjective approach to "difference"

Amanda Kottler, M.A. (Clin. Psych.)

Contemporary self psychologists and relational theorists are currently saying much more than ever before about countertransference and its impact on the work of psychoanalytic psychotherapists. Innovative, creative, and courageous papers have appeared in the literature in which authors disclose aspects of themselves and their selfobject needs in an attempt to demonstrate the effects that their own dynamics have on the way in which therapies unfold. This has also been true of psychotherapists using intersubjectivity theory, who note the significance of the broader context in which each therapy takes place. Those of us who have been able to recognize, in these papers, needs similar to our own will know how they have provided us with a great deal of affirming twinship selfobject experiences that are immensely important to our work.

There is in this literature a conspicuous gap. Few of these pioneering authors have focused on the influence that their own "difference" and therefore their membership of what I shall refer to as a "disadvantaged (supposedly minority) group" against which prejudice is directed, has on their work as therapists. Acknowledging this gap is particularly vital in a country like South Africa, from where this chapter originates, but it also needs addressing globally.

The absence of literature of this kind is not surprising. To engage at this level requires authors to be relatively resolved and comfortable not only with their particular brand of "difference," per se but also with admitting that it is a site of struggle in their professional lives. Nevertheless, the fact is that the paucity deprives colleagues who can identify with this kind of marginalized status, of a range of sorely needed mirroring and twinship selfobject experiences. Said differently, the scarcity deprives therapists of important reciprocal exchanges with fellow professionals (Abramowitz, 2001).

The absence is partly what motivated this chapter. While living and working in South Africa—where one is aware of marginalized groups more acutely—I should perhaps have reflected on working with issues of race, but I decided to focus elsewhere—on another of my own sites of "difference," that of being a lesbian therapist. This should not detract from the fact that much of what I say does not only relate to difficulties that homosexual therapists encounter.[1]

My choice to come out of the closet, so to speak, does not mean that such exposure is comfortable. It is noteworthy that the material used relates to work with a gay male patient rather than a lesbian and that some of the material was first presented at a self psychology conference in North America two years before presenting it to colleagues at home. Certainly, this has to do with a relatively widespread naïve understanding of homosexuality. Attitudes remain largely unchanged, even though South Africa is the only country in the world whose constitution gives homosexuals rights equal to any other citizen in the country, and it is fast becoming internationally recognized as a lesbian and gay center. "Homo-prejudice"[2] nevertheless continues to be alive and well. In South Africa, for example, shared membership of medical aid schemes and reduced university fees for partners require an outing process, which is potentially shaming and therefore not necessarily a choice that the member partner would ordinarily want to make. It also shares the following with the United States, where: "basic adult relationship affirming rituals—family celebrated dating, ... weddings, ... shared retirement benefits and assumed rights of survivorship either are still not considered normative, or occur with extra hardship" (Abramowitz, 2001, p. 1).

This chapter illustrates how the invisibility gives rise to the multiple and contradictory ways in which each of us can inhabit our gender and sexuality and how and why some of these shifts, at least in relation to gender and sexuality, occur. In so doing, I draw on Mitchell's (1993) idea of multiple selves, but more specifically on the postmodern concepts of "discourses" and "discursive practices."

Used in this context, a discourse reflects a set of attitudes, meanings, and beliefs that play a part in influencing the way in which individuals behave in a range of contexts. Discourses therefore make available varied behavior, or discursive practices, which, in turn, shape subjectivity. This is achieved by foregrounding some areas of experience or knowledge, and by creating gaps or silences in others (Davies and Harre, 1990 in Kottler and Swartz, 1995, p. 184). In a slightly more simplified way, discursive practices are similar to Brandchaft's (2001) patterns of attachment behavior or what the intersubjectivists refer to as organizing principles (Brandchaft, 1995, p. 94). Whatever terminology is used, an individual's subjectivity, their behavior, and beliefs about how the world works is a product of: (1) his or her history; (2) the positions each has taken up in particular discourses; and (3) the psychological investment each has had and still has, in taking up these particular positions (Hollway, 1984, p. 238). Individuals, having identified themselves with a particular subject position, "inevitably see the world from the vantage point of that position" (Davies and Harre, 1990 in Kottler and Swartz, 1995, p. 184). A gay, black, Muslim, Jewish, or disabled person then would see the world from the vantage point of being gay, black, Muslim, Jewish, or disabled and a straight or non-gay person will see the world from the vantage point of being straight or not gay. An individual may, however, be positioned within multiple discourses in unpredictable and often contradictory ways. For example, as the clinical material will illustrate, being gay might have different meanings within the discursive practices of heterosexuality, masculinity, or femininity. Our sense of self is elaborated in terms of a series of dichotomous categories, which serve to include us in some groups, e.g. as homosexuals, and exclude us "automatically" from others, e.g. a gay man from being masculine. Gender, sexuality, race, and religion are four such categories, and whether we like it or not, the complex discursive practices surrounding our gender, sexuality, race, religion, or disability shape every social encounter, including our therapeutic encounters.

Complicating things further, it is noteworthy that the positions we occupy in discourses are not simply determined in any rational, conscious, or unitary way, for example, because of biological sex. Discursive practices associated with discourses play a part in influencing which position may be filled by which gender or which sexuality at any particular time. Choices are therefore largely socially constructed and the ways in which they are given expression vary depending on the individual's emotional commitment in being there, for whatever reason. There is always some payoff or protection for the choice and a reason for taking up the chosen position (Hollway, 1984). This is true even though the take-up position might seem irrational and, in terms of other consequences, satisfaction might seem inexplicable. This is evident in the material presented, which draws attention to the effects of the shame involved in being homosexual and how psychologically debilitating it can be to have to try to "pass" as heterosexual, to one's sense of (homosexual) self, one's (homosexual) sense of reality, integrity, and self cohesion. The material also points to the psychologically damaging effects of the need to "pass" in an attempt to accommodate to what I shall refer to as society's pathology. I am referring to the dominant discourse that endorses "heterosexuality as the norm".[3]

Briefly, before going on to the clinical material, I shall contextualize the theories used in this chapter. I come from a very rigid background where ideas or concepts were black or white, true or not true. I was expected to either like or dislike something. There was no room for uncertainty and even less for changing my mind. In my fourth year at university (which was my sixth in therapy) as a mature student and following a change in career from accountant with a multi-national oil company, I discovered social constructionism, postmodernism, and feminist theories. These theories radically destabilized all that I had believed about the way in which the world and everyone in it worked. I recognized myself in them and realized that other possibilities were open to me, and the way I could live my life. The theories changed my experience of, and consequently, the nature of my own personal therapy, and they each inform my daily practice with my own patients. This is illustrated in the material presented.

At the time of these discoveries, I was drawing on Object Relations and Kleinian psychoanalytic theory, which had begun to feel inadequate and wrong for me. At around this time a prominent self psychologist (the late Peter Thompson) visited relatives in South Africa and gave a few public lectures. Discovering self psychology significantly shifted my understanding of my own and my patients' struggles both in relating to and being in the world. It, together with the theories mentioned above, made me realize that different views or perspectives were possible. And, finally, my discovery of intersubjectivity theory provided me with an overarching context within which to link postmodernism, feminist theory, and psychoanalytic self psychology. The combination made me realize that "empathic resonance was available in the world." It was clearly a twinship experience for me—it confirmed for me the feeling that I was, after all, "a human being among other human beings"—the hallmark of Kohut's (1984) idea of twinship. I had come to "see something about the world that was not visible to me before: that something existed which did not seem to exist in my experience before" (Gehrie, 2002, p. 19). This is, according to Kohut (in Gehrie, 2002, p. 17) part of the analytic cure and one of the results of an analyst's empathic understanding. I believe I managed to help Franco whose case material follows in this way. This, disguised, material illustrates many of the issues raised above.

As I started working on this chapter, I became increasingly aware of how Kohut's (1984) concept of twinship was enmeshed in both the therapy itself and the content of this chapter at a number of different levels. I had gently led Franco on a journey very similar to one I had taken so many years earlier—one in which he began to experience the presence of others essentially like himself and thus to feel that he was "a human being among other human beings" (Kohut, 1984). I believe Franco's ride was much smoother than my own with a non-lesbian therapist, and a significantly quicker one. I think this was partly because of the way in which I integrated intersubjectivity, feminist and self theory with postmodern ideas, including the contemporary literature focusing on the notion of multiple selves and the multiple ways in which we inhabit these varied selves. But, it was also because of the presence of an essential dimension of the twinship experience, only implicit in Kohut's (1984) idea and therefore needing much further theorizing, i.e. that, as suggested in Chapter 2, the therapist "recognizes herself in the patient" (Togashi, 2006, p. 1). In this sense, using Togashi's (2006) additional dimension of Kohut's unfinished conceptualization—clearly because I had traveled this path myself—meant that there was an important and significant reciprocal, mutual dimension to this therapy.

Clinical material

Franco's mother referred him to me. He was not at all sure about what therapy could offer. At the time, he was living with his mother, stepfather, and a younger half-sister. When he entered therapy, he was extremely depressed and had been for a considerable time. He spent most of his days in bed, sleeping. At night, he watched TV. A few months before I saw him, he had applied to a local college to study in the hospitality industry, partly, he said initially, in the hope of meeting other gay men. Acceptance was dependent on the quality of a complex project for which Franco had no energy, and dreading doing.

On the upside, Franco occasionally went out with his half-sister to raves. He loved trance music and told me later in the therapy that he sometimes dreamed of becoming a DJ at one of the local trance clubs. When he told me about this, he became unusually articulate and quite animated. This was in direct contrast to our many silent and tortuous sessions in which he said little. I had to work extremely hard with him, initially because he was so insufferably self-conscious and shy. He hardly made any eye contact. He spoke with his face cast downwards and eyes focused firmly on the floor. From time to time, he would raise his eyes and furtively look at me through his relatively short cropped hair. He spoke in short, sharp, almost incoherent sentences peppered with the words "you know" and "like." While still communicating in this way, I discovered that he had had one, in his words, "horrible" sexual experience with a fellow waiter a year earlier. It had ended with a reluctant "outing" of Franco at the restaurant where they both worked. This had shamed Franco terribly partly because, at the time, he was not at all sure he was gay. Feeling betrayed, Franco left the restaurant immediately after this event and had not worked, and hardly socialized since then. In spite of this experience, and inexplicably to me early on in the therapy, Franco had come to firmly believe he was, and wanted to be, gay.

At the time of entering therapy, Franco had only told his mother that he thought he was gay. He suspected that his mother had told his stepfather who remained silent on the subject. But, whenever a good-looking woman appeared on the TV, Franco's stepfather would say something like "Hey, Franco, how about her—do you fancy her?" This would infuriate Franco who believed that, even though it was an act of self-betrayal, he had to say "yes" because this effectively ended the conversation. Franco's mother, although clearly uncomfortable with his announcement about being gay, was extremely concerned for his happiness and prepared to accept that he was gay.

Much of our halted and tortuous discussions in early sessions revolved around the agony arising out of Franco's wish that his stepfather and his half-sister would acknowledge him as a gay man. He was intensely fearful of the anticipated stigma that would follow. In this sense, just as Franco was "embarking upon what is in the best of circumstances, a difficult stage of early adult self-development," he had begun to struggle with the "traumatic loss of cultural selfobject support" (Abramowitz, 2001, p. 4).

Illustrating, at another theoretical level, Franco's struggle with his positioning within or outside of the discourse of "heterosexuality as the norm," and endorsing something of his lifelong struggle with his own sexuality, he told me how he had felt different from other boys for as long as he could remember. As a young boy, he went to a single-sex school and for the most part, at least from an objective standpoint, seems to have managed to fit in with his peers. He was good at sport and is a well-built, conventionally masculine-looking young man, so he could "pass" as heterosexual and hence become a member of what Abramowitz (2001, p. 11) refers to as a "model minority." From a subjective perspective however, the behavior required of him to gain acceptance as "one of the boys" cost him psychologically. From his description, it seemed that at worst, he felt utterly alienated from himself and at best, he felt like a fraud and completely inauthentic. Somewhere in between he felt like a total failure, socially.

Worse, however, than his experience at school, was what lay ahead for him. Franco's decision that he was gay "heightened his selfobject needs, as does any transitional life stage" (Abramowitz, 2001, p. 3) and put him at odds with wider cultural norms. He had decided he was gay at a developmental stage when "ordinarily, vital selfobject experiences of peer twinship and family mirroring are generally found in walking arm and arm with a date of the opposite sex at college or bringing home the right young person for the family to admire and accept" (Abramowitz, 2001, p. 4). In Franco's case, he could find nothing in his surroundings that admired or affirmed him as a homosexual. He certainly did not have the feeling that he was "a human being among other human beings." He was unaware of any cultural institutions from which to derive the selfobject support he so badly needed. And, worse, having decided he was gay, Franco found himself faced with a dilemma of how to *be* a gay man, socially.

Theoretically speaking, he was going to have to begin a process of shifting back and forth between contradictory discourses. Demonstrating his initial positioning, he spent many a session "educating" me with recurring stereotypic but dominant ideas about what gay men looked like, how they behaved, and what discursive practices were therefore available to him. From his exposure to ideas at home, at school, in the books he had read, the

TV he had watched, and the movies he had seen, Franco believed he would have to be either "camp and effeminate" or "butch and aggressive." He decided the latter was impossible because, even though he was a conventionally masculine-looking man, he was far too shy to be an "aggressor." He reluctantly decided, therefore, that he would have to become "camp." He spent hours in his bedroom, looking at himself in the mirror as he tried out various movements with his hands, to see how he could cultivate the "limp wrist" required to indicate to others that he was gay. He had discovered there was a gay language, and he would try out some of the words and speak them with an acquired lisp.

When I asked him why he felt he had to acquire these behaviors, he described a fear that if he did not do so, he would never be noticed as a gay man, and would therefore never find a partner, which he so badly wanted. His experience a year earlier, when he had spent time at gay clubs (which is where he had observed these different behaviors) had been agonizing, mainly because he was so excruciatingly shy and because of what his fellow waiter had done to him. In spite of this, demonstrating in part his vital need for Kohut's version of the twinship selfobject experience, i.e. the need to experience the other as alike, he felt he had to present himself in public "looking gay," so that others—at shopping malls or movies—would approach him and make the "first move." In this way, Togashi's dimension would be present, i.e. the other finding themselves in Franco. However, this was a double-edged sword because dressed and behaving in this way made it likely that his queerness would be "discovered" by other members of his family and old school friends. He knew this would fill him with shame, and he dreaded the traumatic ridicule and stigma that he imagined would follow this discovery.

I could completely identify with Franco's dilemma and I could not bear what he was doing to himself. I could identify myself in this struggle very clearly. Twenty-six years earlier, in a similarly depressed state, an ex-boyfriend of mine had put me in touch with a group of lesbians who, when I met them, dressed mostly in denim jeans, trainers, and checked shirts. None of them wore makeup. Immediately on meeting them, they asked me to join what they called a "lesbian rap group" due to start some weeks ahead. That evening, they invited me to a gay and lesbian nightclub. This was my first experience (and unfortunately, not my last) of such a club!

A model scene evoked by that evening was the horror and confusion I felt when I met Jamie, an extremely butch-looking woman in denim jeans, boots, and a checked shirt. She wore no makeup and regaled us all with stories about her relationship with her partner, who was heavily made-up, wore a pink mini skirt, pink frilly top, and high-heeled pink shoes. The stories included expectations that cooked meals would be ready for Jamie at whatever time she returned home from work and other similar expectations including the putting out of Jamie's slippers and running her a bath. I distinctly remember leaving the club that night feeling despair as to what my growing belief that I was a lesbian was going to mean in realistic terms. Was I going to have to be butch or femme? Which would I choose? At the time, I was an accountant with a multinational oil company. I power dressed as this was expected of me in this position—I wore makeup, skirts, jewelry etc. On the evenings I was due to join the rap group, I would rush home, remove all traces of makeup and change into denims, trainers, and my newly acquired checked shirts! One evening, I went to the theater with a group of non-lesbian friends. I was smartly dressed, I wore makeup, and I bumped into some of the members of the lesbian rap group. I was devastated, confused, and wished that the floor would open up beneath me to enable me to simply disappear. It took me a very long time to work with this issue, helped of course by the fact that discursive practices have changed in the last 26 years, resulting in my having found ample and appropriate twinship selfobject support in my shifting surroundings over time.

Kohut (1959) argued that in order to be truly empathic, the therapist has to find something in herself or her own experience that affectively resonates with what the patient describes. I believe that the experiences described enabled me to understand what Franco felt about having to mold himself into something that truly did not come easily for him, and the psychological dangers involved in doing so. I felt that Franco's, albeit perhaps reluctant, decision to effect a camp and effeminate persona would only lead him down a one-way street to alienation and misery. I felt it was my job to help Franco realize that he did not have to try to reinvent himself into a unitary, camp, and effeminate being in order to find empathic resonance in the world (see Gehrie, 2002). I knew theoretically and personally that for anyone, this would be restrictive, potentially alienating, and likely to be painful and psychologically damaging. It could only lead to the development of more of an alienated self with a greater loss of what I was beginning to see in Franco—a delightfully idiosyncratic and potentially multifaceted self.

Intersubjectivity, postmodern, and feminist theory helped me to formulate the question which came to mind at this point in the therapy and that was: "whose pathology are we dealing with?" Through the lenses of these theories it seemed clear to me that Franco's predominant struggle was with the belief systems and dominant discourses that existed in the context in which he lived. He was struggling with the effects of the dominant discourses to which he had been exposed all his life, each of which cemented the message that heterosexuality was the norm and that anything else was "different" and "other." Being different and other meant that it was deviant, something of which to be ashamed and something which everyone found funny—funny because of the way in which gay men are depicted in movies such as *The Bird Cage*, which was a constant point of reference for Franco.

I felt frustrated and intolerant of these ideas. This led me to conceptualize the foreground of his struggle and his major source of distress and depression not so much as a consequence of his shyness and lack of confidence, or self disorder, but rather as a result of the belief systems or "pathology" to which he was accommodating. This included the beliefs imposed upon him by his long-standing and hitherto unquestioned positioning within the "heterosexual as the norm discourse" and the discourses that dictated the discursive practices of homosexuals. In recognizing this, I decided that initially at least, I needed limited but clearly focused goals for this therapy, one of which involved the introduction of alternative discourses and discursive practices, or put differently, cultural "norms." I hoped these discoveries would enable Franco to discover the kind of empathic resonance he had not yet been able to find in his current context and ultimately to feel like a human being among other human beings (Kohut, 1984).

I found myself having to bite my tongue whenever I was tempted to challenge the ideas Franco presented, and I struggled to carry out my therapeutic goal. But, theoretically and personally, I knew there were other options open to him and I was determined to set about facilitating his discovery of these alternative options, which would enable him to realize that empathic resonance could be available to him (Gehrie, 2002). I wanted to encourage him to play with these alternatives so that he could find his own optimal positioning within these discourses.

In retrospect, and thinking about Togashi's (2006) additional dimension of twinship, it would seem that Franco probably felt something of my recognizing myself in him. However, at a conscious level, he clearly had no idea I was gay, nor did it occur to him, it seemed, that I might see or know other gay men or women. I think he saw a middle-aged, or even very old, straight, professional woman. I decided early on that it would be inappropriate for Franco to discover that I was gay, nor that I knew anything about homo-prejudice from a personal perspective. He was so completely confused and inarticulate about it all that I believed he would have to find his own voice and his own way through the maze that the whole issue of his sexuality presented to him. However, knowing the pain involved in this process, I felt that he, like I had 26 years earlier, needed some help. I also knew this was not initially going to come from other confused gay men like his first sexual partner. This earlier experience had understandably left him mistrustful, fearful, and feeling completely isolated, dreadfully lonely, and confused.

The lack of collective twinship selfobject support had also left Franco with unmet idealized selfobject support (see Abramowitz, 2001, p. 5). He felt this absence acutely. I was concerned that his current depression would intensify and that suicide was possible or that he would become vulnerable to another painful and exploitative relationship of the kind that had seemed to precipitate his depression. It felt important that he meet and experience the presence of others who, like myself, had:

> journeyed through cultural bigotry's rough terrain with intact and productive selves, or who had as they had proceeded along adulthood's developmental path, repaired and restored themselves from this relational wounding and thus developed to their full potentials.
>
> (Abramowitz, 2001, p. 1)

This occurrence, from a self psychological perspective, would act as a mirroring experience for him and hopefully provide him with a developmentally significant twinship (Kohut, 1984; Togashi, 2006) or kinship (Basch 1994) selfobject experience. For this to occur, support was necessary for his attempts at studying with others whose interests were similar to his own and his wish to find a peer group with whom he could identify rather than from which he would feel alienated.

In this process, perhaps attuned to what appeared as "tendrils of psychological growth"—the "forward edge" as described by Tolpin (2006), I hoped that Franco could find a way to develop to his full potential. I wanted him to experience the exploration of the range of selves that seemed to be in his repertoire and to feel comfortable with their diversity and any contradictions. This included, for example, inhabiting and playing with his more camp self, which enjoyed cooking and presenting exotic meals, and wearing jewelry, something I noticed him trying out increasingly as time went on. However, he also loved watching rugby and football and was quite capable of doing odd, traditionally male, jobs around the house, like painting and repair work. He often did this happily and companionably with his stepfather. I hoped he would be able to feel comfortable with all of this and to move in and out of these facets of himself, as his mood and, perhaps, his context changed.

One of my first interventions involved some "bibliotherapy." In retrospect, this catalyzed a shifting of the family dynamic into a cohesive selfobject support system for Franco's emerging identity. I gave Franco a revised and updated edition of a book that, in a similar space to Franco, I had bought in a department store in Cape Town 26 years earlier. At that time, I told the sales assistant it was for a "friend of mine." Perversely, perhaps, she put it into a see-through packet, and I remember walking out of the store desperately trying to cover up the title before I caught a train home.

The book was entitled *Loving Someone Gay* (Clark, 1987). Franco took it home and glanced through it. He found it interesting. Being a particular kind of South African, he especially liked the way in which the author equated homo-prejudice to racism. However, he is not a great reader and he passed the book on to his mother to read. She devoured it and spoke enthusiastically with Franco about much of the content. He loved these discussions with her. Later, he believed his mother must have shared aspects of the book with his stepfather and his half-sister, because it became apparent that they had, as therapy continued, come to know and seemingly accept that he was gay. To his surprise, neither of them appeared horrified. His stepfather stopped the comments about good-looking women on TV and his half-sister became the source of his meeting a number of other gay people, both women and men, one of whom, Dave, was to become extremely significant to Franco towards the end of the therapy.

And so Franco began to discover others close to him who "joyfully responded to him, became available to him as sources of idealized strength and calmness, (were) silently present but in essence like him, and, at any rate, able to grasp his inner life" (Kohut in Abramowitz, 2001, p. 3). He began to feel like a human being among other human beings.

Going beyond the family, with a view to helping Franco find affiliation with others in the same predicament, or who had found a solution to it (Blechner, 1996, p. 232), I told Franco about The Triangle Project that I said I had come across. It is a gay organization that has a library, voluntary HIV-AIDS workers, counseling programs etc. though sadly at that time, no facilitated groups looking at gay issues such as "coming out." I discovered this after Franco had phoned them to find out if there was such a group for him to join. He never explored any other possible activities, e.g. voluntary work, reading in the library, or helping to catalogue gay books donated to the organization.

The apathy with which Franco approached aspects of his life continued but, suggesting something of Tolpin's idea of a "forward edge," there was energy in the room whenever we talked about the hospitality industry and the project that had to accompany his application for the college course. In the process of these discussions, Franco completed the project and gained acceptance into college. This was hugely affirming for him.

Whilst waiting for the course to begin, Franco began to look for a job as a waiter. He told me he knew about "gay-friendly restaurants" and, since he assumed that I did not know, he explained to me what this meant. I sat attentively listening to him, fascinated that he truly seemed to believe this was not self-evident. He said they were the only kind of restaurant he wanted to work in and from a personal perspective, I could completely understand his wish to be with others like himself.

However, he seemed to be getting nowhere. He was only trying small restaurants and he remained painfully shy. This made it difficult for me to imagine him conducting any form of interview, which would get him a job as a waiter. However, since I had no idea how he was outside of therapy and because of my experience of his animation when talking about the hospitality industry and being a DJ, I could not be sure that in other contexts he was necessarily the same as he was in therapy with me. It was perfectly possible that there were slices of his life and his behavior unseen by me. For these reasons, I did not ask questions that might make him question this chosen path, and look for other ways of earning money. Instead, I helped him pursue this idea.

I knew a gay man who is ordinary looking, relatively masculine, neither particularly camp nor particularly butch (in his professional life at least) and who owned a large restaurant. Moreover, I knew this was on Cape Town's "pink map." I told Franco I had come across the map somewhere, and that I had heard the restaurant was owned by a gay man and without having any contact with the owner, I suggested to Franco that he might perhaps try to find work there. I said I had been to the restaurant and liked it very much.

Franco approached the restaurant, which offered him a job following a brief training period. He met the owner in one of his interviews and began to see him on a beach that Franco frequented with a girl friend. He felt good about being able to nod "hello" to such a successful and quite ordinary looking man, who he knew was gay only because I had told him so. This was quite a surprise to Franco who had never met a gay man, who was, from appearances and behavior, not camp and effeminate, nor butch and aggressive and who was successful *and* out. A man who, in Abramowitz's (2001, p. 1) terms had apparently "journeyed through cultural bigotry's rough terrain with [an] intact and productive [self]."

By this time, Franco had begun to look at me when he spoke. He was looking forward to his college course and meeting his classmates, who he remained convinced, would be predominantly gay. He had, through two "old" lesbians (who turned out to be 20 years my junior) met Dave who I believe provided Franco with the kind of idealized selfobject experience he needed. Dave is gay, thirty-something, divorced with two sons. He is a successful professional man who is completely "out" in his professional and personal life. Franco described him as masculine looking and he seemed to be an intact and productive self. For fun, Franco said he fixed cars and "dances topless on his toes at gay nightclubs." Franco loved him. Franco's family seemed to enjoy him and he became a regular visitor at their home. Quite soon after their first meeting, Franco moved in to share digs with him and the two of them began to go out frequently to dinner, gay clubs, and to the movies. Franco clearly felt wonderfully human and filled with energy. In Dave, the lesbian couple he had met and in his family members, Franco had begun to have the kind of developmentally essential selfobject experiences of peer twinship and family mirroring, as described by Kohut (in Abramowitz,

2001, p. 3). Franco had discovered there were others outside there who were like him, and that empathic resonance was after all available in this world. This, according to Kohut (in Gehrie, 2002, p. 6), is the major constituent of a sense of security in adult life.

Kohut (in Abramowitz, 2001, p. 2) also argued that "when the adult experiences the self sustaining effects of a maturely chosen selfobject, the selfobject experiences of all the preceding stages of this life reverberate unconsciously." I believe this is what happened with Franco and in this sense the therapy was, while unorthodox perhaps, transformational and certainly not directive and educational, as some might venture to suggest.

Because of what had occurred in the therapy up to this point, Franco was feeling increasingly confident in the world. This led to talk about terminating therapy, which we did after only six months. While I am aware there was and is much more that can be done in therapy with Franco, which is always true of any therapy, it nevertheless seemed appropriate at the time to end the therapy for a number of reasons, some already mentioned above. In summary, this therapy was not about being a good object. It was not about steering Franco in a direction that might reduce his tension and conflict. I would argue that predominantly because of the twinship experiences, it was developmentally appropriate and transformational. Franco's discovery of the availability of empathic resonance and other cultural institutions from which he could derive collective selfobject support was crucial for him at this critical developmental stage. This enabled Franco to draw vital affirmation and admiration at a time when, feeling severed from collective selfobject support, he was seriously depressed and potentially suicidal (Abramowitz, 2001, p. 5). Finally, according to Kohut:

> The essence of the psychoanalytic cure resides in a patient's newly acquired ability to identify and seek out appropriate selfobjects—both mirroring and idealizable—as they present themselves in his realistic surrounding and to be sustained by them.
>
> (Gehrie, 2002, p. 17)

I believe Franco had learned to do this. In realistic surroundings he had found cultural and relational selfobject support and the relationship between himself and those who functioned as a selfobject for him had changed significantly as a result. Franco had become more of a cohesive self and this increased cohesion had augmented his capacity to use those who functioned as a selfobject for him, for his own sustenance. This had helped facilitate a freedom within himself to choose (appropriate) people in his surroundings who could and would function for him as a selfobject. He had found a comfortable way to come out and to play with his diversity. The diversity had enabled him to find, rather than lose, as he had imagined, "certain representatives of his human surroundings ... joyfully responding to him, ... available to him, ... sources of idealized strength and calmness, ... being silently present but in essence like him, and, at any rate, able to grasp his inner life" (Kohut in Abramowitz, 2001, p. 3). At this point, we agreed he could and would return to therapy should he ever feel the need to do so in the future.

Only after I began to prepare the case material for this chapter did I consciously realize how similar Franco's "coming out" process was to my own 26 years earlier, and what effect this had on the way in which the therapy unfolded.

This raises questions about the implications of therapists working with people from different cultures or whose organizations of experiences or presenting problems are not something with which we can affectively resonate, or without the theoretical tools with which to understand the complexities of the contextual problems with which our patients present.

This chapter focuses on me as a gay therapist. However, because I have foregrounded the importance of the social/cultural field as a vital context beyond the therapeutic dyad that shapes not only the therapy process but the subjectivity of each participant, it also speaks to the general problem of difference and otherness, both in ourselves and our clients. Since most, if not all, of us live in a range of diverse discourses while not being completely at ease with any of them, this possibly enables us to do what Kohut (1959) said we needed to do in order to vicariously introspect and hence be "truly" empathic, and to act appropriately in the therapy. However, to do this, I believe we need the selfobject support from others who can resonate with our particular brands of difference or with the effects of a marginalized status. This is what motivated this chapter; I wanted to fill the conspicuous gap I identified. We, as therapists, need much of what Franco needed in his context and developmental stage in life from our cultural/professional institutions. In our contexts, we need the affirming selfobject experiences, which accompany vital reciprocal exchanges with our fellow professionals (Abramowitz, 2001). I hope this chapter will encourage others to come out and share similar experiences of diversity and difference, both from a theoretical perspective and with regard to our work in the room with "difference."

Notes

1 Obviously, in very similar (but also very different) ways, all that is said in this chapter will apply to individuals whose site of marginalized difference is located in their race, their culture or religion, their marital status, their disability etc.
2 I prefer this term to that of homophobia, a term which is misleading.
3 We could add to this, the dominant discourses of "white as the norm" or "married as the norm." (Don't those women who have actually chosen to be single hate being asked if we are Miss or Mrs, especially as we get older and are forced to take on the stigmatized spinster status in the eyes of the bank clerk attending to us who refuses to hear our answer, "Ms"?)

Chapter 4

Mutual finding of oneself and not-oneself in the other as a twinship experience

Koichi Togashi, Ph.D., L.P.

Among Kohut's (1971, 1977, 1984) three selfobject needs and experiences—mirroring, idealizing, and twinship—twinship has come to be considered the most basic and fundamental selfobject phenomenon by recent self psychologists (Basch, 1992; Ulman and Paul, 1992; Martinez, 1993, 2003; Gorney, 1998; Shapiro, 1998; Togashi, 2009a). Kohut (1984) originally defines twinship as a "need to experience the presence of essential alikeness" (p. 194), and addresses the twinship need as a patient's yearning to experience himself as like his analyst, or as a patient's yearning to experience his analyst as like himself. Then, he expands the twinship experience to include the most basic sense of existing in human society, and he describes the twinship experience as a "confirmation of the feeling that one is a human being among other human beings" (Kohut, 1984, p. 200). As some self psychologists write, this definition of twinship implicitly indicates that Kohut's idea had already moved forward to a two-person psychology with its recognition that there is a reciprocity and mutuality of twinship needs between people in the intersubjective context (Togashi, 2009a; Philipson, 2010).

In Chapter 2, I proposed another dimension of the twinship experience: the patient's yearning for a sense that the analyst finds herself in the patient. I contended that the two dimensions of twinship, "Like-to-feel-we-are-alike" and "Can-you-find-yourself-in-me?" should be differentiated in our clinical practice; they are intertwined and require an analyst to be sensitive to the two different functions. Furthermore, I discussed in that chapter that, in an epistemological sense, the new dimension of twinship experience requires a patient to have enough sensitivity to be aware that his and his analyst's subjectivities are not similarly formed. That suggests that this type of twinship inevitably confronts a patient with a dilemma; he has the yearning precisely because he is aware that his analyst's psychological process is not necessarily contingent on his, but he never proves that she finds herself in him. Given this dilemma, how are a patient and an analyst to organize the twinship experience in their relationship? What interactive processes are going on between them?

I hypothesize, in this chapter, that the twinship selfobject experience takes place in a way by which both participants in an analytic relationship find themselves and not-themselves in the other. Finding oneself in the other includes the concept of finding not-oneself in the other. When a patient finds himself in his analyst, he is expected also to find not-himself in his analyst; and when an analyst finds herself in her patient, she is expected also to find not-herself in her patient. The twinship tie is organized as a balance between mutual findings of oneself and not-oneself in the other. In the relationship in which they find only themselves (or not-themselves) in the other, we can say the twinship selfobject tie is already disrupted.

Before I review relevant literature, I briefly describe my own experience in order to articulate the thesis in this chapter. After the termination of my five-year psychoanalytic training in New York, I went back to Japan; I occasionally visit New York to see my friends and colleagues to, so to speak, keep a sense of a twinship tie with them. When I arrive at JFK airport, I soon encounter an immigration officer who gives me a few brief questions to discover whether I am trying to enter illegally. These questions are very simple and matter-of-fact, but I often feel anxious. This anxiety has to do with a disruption of the twinship experience I proposed in Chapter 2, since the essential feature of this encounter is my lack of confidence in whether or not the officer will find himself in me. Having lived in New York myself, I know how people live there, and I can experience him as being like myself in many ways, large and small; but he, experiencing me only as another in an unending string of others, may see me as a total alien. What interactive processes are going on in the relationship between him and me?

What is missing in this context is my conviction that he will find in me what I find in him. What I yearn for is not that the officer experiences me as essentially like him, since it is obvious to me that he and I are in different positions. I find many aspects in the officer that I cannot find in me. Still, it is easy for me to find myself in him not only in the area of explicit discourse, but also in the area of implicit discourse (Beebe and Lachmann, 2002; The

Boston Change Process Study Group, 2002; Fosshage, 2005, 2009). This includes vocal rhythms, facial expressions, tone of voices, and gaze behaviors, all of which I became familiar with and incorporated into my own way of being while residing in New York. I can find myself and not-myself in the officer, and I am sure that he would find not-himself in me; but the lack of my conviction that he finds himself in me prevents me from experiencing myself fully as being a human being among other human beings.

Once I enter the United States and I am with my friends in New York, I am relieved of my anxiety and feel comfortable. I no longer feel disconnected from the people around me, and I feel secure and vital. I do not have to worry whether my friends can find themselves in me or not, although I find not-myself in them, and I am convinced that they find not-themselves in me in many ways. The twinship tie between my friends and me is organized as a delicate balance of mutual findings of oneself and not-oneself in one another.

Sameness and difference in twinship

When it comes down to the experiential level, a twinship experience includes a sense of sameness and difference simultaneously. Neither a sense of complete sameness nor a sense of complete difference provides a feeling of security, coherence, agency, affectivity, or continuity. Rather, the experience of complete sameness and difference leads to a deep sense of insecurity or anxiety, or it temporarily functions to dissemble a deep sense of insecurity with an unstable connection to others. We yearn to find ourselves in the person who is potentially like us, but basically different from us; we yearn to find not-ourselves in the person who is potentially different but essentially alike.

In Chapter 3 (see also Kottler, 2007), Kottler describes her struggle to deal with her experiencing the patient as alike and different. While she found in her patient a path of life she had already gone through, she recognized some differences between him and her. She states that, in this context, which accords with my definition of twinship (Togashi, 2006, 2009), the analyst's finding herself in the patient, as well as her recognizing his "otherness," can transform the patient's sense of self. In other words, the clinical process provided by Kottler reveals that a twinship experience essentially includes a sense of sameness and difference simultaneously, and a patient's sense of being human among humans takes place through an analyst's finding herself and not-herself in a patient.

Brothers (2008) discusses how psychological trauma destroys a sense of certainty in an individual. According to her, a traumatized individual no longer experiences the world as well known, familiar, or meaningful, and he often creates dualities or dichotomies in which all people and things are categorized into one side or the other. An individual cannot tolerate the differences from others who he believes are supposed to be in the essentially same position with him, and cannot bear any hints of sameness with others whom he identifies as opposed to himself. In this sense, seeking for complete sameness or difference is understood as reactive to emotional trauma. Her discussion indicates that seeking for complete sameness with others does not lead to a sense of being a human being among other human beings. In this paradigm, Kohut's (1984) first definition of twinship, experiencing the other as essentially alike, especially if the emphasis is on the sameness, can be understood as a secondary reaction to emotional trauma.

Stolorow (2009), in his autobiographical reflections on trauma and human existence, also regards "longing for twinship or emotional kinship as being reactive to emotional trauma" (p. 49). According to him, a longing for twinship comes through when an individual experiences himself as disconnected from the world by traumatization. He states: "When I have been traumatized, my only hope for being deeply understood is to form a connection with a brother or sister who knows the same darkness" (p. 49). In contrast to Kohut, Stolorow does not always see twinship as an inherent human longing.

I am not saying here that a twinship need is to be understood as a reaction to an experience of psychological trauma. However, I am saying that Kohut's (1984) first definition of twinship does not necessarily capture the essential element of a twinship experience. In accordance with Kohut's understanding, I believe that twinship is an inherent human longing and the most fundamental longing among all selfobject experiences. What I suggest here is that Kohut (1984) might have defined the two different dimensions in a twinship experience. His first definition of twinship— "a sense of essential alikeness"—can be a secondary reaction to the traumatic disruption of a twinship experience defined as a "feeling that one is a human being among other human beings." Kohut (1984) emphasizes that a twinship tie is present when people are together "in silent communication" (p. 196). In the usual or ordinary case, human beings are enveloped in a sense, without awareness, that they are human beings among other human beings, and so they do not need to take steps to assure themselves of that. Once they experience themselves as not being among humans, they actively yearn for a certain emotional tie with others, which does not manifest itself in a sense of being a human among humans, but in a sense of essential alikeness. In other words, a sense of being "a human being among other human beings" is organized not through a sense of essential alikeness, but through a dialectic between an individual's finding similarities between him and the other whom he experiences as different, as well as finding differences between him and the other whom he experiences as alike.

Finding oneself and not-oneself in twinship

In what interactive processes is a sense of sameness recognized in the other who is experienced as different by an individual? In what interactive processes is a sense of difference recognized in the other who is experienced as alike by him? At the "explanatory level" (Orange, Atwood, and Stolorow, 1997; Coburn, 2007; Pickles and Shane, 2007; Stolorow, 2010), how we can describe the perceptual-cognitive processes that are going on in twinship relatedness?

Benjamin (1988) holds that the issue of sameness and difference should be discussed in the context of the developmental achievement of mutual recognition. She states that "one of the most important insights of intersubjective theory is that sameness and difference exist simultaneously in mutual recognition" (p. 47). In her relational psychoanalysis, mutual recognition is a concept critical to describing how an individual developmentally obtains a sense of being with others without fear or anxiety, but with a sense of autonomy.

Benjamin (1988, 1991) criticizes the classical theories, such as those of Freud and Mahler, which follow a linear developmental model, for not explaining clearly how an individual achieves a sense of autonomy while being with others whom he depends on. For her, these theories regard the psychological development only as a process of separating from or internalizing an object. In these models, the hypothetical caretaker is an "object" whose function is only to fulfill an infant's wishes; and the hypothetical infant "does not *want* to recognize the other, does not perceive him as a person just like himself" (Benjamin, 1988, p. 53, italics in original). In contrast to these models, Benjamin sees psychological development occurring in a context in which a child recognizes the other who is like him, but has a separate center of initiative. The paradox in this relationship is "that the child not only needs to achieve independence, but he must be recognized as independent—by the very people on whom he has been most dependent" (Benjamin, 1988, p. 53). A crucial task for a child in the development of autonomy is to possess a capacity to hold these antithetical ideas in dialectical tension; otherwise, dependency would become a threat to a sense of independency or autonomy, and the other person would induce a fear in the child of the erosion of his developing self.

Although I have been influenced by Benjamin's (1988, 1991) idea, I do not maintain that a mutual finding of oneself and not-oneself in the other is a capacity acquired with psychological development. I posit that it is a psychological process that unfolds in the intersubjective context from birth onward. Neither do I maintain that a finding of oneself or not-oneself is equivalent to recognizing or validating the "otherness" of the other. An individual may or may not be aware in the negotiation of difference that the other has a separate center of initiative; he is always contextually embedded in the mutual process of finding himself and not-himself in the other at conscious and non-conscious levels. By referring to a mutual finding, I maintain that an individual is inherently predetermined to find some aspects of himself in him which are created in the subjectivity of the other, and vice versa. In this sense, I would say that the idea of mutual finding is an explanatory concept that describes the perceptual-cognitive processes that are going on in twinship relatedness, while a sense of sameness and difference is an experiential concept that describes the subjective experience of people who feel themselves connected to others in a twinship tie.

My understanding is influenced by a German philosopher, Karl Löwith (1928), who extends Heidegger's (1927) analysis of "being-with-others" (*Mitsein*) in *Being and Time,* and offers his interpretation of "being-with-others" (*Miteinandersein*) in his early book. Löwith (1928) claims that in Heidegger's framework, the sphere of being-with-others (*Mitsein*) is a priori underestimated. In *Being and Time*, the essence of authenticity is in the selfhood of the self that is radically achieved when the individual confronts finitude in the inevitability of death. In this paradigm, the majority of selves that are defined by a social relationship (with family, friends, colleagues, communities, etc.) seem to be addressed as the "inauthentic everydayness." Löwith posits that the human world that is defined by Heidegger as *Mitwelt*, a co-world, is intrinsically inauthentic. For Löwith, being-with-others (*Miteinandersein*) is not an ignominious episode that should be redeemed toward authentic selfhood or life. The meaning of a self is radically defined by an individual's being in a social relationship. In other words, a sense of self is, in his paradigm, contextually embedded in the complex balance between an individual finding himself in the other and by the other finding herself in him. Löwith states the following:

> Man returns to himself, not primarily from objects, but from subjects, i.e., from Beings who are like him; for the "world" to which he principally turns is the co-world [*Mitwelt*] that corresponds to him. From the outset and without his doing, his own world is ever and always determined through the Dasein of Others, such that it would not be there at all or in this way without the having-been-there of determinate Others ... When we inquire about the Other or the co-world, this question implies inquiring about one's own Self, for whom others are "Other" and a "world"—i.e., one is making inquiries about Being-with-others [*Miteinandersein*].
> (Löwith, 1928, p. 1; translated by Wolin, 2001, pp. 81–82)

My understanding of mutual finding is also influenced by recent infant research and relevant studies of a dyadic relationship in adults (Beebe and Lachmann, 2002; Sander, 2002; Fosshage, 2004, 2005; Stern, 2004; Lachmann, 2008) revealing that, before human beings recognize that they and the other both have a separate center of initiative, they inherently have a capacity for participating in the process of the explicit and implicit relational knowing, and that the two participants in the interaction are embedded in an interactive regulatory process in both dimensions of knowing. The interactive regulatory process is based on an individual's capacity of knowing that the other whom he is communicating with has an aspect of inner process that is not always contingent on an individual's regulatory process. An infant is well equipped to imitate the facial expressions of an adult and to specifically match his affective state to an adult's (Meltzoff, 1985, 1990; Beebe and Lachmann, 2002), while the infant's and the adult's regulatory processes do not match one another exactly. These notions indicate that, regardless of the developmental achievement, there is a psychological area in which they find themselves, as well as not-themselves, in the other.

Case vignette: Midori

Midori is an unmarried Japanese female in her late forties whom I have been seeing for four-and-a-half years on a twice-a-week basis. She came to see me to understand the source of her sense of loneliness in her social and private life, as well as her chronic depression. Although she has a good relationship with her friends and colleagues, she experiences herself as disconnected from them and from the world.

She was born into a wealthy family as the first child. Her father was a very successful businessperson, and he died when she was a child. Her mother, a teacher of a traditional Japanese art form, is a beautiful but controlling woman with a paranoid tendency. She occasionally claims that people in the world see Midori as ugly, and suggests that Midori try to make up herself as beautiful as the mother is. The mother's complaining about Midori's appearance sometimes lasts for several hours. The mother does not like to see any aspects of her husband in Midori. She frequently criticizes Midori by negative reference to the father, saying, "You have your father's nose and eyes. Your way of thinking is sick, just like his."

As her therapy began, Midori did not talk a lot about her relationship with her friends, colleagues, or family members. Rather, she liked to talk about room interiors. She was impressed with my office, which I had decorated in American style rather than Japanese, and she said that it was very close to the style she had looked for for a long time. She said that she did not always like all of the elements of my office, but basically she liked my way of decorating the room. We shared my understanding that it is very important for her to share a sense of aesthetics with others because the feeling itself was the one she had yearned for but did not have in the relationship with her mother. She tearfully revealed that she had been interested in arts and design like her mother, but she had never showed her preference openly because her mother did not like most of the arts she liked. Her mother, a teacher of an art form, often belittled her for not having as good aesthetic judgment as she had. She said, "My mother told me that I am ugly, unlike her, and I live in a different world from her. I don't deserve to be interested in what she likes." While Midori could find herself in her mother, the mother never found herself in Midori, and rather preferred to find not-herself in her.

We can say that during this period of analysis a silent and gentle current of twinship had been flowing between us. I did not think that I was as artistic as she was, but I was able to agree with many aspects of her discussion. As she found herself in her critique of my way of decorating the office, I was able to find myself in her aesthetic sense. The important thing here is that we did not necessarily share the same opinion. Rather, we spent much more time discussing the differences between us. She said, "Your office is a little too classic for me; I like things a bit more modern." I replied, "Good. But it is my style formed through my personal and professional experience. I believe that is also true for your style." Through finding the difference between us in a common concern, we experienced ourselves as connected in the same world.

After two years of sessions, Midori suddenly canceled her session. She called me up to tell me she did not want to see me anymore. I suggested that we see each other in person to talk about what was going on between us, and she came to my office. There she explained that she felt that at the last session I had tried to come too close to her emotionally, and within a distance where she felt uncomfortable. In that session, she had been talking about her mother. As she recalled that her mother had barged into her room and blamed her for having an ugly face, Midori cried. Toward the end of the session, I felt that she looked deeply depressed. I was worried about her psychological condition and said, "Are you okay? If you want another session before the next regular session, I can set it up." After she left my office, she said now, she found herself feeling insecure and depressed. She experienced herself as losing an essential aspect of the emotional connection with me. She said, "It was okay with me that you worried about me. But we are no longer on the same wavelength."

I then carefully looked back at my own feelings in the previous session. I saw that I had found myself in her story because her story had enough in it to remind me of a similar experience of my own. That reflection probably involved me too much in her story, and so I ended up thinking she was more devastated than she experienced herself to be. In other words, the depth of my concern did not match her feeling. I found myself in her, and I lost a sense of difference in this intersubjective context. I experienced her as completely the same as I was at that moment. The part of her subjectivity in which I could find not-me became very narrow, and the part of her subjectivity in which I could find myself became too wide.

I told her that I had found my own experience in her story, but I might have forgotten about the importance of recognizing some differences between us. She was more resilient than the "myself" that I had found in her story. As she listened to my interpretation, she was upset: "If you claim that you found your experience in me, you were already in a different world ... temporally and spatially. You are a man; your experience cannot be the same." She remembered that her mother sometimes was extraordinarily excited about finding some similarities between her features and Midori's, such as lips and hands, and occasionally lost control in a manic episode. Midori also thought that these features were, in fact, her mother's. However, her finding herself in her mother in this way did not lead to a sense of twinship; rather, the similarities led to a fear for the erosion of self and enhanced a sense of difference—"we have some similarities, but we are so different!" The more the mother emphasized the similarities, the more Midori experienced herself as different from her. In this context, neither my finding myself in her nor her finding herself in me enabled her to feel herself as being a human among humans. For her, a sense of twinship is organized as a delicate balance of mutual findings of ourselves and not-ourselves in the other.

After this session, we discussed how men and women differently experience how someone else looks at them in this world. Working through this theme got our relationship back on track, and she now experiences our relationship as warm, gentle, and a bit evocative.

Conclusion and discussion

My case vignette confirms the validity of my hypothesis that a twinship experience takes place while both participants in an analytic relationship are finding themselves and not-themselves in the other. In other words, a twinship experience is organized by a delicate balance of mutual findings of oneself and not-oneself in the other. Finding only oneself in the other, or finding only not-oneself in the other, cannot provide a twinship experience. In order for one person to experience herself as being a human among humans, they have to be the "thou" in whom she finds not-herself.

This vignette also indicates that the mutual finding of oneself and not-oneself in the other is not a developmental achievement, and the finding of oneself or not-oneself is not necessarily equivalent to recognizing or validating the otherness of the other. It is a psychological process in which two participants, consciously and non-consciously, regulate a sense of sameness and difference in their effort to match some aspects of their subjectivity. Midori was born into an environment in which her mother looked forward to finding many aspects of Midori's father in Midori as well as finding herself there. In this environment, Midori's effort to find herself in her mother must have been reorganized in her mother's conflicted psychological process, and her mother's effort to find herself and not-herself in Midori must have been reorganized in Midori's psychological process. Midori and her mother have been embedded in the mutual finding process since the very moment Midori was born—namely, before Midori recognized that her mother had a separate center of initiative.

Mutual finding always runs as an ongoing process of human interaction when people experience a twinship selfobject tie to each other. A sense of being a human being among other human beings, based on the dialectic between a sense of sameness and difference at the experiential level, can be organized as a delicate balance between mutual findings of oneself and not-oneself. This balance is always context sensitive—determined at a particular moment in a particular dyad. As a dyadic relationship continues, the participants' subjectivities are being reorganized through one participant's influencing the other and by being influenced by the other interactively. In his partner's subjectivity, an individual finds the aspect that is being organized through his finding himself in her and the aspect that is not being organized through his finding. His partner also finds, in his subjectivity, the aspect that is being organized through her finding herself in him and the aspect that is not being organized through her finding. The quality of twinship relatedness is determined through this interactive regulatory process. That people are in a twinship relatedness does not suggest that the balance of finding oneself and not-oneself in the other is maintained at a constant level. Toward the beginning of our therapy, in a twinship relatedness between Midori and I, the balance of mutual finding was tilted toward finding not-ourselves in one another more than finding ourselves in one another, and toward the end of our therapy, the balance became tilted in the opposite direction. As Bacal (1998, 2006) illustrates, the balance of mutual finding that is organized in twinship relatedness changes moment by moment in the specificity of interaction between a particular patient and a particular therapist.

In this chapter, I only focus on the mutual finding process in twinship relatedness. However, I believe that this process can also be found in other types of selfobject relatedness. As Orange (2008) discusses, "Kohut's (1971, 1977) description of the 'narcissistic transference' placed the spotlight on developmental processes of mirroring and idealizing that created opportunities for the parent to recognize the unique qualities and talents of the child, and thus to participate in bringing them into being" (pp. 80–81). Kohut (1968, 1971) describes a mirroring experience as a child's finding "the gleam in the mother's eye" with great joy. In this process, the mother is excited by seeing the existential uniqueness of her child, as well as by finding herself in him, and the child is excited by finding himself in his mother's eye and by finding an aspect of being the other in his mother. In his discussion of the healthy Oedipus period, Kohut (1977) also describes a mirroring and idealizing relatedness as follows:

> [If] the parental selves have formed stable patterns of ambitions and ideals, and the parental selves are experiencing the unrolling of the expression of these patterns along a finite life curve that leads from a preparative beginning through an active, productive, creative middle to a fulfilled end ... the oedipal child then is the beneficiary of the fact that the parents are in narcissistic balance. If the little boy, for example, feels that his father looks upon him proudly as *a chip off the old block* [italics added] and allows him to merge with him and with his adult greatness, then his oedipal phase will be a decisive step in self-consolidation and self-pattern-firming.
>
> (p. 234)

In this mirroring–idealizing selfobject relatedness, a father finds his former self in his son, and a son finds his future self in his father. A father's finding his former self in his son includes his recognition that his son is different from him as he is now, and a son's finding his future self in his father includes finding that his father has an aspect that the son is not able to find in himself. The mutual finding process could be addressed as a significant aspect of mirroring and idealizing selfobject relatedness.

Another important thesis that we need to explore further would be the relationship between a twinship experience and empathy. The concept of twinship, which was originally addressed as a subcategory or a special form of the mirror transference (Kohut, 1971), is finally defined by Kohut (1984) as a "feeling that one is a human being among other human beings" (p. 200). At the same time, in his final discussion on the existential anxiety caused by the lack of a fundamental empathic environment, Kohut (1981, 1984) exemplifies the experiences of the astronauts when their space capsule lost power in outer space, and describes their yearning as the "ultimate deepest desire the wish to be symbolically reunited with the earth: the symbol of human meaning, human warmth, human contact, human experience" (Kohut, 1981, p. 545n). In other words, Kohut (1981, 1984) uses the concept of "feeling that one is a human being among other human beings" as a representation of the twinship experience and an empathic environment interchangeably. In our understanding, toward the end of his life, Kohut's "psychology of the self" moved toward the "psychology of being human." I believe that twinship and empathy are key to our understanding of Kohut. They will help us to understand in what environment and in what processes an individual experiences himself as human and as being treated as a human being by others; or, consider the contrary. What did Kohut see in twinship and empathy in the final stage of his life? What essential psychological process in being human did Kohut see in twinship and empathy? These are questions that require further elaboration.

Chapter 5

Trauma, recovery, and humanization

From fantasy to transitional selfobject, through a twinship tie

Amanda Kottler, M.A. (Clin. Psych.)
Koichi Togashi, Ph.D., L.P.

Our frequent encounters with patients who have not experienced the feeling of being "a human being among other human beings" (Kohut, 1984) and who, instead, feel at odds with and alienated from others is the subject of this chapter. Our focus is on those patients whose style of relating prevents this feeling, primarily because it impedes their capacity to experience others as "real," "live" human beings.

We believe that instead of participating in interactive emotional exchanges, these patients often create objects in their imagination or shape others into "objects" with which they then imagine an emotional tie. This eases the utter alienation that they feel in relation to the human world, but, because their creation is an imagined fantasy, the relief can only ever be temporary. However, as we will demonstrate, there is potential for a different outcome. The created "object" can acquire the qualities of a transformational fantasy selfobject (Bacal, 1981), which can be experienced as more than an "object" with no agency. Whether this happens depends on whether the patient is able to first, position, or in Togashi's (2009) terms, find herself in the "relationship" with the fantasized object, and second, to participate in discussions about the "relationship" that she has created around the fantasized object. If this occurs, the fantasy can both sustain the patient's sense of self—beyond the moment, and generate experiences of being alive, secure, solid, and "at home" in the human world. Equally significant is whether the fantasy is accessible to others and whether its organization allows for expansion and growth in collaboration with others. If it is, we believe that this emotional experience with (albeit initially) an imagined fantasy selfobject, has both the capacity to transform itself along a forward edge dimension (Tolpin, 2002) and the potential to develop into a selfobject tie with a real human being, as opposed to the fantasy.

Bacal (1981) originally introduced the concept of a "fantasy selfobject" to describe a selfobject tie "that is created by the patient almost totally out of his own fantasy in a nuclear environment, when, in fact, such a real selfobject barely existed, if at all" (p. 36). To illustrate how this kind of patient develops "the capacity for a type of sustaining fantasy that they attach to potential selfobject figures" (p. 36), Bacal (1981) describes a traumatized patient who was often in a regressed state, but who was able nevertheless to function professionally and socially. He concludes that this demonstrates the existence, unbeknownst to others, of an unarticulated fantasy selfobject tie, which enables this kind of person to psychologically sustain themselves for long periods of time, without therapy.

As psychoanalytic psychotherapists with our particular theoretical interest, we have increasingly noticed the extent to which so many patients rely on an imagined, fantasy selfobject. This is evident in Kohut's (1984) inspirational understanding of his patient's creation of a "genie in a bottle," a case he used to introduce and illustrate the concept of twinship. Kohut's unnamed patient, Ms G, invented a "twin," which she referred to as her "genie," who lived in a bottle with a tightly fitting lid. She created this fantasy when she was six years old, following her family's relocation and the developmental arrest that occurred as a result of traumatically losing her grandmother with whom she had spent many comfortable, self-affirming, self-maintaining, and self-sustaining hours (1984, pp. 196–200). The genie was someone "just like herself, and yet not herself to whom she could talk, who kept her company and made it possible for her to survive the hours of loneliness when she felt that no one other than her companion in the bottle cared for her" (p. 196). It was a replacement for her grandmother's reassuring "silent presence" (p. 196), which at the time provided her with what Kohut isolated as a self-sustaining twinship selfobject experience. Although we do not have the details of her therapeutic process with Kohut, the genie clearly provided a fantasy selfobject experience for Ms G that had undoubtedly sustained her throughout her life, and well into her analysis with Kohut.

This example intrigues us because Kohut describes Ms G's twinship tie with a non-human object even though he defines twinship as a "feeling that one is a human being among other human beings." It forces us to ask: why and how did Kohut understand that an emotional connection with a fantasy object could be transformed into a human, rather than a fantasy connection with human beings?

Our aim here is to extricate the processes involved, and to explore the more elusive details of how this occurs. We draw on the concepts of both fantasy and transitional selfobject experiences, and on our evolving ideas of twinship selfobject experiences. We posit that a fantasy selfobject experience can be transformed into a real *human* selfobject experience by working through a transforming selfobject experience. We connect these ideas to the movie, *Lars and the Real Girl* (2007), through which we attempt to generate a hypothesis using two therapeutic vignettes. We relate this to our thesis, drawing attention to the way in which the transitional process of a selfobject experience can facilitate a person's emergent discovery of their own subjectivity, their recognition of the subjectivity of the other, and finally, their capacity for mutual recognition and regulation. We argue that this process leads to the experience of the humanizing feelings which we, like Kohut, believe are the essential components of living with a solid sense of self, with a sense of vitality, initiative, agency, and authenticity, in a relational world.

The function of a fantasy and a transitional selfobject

1. Fantasy selfobject

A fantasy selfobject, which many post-Kohutian self psychologists have referred to as a clinically useful concept (Bacal, 1981, 1985, 1990, 2007; Hagman, 1996; Lachmann, 1993; Lachmann and Beebe, 1995; Coburn, 2007c; Shane, 1992; Shane and Shane, 1993) is "created by the patient when the environment provides almost nothing around which he can elaborate a need for the responsiveness he requires" (Bacal, 1985, pp. 221–222). They evolve "out of an internally generated and organized selfobject that apparently has little to no referentials in the environment" (Coburn, 2007). The creation, out of imagination, represents a striving for health and psychological stability in the face of the kind of fragmentation that follows trauma. In Bacal's view:

> Elaborations in *fantasy* of positive images of the object may contribute to its being experienced as a selfobject and, in this way, [they] become integral components of the selfobject experience. In this sense, of

course, all selfobjects are to some extent "fantasy" selfobjects. However, the term is worthwhile retaining, I believe, to designate selfobject relationships that are inordinately determined by the elaboration of fantasy. These "fantasy selfobject relationships" are, in effect, created as psychologically lifesaving responses to otherwise unmanageable trauma, and they are particularly vulnerable to severe disruptions.

(Bacal, 1990, p. 215; italics in original)

In this sense, we believe a fantasy selfobject can include both a forward and a trailing edge dimension. Both dimensions can occupy the foreground or background at different times in an individual's selfobject relationships. Which dimension is in the foreground at any one time is entirely context embedded.

If the forward edge dimension is in the foreground, a fantasy selfobject not only generates a patient's experience of himself as energetic, secure, and solid in the relationship he has created as a fantasy, but can also be transformed into a relationship with a living person. If the trailing edge dimension is in the foreground, the opposite will occur. The fantasy selfobject experience will interrupt and suspend emotional development, effectively leaving the patient walled off from the outside world, while he continues a "relationship" with the object created in his fantasy. For as long as he remains enveloped in such a relationship, he is "shielded" from experiencing the subjectivity of the other, something he will have experienced earlier in his life, traumatically, and something he now wishes to avoid.

We are not suggesting a qualitative distinction between a fantasy selfobject in the forward edge and one in the trailing edge dimension of the fantasy, nor that there are two types of fantasy selfobjects. We are, however, suggesting that the difference between the two edges depends on how, and in what context they evolve. If the fantasy selfobject is organized in a way that allows both patient and therapist to find themselves in it, it is potentially transformative. In this case, the forward edge dimension will come to the foreground. However, the quality of the fantasy itself does not determine whether or not there is room in it for a particular analyst and a particular patient to find themselves. Rather, it depends on a therapist's capacity to find, and to work with herself in the particular fantasy selfobject that the patient has created around them both. And, obviously, a fantasy in which one analyst might easily find herself might be one in which another analyst cannot.

2. Transitional selfobject experiences

Transitional selfobject experiences result in a shift from a state of engaging with a fantasy selfobject to a real person who provides a selfobject function. Bacal (1985) defines a transitional selfobject as "created by the patient, partly out of himself (in fantasy) and partly out of a sense of pliable surroundings" (p. 221). Bacal (1985, p. 223) argues that a transitional selfobject comes about as a result of an individual's creation of a fantasy selfobject in response to selfobject failures. They involve the creation of highly crafted fantasies of objects that are used to shape an invented, self-sustaining, relationship. Yet, their ongoing aim is to create a new kind of relatedness. Once patients feel understood and responded to appropriately by a live person, their fantasies have the potential to begin a transitional shift.

This idea is potentially problematic because all selfobject experiences could be considered transitional since fantasy is involved in every selfobject experience (Lachmann and Beebe, 1993), and because all subjective experiences are organized between both fantasy and reality (Bacal, 1981). However, the idea is useful to draw attention to the essential role of the therapist's participation in the transformation of a fantasy selfobject to a live person providing a selfobject function. This idea must, however, be understood in terms of an experiential and not a descriptive dimension.

In a transitional state, the patient's needs to experience the therapist as someone who can provide an archaic selfobject function, specifically designed by, and for, him will be in the foreground. But therapists need to understand that as an effective means of surviving, fantasy selfobject relationships are extremely precarious. They can be "more seriously undermined than real selfobject relationships" (Bacal, 1985, p. 217). However, it is essential to be aware that because the fantasy is not an entirely inaccessible fantasy, the fantasized experience can develop as a co-creation between a patient and an analyst. This depends on whether the patient allows his analyst to participate in the ongoing co-creation of his fantasy. For transformation to occur, a collaborative fantasy must evolve in which the patient must locate herself and her therapist, and equally significant, the therapist must be able to discover both himself and his patient. It requires exquisite sensitivity to, and an understanding of, the forward edge dimension involved in the therapeutic process. Without this understanding, given the vulnerable nature of the fantasy selfobject relationship at the time, re-traumatizing of the patient is likely.

Ulman and Paul (1995) have suggested that Kohut's reference to the shifting subjective experience of a selfobject from "subject" to "object-oriented" is consistent with, and parallels Winnicott's (1951, 1959) description of transitional objects. These phenomena are subjectively experienced as existing in a psychological space of illusion and fantasy between "me" and "not me," that is, between subject and object. However, drawing attention to the idea that a transitional object is not compatible with self psychology (1992, p. 113), they cite Adler's work (2006, p. 34) to introduce the idea of a transitional selfobject, which "constitutes a legitimate blending of Winnicottian object relations theory with Kohutian self-psychological theory" (2006, p. 459).

We suggest that every fantasy selfobject in its transitional state includes a twinship experience. A fantasy selfobject is created when a person's archaic longings have not been met. The person imagines or fantasizes himself in a relationship that he has not experienced in his real world, creating an alternative world for himself, in the fantasy. If a patient can recognize his creation of himself in the fantasy he has created, it is possible for the fantasized version of himself to evolve into a person who recognizes his longing for the responsiveness he requires, and can ensure it is met. It is noteworthy that when a patient inserts someone else into the fantasy, that "person" is his own creation, and is organized by a part of his own subjectivity. The "other" in the fantasy is literally an extension of himself. In this sense, a fantasy selfobject is in fact, an archaic twinship selfobject experience, even if the fantasy involves an idealizing or mirroring selfobject. In a fantasy selfobject, a patient experiences himself as a human being among other human beings *who are all inherently parts of himself.*

Lars and the Real Girl

In the movie, Lars "presents" as an extremely shy young man who works in an office with others. His mother died giving birth to him and his only connection with her is a blanket she knitted for him before his birth. Lars' father, who in Lars' words, "didn't want anyone around" withdrew emotionally when Lars' mother died. His father's withdrawal was so unbearable that Lars' older brother, Gus, left home as soon as he could, abandoning Lars to a lifeless and lonely existence.

We meet Lars after his father has died and Gus, with his pregnant wife, Karin, have returned to live in the family home. Lars has moved into a rundown garage on the same property. He is obviously well liked by people in the community, all of who persist with minimal success, in trying to engage him.

These pressures to participate socially make Lars extremely anxious. His dread of engaging is apparent in a number of ways. He assiduously avoids eye contact of any kind. When Karin approaches the garage to ask him to join them for a meal, he, like a terrified young child clinging on to his mother's skirt as a stranger approaches, hides behind a curtain, hanging on to his mother's blanket which, throughout the movie, he wears as a scarf. Not surprisingly, he is clearly very lonely.

Through a colleague, Lars buys a life-sized blow-up, anatomically correct plastic doll, online. Lars excitedly asks Karin if a friend—Bianca, the name he gives to the doll—can stay with them. Gus and Karin, equally excited by this arrival, agree. Lars proudly carries and places Bianca at the dining table and talks to all of them as if she is human. Making eye contact now, he excitedly explains that they met online, that her mother died when she was born and that she, like him, is very shy. He describes a number of other similarities between them.

Gus is convinced his brother is "crazy." Karin suggests they take Bianca to the local doctor "because her trip must have been stressful." Lars agrees. The doctor, also a pyschologist, suggests weekly visits because "Bianca seems to have something medically wrong with her" and advises Gus and Karin to "go along with it … because Bianca is in town for a reason." Very reluctantly, they follow this advice, and slowly the community, also very reluctant initially, begins to creatively participate in the fantasy by including Bianca in many activities with and, later, without Lars.

Following Bianca's arrival, Lars spends many comfortable, anxiety-free hours with her. He clearly feels completely "at home" with her, and in this safe space he shows her his childhood haunts, which significantly are all connected to activities he shared with Gus and Gus's friends before Gus left home. He sings unselfconsciously, and shows off his skills while he chatters away to Bianca. As the devoted boyfriend, Lars attends her weekly treatments with the doctor who asks him about Bianca's background. Lars responds reluctantly and with little eye contact initially. When he tells her that Bianca's parents died when she was a baby, the doctor says, "That's not fair," to which Lars responds: "Yeah, but she does not feel sorry for herself or anything, she just wants to be treated as normal." At the same time he picks up an ornament, which he begins to swivel on the tip of his middle finger. The doctor says: "I admire Bianca's wishes" and Lars agrees. He points to a picture on her bookshelf and asks: "is that your husband?" to which the doctor says: "yes ... he died." Lars is moved and says emotionally: "I'm sorry ... do you have kids?" The doctor says: "no." Lars looks up, drops the ornament and says: "you must be very lonely." She replies: "sometimes I feel so lonely that I forget what day it is and how to spell my name." He looks at her first disbelievingly and then when he realizes she is serious he laughs, looks down, and picks up the ornament. A relatively long silence is followed by the doctor asking, apparently casually, "you?" Lars sits back, wags his finger with a smile and says "you're funny" communicating quite clearly that he was not going to fall for that trick—to get him to talk about himself. As the movie continues, the content of their conversations, all focused on Bianca's experiences, made up by Lars, become increasingly intimate. They reveal similarities between all three of them, particularly Bianca's experiences (made up by Lars) of loneliness and isolation, in which Lars and the doctor are both able to find themselves and each other.

This intimacy is evident when the doctor, referring to his sister-in-law, Karin, comments: "you must be excited about a baby on the way," which Lars does not confirm. Instead, after she asks if he wants to be an uncle, he asks her if she ever wanted to be a mom. He challenges her with eye contact when she says, "I don't know." This prompts her admission: "yes, but I am not able to have children now." Distressed and crying, Lars says "that's too bad ... Bianca is like that too ... she cannot have babies either."

He tells the doctor that when Bianca was a baby her mother died in "the middle of things" to which the doctor replies: "like yours."

As these conversations continue, and while Lars is in a "relationship" with Bianca, he grows more and more able to participate and engage in intimate conversations with others beyond Bianca and the doctor. He begins to ask questions, which help him to discover aspects of his own life that, from the frozen and bewildering place he inhabited, he had obviously never been able to ask. For example, he asks Gus about what their father did. And, following Bianca purportedly describing her culture's rituals around transitions between boy and manhood, Lars asked his brother how he knew he had reached manhood. These conversations reveal to Gus for the first time how his leaving had traumatized Lars and how Lars, like himself, felt in the face of their father's depression. Towards the end of the movie he explains that he left home because he too could not bear the emptiness of his father's depression.

Lars begins to witness how people relate to and find similarities between themselves and Bianca through a variety of social interactions. Ultimately, and again significantly, by their active participation in the life Lars has created for Bianca, the community facilitates a process in which Lars learns to recognize her as a separate center of initiative. One evening, he comes home to find a woman from the church and Karin getting Bianca ready for a charity function. He says he and Bianca had an arrangement to play scrabble and they ask him if he consulted "the roster" of Bianca's commitments. He said he hadn't and asked them to give him some privacy with Bianca. We hear him shouting—he should not have to check a roster to know Bianca's movements; she was his girlfriend. The women reprimanded Lars for the way he shouted at Bianca who they explain has a life of her own and is making valuable contributions in the community, suggesting he should be proud of Bianca.

As the film develops, Lars manages to tolerate these externally led reorganizations of the fantasy he created around Bianca more and more. The responses and modifications by the community enable Lars to engage with others besides Bianca, including Margo, a young woman at the office who has, throughout the movie, obviously been attracted to Lars.

While this is all taking place, Lars announces that Bianca is unconscious. After a consultation with the doctor, Lars sadly tells everyone that Bianca is dying, which she does shortly afterwards. The local community feel the loss in very moving ways. The movie ends with Lars and members of the community standing at Bianca's grave. Lars asks Margo if she would like to go for a walk. She happily agrees and the movie, and the fantasy, both end.

Interpreting the movie

Prior to Gus's leaving, Lars had clearly shared with Gus a healthy relational beginning. Gus's leaving constitutes a devastatingly traumatic selfobject failure, which left him exposed to a disillusioning world of people, none of whom provided him with the selfobject responsiveness he required. It forced Lars to live an incredibly lonely life feeling agonizingly uncomfortable, panicky, and with little idea of how to "be" in the presence of other human beings. This is evident in his assiduous avoidance of any kind of human exchange. We suggest that the blanket/scarf, his constant comfort and companion following the loss of his mother and brother, became an antidote to the crushing feelings of loneliness that he felt when Gus left. As such, while it might have functioned to sustain his self-state for long periods of time, occupying the trailing edge dimension, it was never going to facilitate the kind of relational transformation we examine in this chapter.

Lars' creation of Bianca can be understood as an attempt to create a new kind of relatedness; but whether she is going to perform the function of a forward, rather than a trailing edge "fantasy selfobject" is, initially, uncertain. Lars enjoyed discovering himself as alive, vital, and solid in Bianca's presence but notably, she is not a subject and she is not human. She is organized initially as an "object" with no agency of her own, providing the same pacifying relief that the blanket did.

Lars' creation of Bianca and his organization of who she is in his life is, however, very different to the blanket. The very fact that she is not a human means she starts off as a safe and non-intrusive "other" with whom Lars begins to "relate" and, in "conversation," discover himself and his own subjectivity. Unlike the blanket, he "talks" to and "communicates" with her, but more importantly for transformation, he can talk about her to others. This, significantly, gives these others access to his fantasy. His creation of Bianca's background enables him to find similarities between the two of them which means he can, and does, find aspects of himself in this fantasy. Lars might fantasize that Bianca experiences him as alike, too. He enjoys her watching him sing and chop wood and, his renewed energy, happiness, and cohesion appear to rest simply on his newfound capacity to feel, to exist, and to "be" in the presence of this initially safe, fantasized, self-sustaining other. As long as he is with her, it is clear that Lars experiences himself as human, vital and filled with energy, enthusiasm, and a confidence that was not in evidence before she "arrived."

The central feature of this early relationship is that it is an archaic selfobject experience that unfolds in a one-way fashion, there for Lars and Lars only. It is located in the trailing edge dimension. Its rigid initial organization, while seemingly self-sustaining, clearly indicates that it is not a mature and mutual form of relating. For longer than Gus is comfortable, transformation seems unlikely. However, as the movie continues, we become aware that there is indeed a window for transformation. It begins with the doctor's understanding that "Bianca is in town for a reason" and the way in which she treats Bianca as human, engages with Lars as if Bianca is human, and encourages others in Lars' context to do likewise.

The doctor's capacity to participate in the fantasy for as long as it is needed is an essential aspect of Lars' recovery. Her familiarity with the crushingly painful feelings of loss and loneliness, having lost her husband and being childless, enables her to find herself in Lars' creation of Bianca's loneliness. This helps her to profoundly recognize Lars' loneliness and his need for Bianca.

What is key in this process is the fact that Lars' fantasy tie with Bianca was created in a way that makes it accessible to others in his context, who can, and become willing to find themselves in the fantasy. The doctor is the first to do this, but initially, Lars only allowed her to do this with reference to Bianca's subjectivity. Whenever she enquired into Lars' subjectivity directly, he effectively sidestepped the question, e.g. when, following her direct question about his, and not Bianca's, loneliness, he wagged his finger at her "warning her" not to intrude.

The doctor's empathic understanding of his need for this fantasy enabled Lars to safely find and discover his subjectivity in a relational world without threat to his fragile self-state and without the intense anxiety of being abandoned again to the intense isolation and loneliness he knew only too well. The co-created fantasy of Bianca, which can also be described as shared "reality," suggests "transitional selfobject relatedness"

(Bacal, 1985; Basch, 1986; Ulman and Paul, 1992), this time in the forward edge dimension. While Bianca began as a fantasy selfobject, with a "subjectivity" created by Lars alone, significantly, its organization allows for its evolution to a fantasy, which is influenced and reorganized by the doctor and later, others in Lars' surroundings. He began, through Bianca, to ask Gus questions about his father and masculine development. Gus's realization of how naive Lars still was about life and movingly, the way in which Gus discovers similarities between them ushers in a new way of relating between himself and Lars. This revives the archaic selfobject experience that Gus had begun to provide for Lars before he left home. It stirs Lars' developmental yearning for confirmation that others can find themselves in him (Togashi, 2009a, 2011a or see Chapters 2 and 4). The new experience of receiving the responses he requires, as he did in the movie, provides Lars with a humanizing experience, i.e. one of feeling human in the company of, as he has begun to discover, other essentially alike, human beings.

In the process of the co-creation of Bianca as a fantasy selfobject, a space was created for her "subjectivity" to emerge. This happened because others involved were allowed, and able, to find a space for their own subjectivity in Lars' creation of Bianca. Her "subjectivity" emerged in conversations about her and as a result of how the doctor and others were able to find themselves in her. In other words, they created a psychic function in Bianca, which was not necessarily related to the one that Lars intended and created initially.

In this way, Bianca became more human to Lars and to the community who in these conversations, elaborated on who she was and her involvement in community activities. This gave her a function in the community not only in relation to, and for, Lars. Bianca was no longer merely a plastic doll, an object, with no agency, which Lars could control and use whenever, and however, he needed to. She had become someone in the community who was being consistently treated as a woman with an independent and separate center of initiative. For Lars, this ushered in a reluctant understanding that Bianca had different needs to his own. She required space away from his control, which was initially very difficult for Lars' vulnerable self-state.

For us, Lars' experience of Bianca is best described as a transformation of experiences from a trailing edge fantasy selfobject to a forward edge selfobject experience, which, in the transformation of what was until then a traumatized system, became a mature system of relating. This was only possible as a result of the way in which the community participated in the development of who, rather than what, Bianca was and what she needed, as a separate subjectivity.

In so suggesting, we posit that transformation of a fantasy selfobject is possible as a result of a process in which the patient's organization of the fantasy is such that it allows others to participate in, and to find themselves in it. We believe that it is through the mutual finding process (Togashi, 2012a) of the selfobject fantasy, that patients come to recognize the subjectivity of the fantasy selfobject, because it is rooted in the recognition of both their own subjectivity and that of the other participant. A transitional fantasy selfobject, therefore, functions as a way of maintaining the individual's fragile sense of self, regulating his affect, while at the same time also providing a safe enough space for him to recognize the subjectivity of the other. It generates what we would describe as a relationship in which, like Lars, the patient begins to participate as a human being among other human beings.

Case vignettes from Kottler's work with her patients

1. Aakifa

Aakifa's childhood was one of chronic exposure to a disillusioning and traumatically interfering world of people who failed to provide her with the selfobject experiences she needed. She was the youngest child in a large family of boys, all of whom bullied her. One of them was both physically and emotionally crushing. Her father was critical, unsupportive, and verbally violent in unpredictable, often humiliating ways. There was little affirmation of her adventurous, curious, and creative nature, which seems to have been evident from a young age. Her mother, a devout Muslim, acknowledged her substantial achievements, but being extremely religious, encouraged her never to take pride in them because "God had blessed her" with the talents she obviously had. The rest of her family ignored, demeaned, trivialized, or ridiculed the many products of her creativity. This left her constantly feeling humiliated and misunderstood by them and, in a confusing way, embarrassed rather than proud of her talents. She concluded that there was something inherently bad about her, especially when she was enjoying herself in the presence of others.

Nevertheless she kept trying and succeeded in many ways. She did very well academically and had a number of good friends. She had a part-time "business" at school, which drew unmerciful teasing, and was constructing artworks of note when her father accepted a job in his country of origin. She was sent ahead to live with unknown grandparents to complete her schooling. What she imagined would be an incredibly exciting adventure turned into a traumatically alienating nightmare, the extent of which we are only now beginning to understand. She found herself alone in a new town, at a new school, surrounded by strangers.

We have, in the course of the therapy, discovered that Aakifa grew up believing that acceptance, love, and relationships were entirely dependent on the agendas of others. Her function was to please by doing only what others expected and demanded of her. Her childhood and adult relational life have been filled with what she has come to describe as her "doing" rather than "being" human while keeping wishes or desires of her own, secret or hidden. Very early on in the therapy, Aakifa told me of a dream in which "I swam up to a glass barrier beyond which I could see a vast ocean filled with the most beautiful sea life. I was frustrated because I could not find a way to get beyond the barrier."

Aakifa began to keep a diary about ten years prior to entering therapy. Like Ms G's genie (Kohut, 1984), it functions for her as a fantasy selfobject in the trailing edge. Initially mistrustful of the therapeutic process, and of me, she kept the contents of her diary very much outside of the therapy process.

Treating me somewhat like Bianca, for a long while Aakifa did not want me to talk too much and for the most part kept me at a distance and as a somewhat invisibly created object—there to listen but not to speak. Slowly, however, with an increasing sense that I was not sitting in constant judgment of her, she began to share the contents of her diary with me. In it were conversations with "herself" and the most delightful drawings, which she used to visually make sense of who she was, her way of "doing" in the world, and how this was influenced by others in the context in which she lived. This allowed us to elaborate and comment together on the contents in what were now becoming for Aakifa safe, comfortable, self-affirming, self-maintaining, and self-sustaining hours (Kohut, 1984) with me.

Some way into the therapy, while her diary entries remained devoid of the subjectivity of others in her world, Aakifa told me that when she wrote in her diary I was very present for her and that she sometimes wondered if she needed to continue with me as the diary provided much of what she felt she needed. This is not surprising. As a largely visual person myself, and someone who loves splashes of color on a page, it wasn't hard for me to relate to these drawings and to make sense of them in very similar ways to the way she understood them. There were often uncanny similarities between what was going on in us, so it was not difficult for me to find myself in the "conversations" she was having with her diary about herself and to elaborate on them in ways that resonated with and excited her. This facilitated a growing discovery of who she had been and who she was becoming in the world. She began to define what she described as an increasingly "authentic" self, "being" rather than "doing" in the world. I clearly became more alive for her in this collaborative process. This prompted a sudden wish to know a little more about me beyond the silent mirroring presence, which bore witness to her discovery of herself in relation to the "conversations" she had with her diary. She tentatively said she wanted a sense of how I saw the person she was discovering through her diary, rather than how she had always already imagined I saw her. Our backgrounds were, while very different in many ways, remarkably similar. I shared some of these similarities. In this process, it was noteworthy that she regulated how much I could share and say about how I saw her.

This phase of therapy was powerfully transformative developmentally. Her creativity and energy escalated, and she began to talk about venturing out beyond the "glass barrier" into the world she had dreamed about, taking little with her. She had yearned to do this for a long time.

She began to trust others with a little more of herself and her professional life was growing in leaps and bounds. But there remained a noticeable struggle with the subjectivity of others. She had for a long time contemplated ending a relationship, which "curtailed her self-discovery and development." She complained that her partner was too different from her and that the differences inhibited her own vitality.

She said she wanted to go and "test" herself alone, reminded as she was now of a time when she had felt like a lone leopard: "I was happy and I felt powerful." For this reason, she began to talk also of ending therapy. My suggestion that we find a way to continue with the therapeutic relationship at the same time as the adventures began, and a reference to the similarities between the freedom she seemed to be wanting from the constraints of her partner and from therapy was devastating for her. She felt completely misunderstood. She questioned her belief in me as the person she had come to feel I was. It seemed like I, too, had an "agenda, just like all the others who said they believed in me but who made me conform to what they needed from me, not the other way around." She felt demolished by what she heard and understood as my suggesting she "still needed" me and was "unable to grow" without me. Entries in her diary escalated—of her achievements, and of how strong and independent she felt. She increasingly challenged much of what I said, let me speak less and when I did speak raised her voice as if to drown me out in much the same way Lars had wagged his finger at the doctor to stop her from engaging with his subjectivity.

It was an extremely difficult phase. I struggled with the intensity of the feelings I was experiencing in relation to the way in which the fantasy selfobject that Aakifa had created was at this point being reorganized. She was disappointed in me, and clearly, although I was not aware of it at the time, the fantasy selfobject experience was in a precarious state.

I felt frustrated with the discovery that the "we" that she and I had (until then) been delicately co-creating had catapulted back into the antidote repetitive, trailing edge dimension, and that her archaic selfobject needs required more of my participation. As her desires to leave therapy escalated, I was tempted to make it easier for myself by letting Aakifa go. However, I knew that if I allowed her to go, thereby erasing my subjectivity from the relationship, the fantasy selfobject experience as an archaic one would only interrupt and, worse, suspend further emotional development.

In the months that followed this disruption, we struggled through what has turned out to be an incredibly collaborative attempt to make sense of what had emerged between and within each of us. Aakifa refers to the significance of "that session," which we agreed was "scary" for both of us, especially when Aakifa, invoking the metaphor of the leopard again, thought: "I am going to kill you if you push me one bit more, and I will carry on without you." When I suggested that this might have been liberating for her she agreed:

> For two days after our fight I was in some kind of resistance. I thought, "this is not what is happening ... no! ... we are not going to go along this route ... if we do then I am out." Then I had a chat to myself and said: "Amanda is human and I am human ... I said things, and Amanda said things, and thank god we are human ... Amanda is not Ultra God on a pedestal and we are in a relationship, and we will get there ... Amanda is reasonable and rational and we will get there." The minute I had that conversation I felt free. But, I had to ask myself if I was giving up again and not being completely authentic just to protect this relationship from going the way that the others went.

These thoughts facilitated an increasing recognition of, until then, hidden aspects of Aakifa's subjectivity, particularly her fears of the travel she had insisted she wanted to do alone. A forward edge therapeutic revival of earlier relationships with a transitional selfobject experience appeared, which has helped Aakifa develop a capacity to acknowledge differences between people. Significant, too, is the appearance of the tendrils of recognition of the subjectivity of the other.

2. Taurik

Taurik was struggling with his relationship and was referred by his general physician for depression. He could not understand why his boyfriend, Gavin, to whom he gave his all, did not reciprocate his love and efforts. Very early into the treatment, he said that although I was much older than he was and a woman, he felt "completely at home" with me. He insisted he knew me inside out, that I was just like him, that I liked the same food and that he knew what car I drove. The fact that he was often accurate was unsettling to say the least and led to my enquiring as to whether he had seen me outside of the therapy room when I had not noticed him. He denied this, simply insisting that he could tell what kind of person I was just by being with me.

He believed I was the "best therapist in town" and insisted that our relationship would never end—he believed we would eventually become friends. Suggestions of anything to the contrary were knowingly brushed aside as if to say that I would ultimately discover that he was right and I was wrong. He "knew" we would in due course regularly meet for coffee. I found this unswerving confidence both fascinating and extremely uncomfortable. At times, the absoluteness of the objectification of me was unbearable, and I struggled to find myself in his creation of me.

He came to therapy twice a week and in this time there were significant changes. His professional life, which was already successful, had nevertheless improved substantially. He had bought his "dream house." Although separated from Gavin, the loneliness he had experienced when he first came to therapy had disappeared. He was enjoying a rich social life with newfound friends. Whereas previously he was intent upon bringing me gifts, these had diminished as it felt he was finding himself much more comfortably in the world and in relation to me. Three years into the therapy, Taurik announced that he did not need the therapy anymore but did not want to stop seeing me. He said there was too much "analysis" going on; he "just wanted to come and chat with me about ordinary things."

Clearly influenced by the movie *Lars and the Real Girl*, which I had not yet seen, he half jokingly suggested that a life-size cardboard cut out picture of me in his house would for the most part provide him with what he needed from me. This was a clear indication that he remained far from comfortably able to find himself in the presence of others and that a capacity to mutually relate had not yet developed. Many of our conversations indicated that he was still struggling with accepting, on a more intimate level, that others might have different needs to his, with voices and minds of their own. I believed there was still much work to be done but should have recognized that the trailing edge repetitive dimension of the fantasy selfobject was still very much in the foreground. Although this perturbation most likely signaled a developmental preparedness for a transition, he needed my participation to enable this. What I did illustrates my lack of understanding of Taurik's need for me to facilitate and not to challenge, for as long as it was needed, the emergence of something new, and the further unfolding of his transitional selfobject fantasy, which had been organized in the form of a twinship tie.

I did the opposite of what was needed. I upped the "analysis" without recognizing the damage this was doing to Taurik's still extremely vulnerable fantasy selfobject experience. At precisely the wrong time,

Taurik's "Bianca" (in the form of Kottler) came "alive" with an unwelcome, separate, and unexpected voice that he could no longer magically control (Ulman and Paul, 1992), and in which he could no longer safely maintain and sustain his self-state.

The "we" of our relationship, the unbeknownst to me until then, co-created fantasy selfobject, became intolerable. Taurik was no longer able to spontaneously conjure me up whenever he needed his creation of me to provide relief from unbearable affect states such as the one he would have felt at this point in the therapy. From wanting to always be my friend and to have coffee with me, he decided that it was time to terminate the therapy. Clearly, my response to his request demonstrates a total misunderstanding of what we have described above. I believe that he experienced the rupture to his creation of me and of our relationship as retraumatization. My failure to find myself in his fantasy had maintained Taurik's need for it to continue in its still archaic state. Further, I had failed to understand that I was participating in his creation of this self-sustaining relationship—as an antidote in the repetitive dimension of the transference, in which the trailing edge dimension was in the foreground.

Discussion

We have drawn attention to the distinction between the trailing and forward edge dimensions of a fantasy selfobject. We have expanded the concept by demonstrating the crucial role of the therapist's participation in the creation of the fantasy. This is essential for it to function effectively in our work with developmentally traumatized patients, their recovery, and their process of humanization, or of becoming human in the relational world. Our case illustrations reveal significant clinical implications:

1 Traumatized patients often organize therapeutic relationships by creating a fantasy that provides the conditions necessary for them to find or discover themselves.
2 The organization initially prevents the therapist from being able to do likewise, for fear of recreating the trauma that necessitated the use of a fantasy selfobject in the first place.
3 Whether aware of it or not, therapists are always already participating in the patient's fantasy creation of this developmentally enabling

environment—the "we" within which patient and therapist work. This process can facilitate the shift into the forward edge transformational dimension. However, as demonstrated in the cases of Aakifa and Taurik, fantasies are not always as transparent as Lars' creation of Bianca.

4   The lack of transparency makes successful participation in the process extremely challenging, particularly because the fantasy rests on a very fragile and tenuous base.

5   Whether or not a therapist comes to function as a successfully participating person in the creation of a humanizing transitional selfobject experience will depend on the therapist's ability to recognize and distinguish between the forward and trailing edge dimensions of the fantasy. Without this recognition of the vicissitudes of the meaning of a fantasy selfobject, it is difficult to respond in a way that will facilitate its potentially transformative nature. Recognition facilitates an understanding of the need, as difficult as it might be, to participate in the fantasy for as long as it is required.

Our analysis of Lars reveals another essential developmental need for such patients to experience, that is, the ongoing and fluid nature of the particular form that each patient's fantasy takes. If the forward edge dimension and meaning of the fantasy is not empathically understood, the essential features of a twinship selfobject tie cannot occur and, as we have demonstrated with Taurik, there is a danger of retraumatization. Taurik's feeling that there was too much analysis going on and his wish to meet to chat as friends was indicative of the fantasy remaining in the trailing edge, and as still extremely delicate and vulnerable in spite of the vitality he was experiencing in his relational world. Discovering the existence of Kottler's subjectivity was something his fantasy could not yet absorb. Further, because he left therapy, the equally essential need to facilitate a co-created transformation of the fantasy—including the incremental and inevitable disruptions—was denied him, at least with Kottler. The moments in which similar disruptions occurred between Lars and the community over the scrabble game, for example, were empathically understood, explained, and responded to, by the doctor and significant others in his environment. This also happened with Aakifa.

Our case material suggests that a person who is not able to experience or treat others as being human can only come to experience himself and the other as being human in the context of a delicately negotiated transformation of a fantasy selfobject. In this process, the originator of the fantasy has to allow access to the other participant. For it to succeed, the other must be willing and able to find herself in the fantasy. Without this, it will not move into the forward edge dimension. Through this mutual finding process (Togashi, 2012a) in the selfobject fantasy, patients come to recognize the subjectivity of the fantasy selfobject, which, as we have seen, originates in the delicately unfolding subjectivity of the other participant.

A fantasy selfobject, which has the capacity for transformation, can only evolve in the forward edge, not the repetitive/trailing edge dimension. A fantasy selfobject occurs in a space in which patients like Aakifa create their own fantasy, in which, for transformation, therapists need to be able and willing to participate by establishing in them their own subjectivity. As Taurik's case material demonstrates, when therapists cannot find themselves in the fantasy, or resist doing so, the fantasy, created for psychological survival, cannot transform. They will continue to exist as an antidote, in the trailing edge dimension of what Stolorow (1988), and Stolorow and Atwood (1994) describe as the repetitive dimension.

It is noteworthy that the transformation of a selfobject experience, which proceeds from a fantasy selfobject to a transitional selfobject experience, involves struggles with similarities, differences, and otherness in each of the cases described. As discussed, a fantasy selfobject and its transitional state involves a twinship experience to the extent that, in the fantasy selfobject, a patient creates an alternative life for himself with others who are extensions of his own subjectivity. In this sense, the difference between a fantasy selfobject and a traditional selfobject is the degree to which otherness is recognized. If, in the therapeutic process, an analyst is successfully allowed to participate in the co-creation and evolution of the fantasy, the fantasy will come to include some aspects of the otherness of the analyst. At this point, we would no longer refer to it as a fantasy selfobject. It has become a transitional selfobject. The patient no longer experiences himself as a human being, among other human beings who are actually intrinsically parts of himself. Instead, he experiences himself as a human being among other human beings *with some quality of otherness*, as separate and different beings, that is, human, human beings.

In human relationships, our similarities and differences are immediately evident, and we can hold on to ourselves as separate but able to relate nevertheless. However, as described in Chapter 8, victims of relational trauma are afraid of, and do not trust, this possibility. This illuminates another crucial expansion beyond Kohut's idea that the essential point of a twinship selfobject tie between two people is that a person's self–state is vitalized and solidified as a result of the way he or she is experienced by the other. Considering Kohut's final definition of twinship, in Chapter 4, Togashi (see also 2012a) states that for a twinship tie to be a mature one, it must have been organized through a delicate balance of empathic negotiation of a sense of sameness and differences in a dyad, i.e. twinship is organized in the mutual finding of oneself and not-oneself in each other. For us, then, the essential feature of a transitional selfobject experience lies in this indirect process of mutual finding within a twinship experience. However, as is evidenced in the case of Aakifa, we need to be sensitive to, and with, the tentative nature of the evolution of the forward edge aspect of a fantasy selfobject. We also need to be aware of how often, as demonstrated in the case of Taurik, this can mimic and feel like intolerable, untreatable, severely narcissistic, or even psychotic pathology.

Chapter 6

Contemporary self psychology and cultural issues

"Self–place experience" in an Asian culture

Koichi Togashi, Ph.D., L.P.

Self-psychological and intersubjective theories are now recognized by clinicians internationally. Some theorists argue that cultural and ethnic issues have not been sufficiently addressed in these theories (Orange, Atwood, and Stolorow, 1997; Togashi, 2010; Frie, 2013). Understanding how theories that arise from experiences in different cultures can lead to new understanding is the point of this chapter.

Self psychology is often regarded as the antithesis of the modern Western perspective, in which it is believed that an individual mind is organized independently and that a narcissistic tie with the other is primarily pathological. It recognizes that a sense of self is always understood in the context of relationships with others, groups, and society. Contemporary self-psychological system theories—such as intersubjectivity theory (Atwood and Stolorow, 1984; Stolorow, Brandchaft and Atwood, 1987; Stolorow and Atwood, 1992; Orange, Atwood, and Stolorow, 1997; Stolorow, 1997), dyadic systems theory (Lachmann, 2000, 2008; Beebe and Lachmann, 2002), complexity theory (Coburn, 2002, 2007a, 2007b), and specificity theory (Bacal, 1998, 2006, 2011)—more clearly avoid describing a human mind as static, isolated, and separated from others. They posit that an individual's mind is organized as it is influencing and being influenced by the other's, and that all psychological phenomena, such as symptoms, fantasies, and transference–countertransference, should be understood as unfolding in the intersubjective field co-created by him and the other. By avoiding the myth of a static and isolated human mind, these theorists open the door to non-Western perspectives in self psychology.

These theories are well understood and useful, but I would say that they are not necessarily sufficient to ground a discussion of the various cultural issues and experiences in self psychology. An individual is embedded in the intersubjective context; these theorists are also embedded in cultural, ethnic, and social contexts through which he or she experiences the world. These theories have not been sufficiently worked out for an individual's subjectivity that is embedded in a non-Western or non-North American cultural context.

Satoshi, a Japanese man whom I have seen for five years, occasionally claims that he is not able to say what he wants to say. He often remarks, "I do not think that the topic I am thinking of is suitable to this place" or "I am unable to read what this place wants me to say." When he feels that he can discuss the topic that the place wants him to talk about, he can freely talk about it; otherwise, he feels he is talking about something inappropriate in that place. At the beginning of therapy, I thought that he was searching for the topic that "I" wanted him to talk about. His answer was no. He emphasized that he knew that I wanted him to talk; stated differently, he knew that I wanted him to talk about anything coming into his mind. What he did not know is whether or not the topic coming to mind could be blended into a place that included everything relating to the analytic dyad. His sense of self is organized in his experience of place and in his awareness of how the place experiences him. In this context, it does not matter how his analyst experiences him, for he experiences his analyst only as a part of the place.

Such an episode is not unusual in practice with Japanese patients. They sometimes experience themselves and others as a part of the place, or they experience the place as a part of them; the sense of self is organized in relation to "the place" more than it is to "the analyst." This manner of self-experience does not necessarily indicate a defense, a pathology, or a devaluation of the human in this culture, but indicates a significant cultural form through which people experience themselves. Unfortunately, this manner of experience cannot be adequately described in traditional or contemporary self-psychological theories. It is what I would call a "self–place experience"—a term modeled on Kohut's naming of the selfobject experience (Kohut, 1971, 1977, 1984).

In this chapter, I first briefly review some experiential concepts advocated by traditional self psychologists and discuss some explanatory concepts provided by our contemporaries, because self psychologists tend to differentiate traditional ideas from contemporary system theories in the dimension of description. They identify the former as experiential description, and the latter as explanatory (Orange, Atwood and Stolorow, 1997; Coburn, 2007a, 2007b; Pickles and Shane, 2007; Lachmann, 2008; Stolorow, 2010). From this perspective, the former is understood as aiming particularly to describe how a patient (and an analyst) experience the world; the latter is defined as theories aiming to reveal how interactive psychological processes are proceeding in an analytic dyad and how a relationship transforms through an analyst's (a patient's) effort to put himself in his patient's (an analyst's) position (Lachmann, 2008). After this review of papers, I present the "self–place experience," which is deeply connected to Asian and, especially, Japanese culture. An analyst who treats a Japanese patient is often required to be sensitive to this dimension of experience. Satoshi's case vignette, which then follows, will make my point clear. Finally, I conclude that a patient's working through a self–place experience leads to the dialectic between committing himself to fate and experiencing himself as an independent center of initiative. This dialectic could be through a patient's recognizing himself in the place and his therapist, and recognizing the place in him and his therapist.

Self-psychological concepts in the experiential discourse

Kohut (1971, 1977, 1984) claims that the self is not a product of psychological separation from his caregiver, and that a sense of self is always organized in relation to the way he experiences how his caregiver experiences him. A child experiences himself as vital, cohesive, and consistent through finding a gleam in his mother's eyes (mirroring); he experiences himself as protected and strong through finding his caregiver as idealizable (idealizing). He experiences himself as connected to the world by experiencing himself essentially as like his caregiver (twinship). Kohut emphasizes that a self-experience endures by maintaining an affective tie to others who are experienced as providing a certain function, namely, a selfobject function.

Self psychology reveals that a human being unavoidably finds himself in a difficult position. In order to maintain his psychological health, he needs the other, whom he experiences as providing a selfobject function; but he cannot control how the other experiences him. Thus, in this model, a conflict takes place between his selfobject need and the way he sees how the other experiences him, rather than between agencies within the ego as Freudian ego psychology claims.

When Japanese psychoanalysts treat their patients, this model is useful. Among Japanese, it is self-evident that an individual's experience is always influenced by how the other experiences him, and that a sense of self is embedded in a relational (sometimes a familial) context. Nevertheless, I would say that this perspective does not fully describe and capture a Japanese patient's self-experience. A Japanese patient will occasionally complain about a conflict between his selfobject need and a spatial system that exists beyond the relationship between him and his analyst. He often calls it "place," "circumstance," or "situation." As I have discussed elsewhere, Japanese people tend to experience themselves "as within nature or a part of the cosmic tide of time" (Togashi, 2010, p. 114)—and to perceive all human beings and even things as a part of it. Self psychology has not sufficiently focused on this type of subjective experience.

Self-psychological concepts in the explanatory discourse

Contemporary self-psychological system theorists and relational psychoanalysts criticize Kohut's self psychology for adhering to a Freudian linear and one-person perspective in its theoretical framework (Hoffman, 1983; Bromberg, 1989; Aron, 1996; Stolorow, Brandchaft, and Atwood, 1987; Orange, Atwood, and Stolorow, 1997). They insist that Kohut's theory only focuses on how a patient subjectively negotiates the other's experiences, and does not focus on the influence of how the other actually experiences a patient.

Contemporary self-psychological system theorists directly focus on a psychological interplay between an analyst and a patient. Intersubjectivity theory (Atwood and Stolorow, 1984; Stolorow, Brandchaft, and Atwood, 1987; Stolorow and Atwood, 1992; Orange, Atwood, and Stolorow, 1997; Stolorow, 1997) states that the two subjectivities are always embedded in the co-created context, each influencing and being influenced by the other. Specificity theory (Bacal, 1998, 2006, 2011) maintains that a selfobject relatedness is specifically determined in an interaction between a particular patient and a particular analyst. Dyadic system theory (Lachmann, 2000,

2008; Beebe and Lachmann, 2002) advocates that a psychoanalytic relationship is always co-constructed in a psychological interplay coordinated in self-regulation and an interactive regulation involving implicit and explicit processes. In these models, any clinical issues are understood, not as a representation of a patient's isolated mind, but as a co-construction arising in the interaction between a particular patient's mind and a particular analyst's mind.

Yet these contemporary self-psychological system theories do not deny the importance of experiential concepts provided by Kohut's self psychology, such as self, selfobject, and empathy. As Lachmann (2008) describes it, experiential concepts are clinically useful and make it easy to follow a patient's experience, even though they do not actually explain what exactly is going on between a patient and an analyst. For example, a description such as "fragmentation of the self" or "selfobject experience" is clear and experience-near, which makes an analyst easily empathic to his patient's subjective experience, even though a theory is still needed to explain how and in what process a patient's experience emerges and changes. Both theories are supposed to work together collaterally. The development of explanatory theories does not immediately mean that it is not necessary to elaborate self-experience that is embedded in a certain culture at the experiential level.

Self–place experience in Japanese people

Contemporary self-psychological system theorists and relational psychoanalysts struggle to theorize how an individual negotiates his yearning for connectedness and the other's having an independent center of initiative (Benjamin, 1991, 1998; Teicholz, 1999; Pickles and Shane, 2007; Orange, 2010). Despite some differences of emphasis, these theorists advance the view that an individual's failures and successes in recognizing the otherness of the other are connected to his psychological health. They believe that one proper therapeutic goal is to enable a patient to experience himself as having his own initiative in the presence of the other on whom he has been most dependent (Benjamin, 1990). In this paradigm, the basic conflict takes place between the patient's selfobject need and the other's will.

To the contrary, as I mentioned at the beginning of this chapter, a conflict in a Japanese patient often emerges between his selfobject need and "place." "Place" here does not mean Newtonian absolute space; it would be defined as a space subjectively bounded by, and leading to, the participant's roles, positions, needs, expectations, the form of relationship of the two participants, and other external factors. It is experienced by an individual as a dynamic system, self-organized around nonlinearity and unexpectedness in a particular therapeutic process. It includes, for example, an analyst's office, all the subjective experiences and cultural background of a patient and an analyst, those aspects of the people around them, the history of their therapeutic journey, the time appointed for the session, the order in which patients are seen, a patient's and an analyst's feelings and thoughts, the flow of the session, the weather, the unspoken mood in the office, the emotional states of people whom a patient and an analyst have seen just before the session begins, the topic an analyst has discussed with a previous patient, and so on. In this perspective, a conflict does not take place between a patient's selfobject need and the other's will, but between a patient's selfobject need and the suitability of the place.

Roland (1994, 1996) differentiates self structure in Eastern culture from self structure in North American culture. In Japan and India, he says, it is manifested in a "we–self" structure, in which selfhood is often formed in the relational and situational context. According to him, in Western or North American society, self structure is formed in "I–self," in which people wish to experience their own needs as an entity independent of others. He finds that self structure is colored by a culture, and that culturally determined communication style facilitates the creation of a culturally unique self structure.

From his cultural perspective, Roland (1996) posits that previous self-psychological and intersubjective studies have not sufficiently revealed the culturally unique reciprocity of the self–selfobject experience as manifested in the Asian interpersonal relationship. I fundamentally agree with his perspective; however, I would posit that Roland's discussion of I–self and we–self still includes a Western perspective. First, the dichotomy already includes Descartes's dualism, in which it is seen that an independent self is related to an individual's inner experience, while an interdependent self is related to his outer experience. Recent cultural researches (Sober, 2000; Markus and Kitayama, 2003a, 2003b; Frie, 2010) suggest that there is diversity in self-experience within and across cultures, and both an independent sense of self and an interdependent sense of self are seen in many cultures and generations. Furthermore, the term "we" indicates an individual self that is organized in relation to an analyst and a patient, or to people around them. His discussion fails to take into account that self-experience in the Japanese patient is embedded in the situational context beyond human relationships, that is, in "placeness."

"Place," *basho* in Japanese, is a concept that has been studied by Japanese philosophers (Nishida, 1946; Nakamura, 1989; Ueda, 2000; Kimura, 2005). Nishida (1946) draws attention to place or topos in the understanding of "being" in his epistemology. For him, focusing on a predicate logic in Japanese language, in which "the predicate is predominant and the subject can often be omitted" (Sakabe, 2010, p. 13), and which is often contrasted to a subject logic in Western language, the infinitive, "to be" means "to be within." His question concerning how self-awareness is grounded in human experience leads to a consideration of the place in which what is reflected, is reflected. He attempts to redefine self-awareness in place terms, and emphasizes that it refers to a process in which a self mirrors itself within itself. In other words, knower is within known. In order to acquire such awareness, for itself and from within itself, self should have a place of its own.

Self-awareness in his philosophy does not refer to a pre-given personal self which can often be objectified in a subject logic. Rather it indicates a self which can manifest itself in such a way as to place itself within itself. He refers to it as "self-identity in placeness".

"Placeness" in Nishida's philosophy is not necessarily the same as the placeness I discuss in this chapter, His place is the absolute nothingness in which self-consciousness as place is within the place. Our place is, however, a broader concept including relative nothingness in which place can be known and objectified occasionally; our self is a clinical self of a patient and/or a therapist, which can be experienced in the process of referring to the place of which the self is a part. Still, Nishida's discussion indicates that a unique aspect of the Japanese language, the "logic of place," is deeply embedded in Japanese culture.

Nakamura (1989), in his phenomenological reflections, clarifies the psychological meaning of place from a variety of different angles. He posits that place is the basis of being, and is a symbolic and non-Euclidean space embodying the principles of nonlinearity and self-organization; it includes a cosmic rhythm that can be found in any of the elements of place.

Isobe (1976, 1983), through his phenomenological and anthropological study of Japanese culture, emphasizes that Japanese people tend to see themselves within nature or as a part of the cosmic tide of time. He does not discuss placeness directly, but his discussion beautifully describes how a sense of self in Japanese people is organized in relation to a dynamic system beyond the human world. He stresses that in Japanese culture, in contrast to the modern Western perspective, self-experience is organized in the process of an individual's finding himself in nature and finding nature in himself. All entities in this world can be seen as surrounded by a certain cosmic rhythm and as having the same rhythm within them.

Japanese patients often experience place as if it has its own will. This experience can be seen at many levels, ranging from a pathological sense of hopelessness to a healthy level of fatalism; at the extreme, it could be the absolute nothingness in Buddhist enlightenment (Nishida, 1946). I would say that while a hypothetical Western self emerges when an individual finds a certain thing in himself that he finds in the other, a hypothetical Japanese self emerges when an individual finds a certain thing in himself that he finds in the place. In this paradigm, one therapeutic achievement is the negotiation between selfhood and placeness.

Case vignette

Satoshi, a successful researcher in a scientific institute in his early thirties, came to see me in search of an understanding of his chronic sense of loneliness and a feeling of disconnection to the world. He had a good reputation in his institute and professional field; but he was not able to experience himself as secure and safe and vital. He felt that his research belongs outside of the mainstream of his professional field, and he described himself as belonging nowhere. A month earlier, his mentor had died in a traffic accident. The mentor had recognized Satoshi's ability, and Satoshi had idealized him. They had only recently started a big research project together. Now Satoshi was seeking psychoanalytic therapy.

At first I thought that he suffered from the tragic loss of a very special person. However, he described the relationship with his mentor as being only an immature dependency. He emphasized that he would not have been so dependent on the mentor if he had experienced himself as affirmed by his professional field. Asked whether affirmation by the mentor, who was in the same field and who recognized his work, had not been helpful in changing his feelings, he answered immediately, "I feel I am not suited to the professional field if the field does not recognize me." However, he was unable to name those of good reputation whose recognition he sought. And even if the most famous person in the field recognized him, he said, his feeling would not change. For him, no one could represent the field; he was only concerned about recognition by it.

Satoshi often did not feel he could talk about the topic he would most like to talk about. He had talked about unimportant topics that came to mind. He described the feeling by saying: "I do not feel that the most urgent topic is suitable to this place, but another one seems to be okay." When he felt that it was suitable to the place, he could talk about even the most urgent topic without hesitation.

One day, I canceled a session in order to attend a Buddhist memorial service for one of my relatives. He expressed his upset at this, and I asked him to tell me what aspect of my cancellation might have upset him. Was he upset because I was not concerned about how he felt? Was he upset because I put my plan ahead of his? Or was he upset because I did not tell him about the cancellation earlier? He denied all the hypotheticals I presented and said, "It does not matter what you did. What matters is that the memorial service is being held next week. You cannot help attending it, because it was scheduled so. But why now? It is really bad timing." I simply thought at that time that he was trying to avoid accusing me for a fear of losing me, but I did not verbalize that thought.

Satoshi was born into a wealthy family; he has an older brother born a year before him and a younger sister born two years after him. His mother is warm and empathic, and his father is intelligent and idealizable by others. He was treated by both parents with care and was warmly protected and fostered, and he has never felt judged by them or compared to other siblings. However, he knows that he was born unexpectedly. His parents did not plan to have a second child immediately after the first son was born. His parents did not say anything about having him unexpectedly. Yet Satoshi often felt that his birth was meaningless. The birth of his brother, the first son in the family, had obvious significance for the family. And his parents surely had planned to have the third child because they wanted a girl. His sister met their expectation. A year after his sister's birth, he lost a grandmother who had taken care of him and whom he was especially attached to. Although he felt that his parents took good care of him, he often deplored his fate. "I cannot escape from fate. What does the world expect from me?" Within the cosmic tide, he saw himself as powerless.

In the meantime, a week after Satoshi canceled a session, he met a female patient at my door whom I would see after him. A patient who arrives at my office usually waits for the session in the waiting room, and a patient who finishes the session leaves my office and does not pass through the waiting room. Patients do not encounter each other in person; but a patient can determine whether I am seeing someone else before him because every patient takes off his shoes at the door. The patient after Satoshi knew that he had canceled the previous session, because she had not found his shoes. The patient who met him accidentally at the door simply said to him, "Oh, you've come to your session today. Hello." He was struck by her words. As soon as he came into my office a week later, he excitedly told me how wonderful it had been for him that she recognized him. When I asked him in what sense the female patient was important to him, he said that the patient was observant. It was important for him to see that there was a place for him. The female patient's simple words made him realize that he was a part of my office, and my office was a part of him. He continued, "Even if you had said that I am important to you, I would not have had such a wonderful feeling. I would have felt happy, but it would have been a temporary feeling like I had in the relationship with my mentor."

After this session, he was able to talk about any topic freely, and I experienced him as being closer to me. He described his experience, saying, "I did not feel that I was a part of the world. To me, the world worked in a rhythm different from mine. Everybody but me could find the same rhythm in themselves, but I could not find it in me." Through the female patient's recognizing him, he saw himself as a part of a "place"; through his canceling a session, he experienced himself as a person who has an ability to influence "place," as my cancellation affected him and other patients in many ways.

He continued to say that he did not like the term "fate" because he experienced himself as completely powerless in its presence. When he faced the two traumatic losses of special people, his grandmother and mentor, all he could do was to deplore his fate. "Why does the world steal such important figures away from me at the worst possible time?" But now he experienced people as having the same rhythm, more or less; the rhythm was the one he found in the world and in himself. He believed that fate tells him his role. The more he experiences himself as a part of the world, the more he sees me as sharply etched and emotionally close. He no longer feels that his research belongs outside of the mainstream of his professional field.

Discussion

Contemporary self-psychological system theories are often considered the antithesis of modern Western culture because they do not define a human mind as static, isolated, and separated. They posit that an individual's mind is organized by influencing and being influenced by the other. However, these theories do not sufficiently explore a non-Western patient's unique psychological experience *at an experiential level*. A sense of self in a Japanese patient is often organized through the way he experiences how a place experiences him, that is, through a "self–place experience." In a traditional self-psychological model, this seeking for a self–place experience might be misunderstood as resistance, avoidance, or self pathology. An analyst's sensitivity to this type of experience helps him to understand and be empathic toward the self-experience of a Japanese patient.

Our case vignette reveals that a patient's working through a self–place experience leads to the dialectic between committing himself to fate and experiencing himself as an independent center of initiative. This dialectic could be through a patient's recognizing himself in the place and his analyst, and recognizing the place in him and his analyst. In my self-psychological study of a Japanese patient addicted to an archaic narcissistic fantasy, I (Togashi, 2009b) revealed that there is a process in which a patient attempts to envision himself as living in a flow beyond human consideration, as in the cosmos or fate. My finding in this discussion is consistent with the previous article.

I do not limit the self–place experience to Japanese patients, for I maintain that we can find a similar experience in non-Japanese or non-East Asian patients. I would stress, however, that this experience is deeply embedded in the cultural aspect. As Atwood and Stolorow (1979) indicate, psychoanalytic theories cannot avoid being influenced by the theorist's subjective experience. Most self-psychological theories have been advocated by analysts within North American culture. I believe that the intensive study in the experiential discourse by non-North American or non-Western analysts would reveal other types of self-experience embedded in other cultures.

The self–place experience is an experiential-level concept. In this chapter, I have basically focused on a patient's subjective experience; I have not focused on the psychological interaction between an analyst and a patient. For the next step, this concept needs to be elaborated through the study of how and in what processes the experience is organized between an analyst and a patient in the explanatory discourse. Complexity theory proposed by Coburn (2002, 2007a, 2007b) would be helpful in illustrating the process. This theory is concerned with the process of emotional experience through the self-organization and cooperation of many parts in systems. It does not see a psychological phenomenon as an attribute only of one's history, current mental state, or immediate environment, but sees it as an emergence in complex mutual influencing processes between many parts of systems. In this model, "we can no longer think of our world, including our experiential world, as containing disparate, unrelated parts. Not only is the world greater than the sum of its parts, as systems theories are wont to say, but the parts— *all* the parts, *without exception*—are inextricably intertwined and ceaselessly embedded in a larger context" (Coburn, 2007b, p. 6; italics in original).

The mutual finding process (Togashi, 2012a) may also be helpful in elaborating self–place experience in the explanatory discourse. In Chapter 4, my effort to explore the psychological processes that are operating in a twinship experience, I present that "a twinship experience is organized by delicate balance of mutual findings of oneself and not-oneself in the other" (p. 68 in this book, see also Togashi, 2012a, p. 362). When a twinship tie is established in a dyad, an analyst finds himself and not-himself in his patient, and a patient finds herself and not-herself in her analyst. A human being is immediately embedded in this process when he meets the other. As Satoshi's case indicates, the self–place experience is organized by an individual's finding a thing in himself that he finds in the place and in all elements of the place. The mutual finding process may give us a perspective that will permit us to elaborate how an analyst and a patient both contribute to the self–place experience.

Chapter 7

Placeness in the twinship experience

Koichi Togashi, Ph.D., L.P.

Twinship was originally defined by Kohut (1971, 1984) as a patient's yearning to experience himself as like his analyst, or as a patient's yearning to experience his analyst as like himself. Then it was expanded to include the most basic sense of existing in human society, and he described the twinship experience as a "confirmation of the feeling that one is a human being among other human beings" (Kohut, 1984, p. 200). In this theoretical endeavor, the essential aspect of a twinship experience came to be understood as a sense of being a human among human beings more than as a sense of commonality or alikeness.

In a series of studies on a twinship experience from a contemporary self-psychological perspective, referred to throughout this book (see also Togashi, 2009a, 2011c, 2012b; Togashi and Kottler, 2012a, 2012b), I have proposed that a twinship tie is not organized in the way of sharing mere sameness or alikeness (Togashi, 2012a). Rather, it can be described as based on the dialectic between a sense of sameness and difference in the dimension of both participants' subjective experiences, and I maintain that it is organized as a delicate balance between mutual findings of oneself and not-oneself in the other in the dimension of cognitive-perceptive processes. This mutual finding process is not a capacity or achievement acquired through psychological development. Throughout his life, the individual is "always contextually embedded in the mutual process of finding himself and not-himself in the other at conscious and non-conscious levels" (Togashi, 2012, p. 358, see also Chapter 4). As long as people experience themselves as being in the mutual finding process in relationship with others, they will experience themselves as being among other human beings.

Yet I believe it is important to consider the affective quality of deep joy and excitement that is hypothesized as being evoked by a sense of commonality or alikeness in Kohut's model. For this joy and excitement is a significant aspect of a type of twinship, and can be distinguished from a sense of security and relief that comes with feeling that one is a human being among other human beings. In Gardner's understanding (2011, personal communication), that is why Basch, in his attempts to clarify this affective experience (1994), prefers the term "kinship transference" rather than "twinship transference," and redefines it as "the need to belong and feel accepted by one's cohort" (Basch, 1994, p. 4).

What I maintain here is that this deep joy and excitement is not always a central aspect of a sense of commonality or alikeness. I hypothesize that for a therapeutic relationship between a Japanese analyst and a Japanese patient, this affective experience can be connected to another subjective experience for human relatedness. A sense of twinship or kinship in Japanese culture, as I discuss elsewhere (Togashi, 2009a, 2011a, 2012b), is organized in ways that go beyond a sense of commonality or alikeness. Good examples of culturally unique types of relationship among Japanese people have been described as follows: the "teacher–student" relationship (Taketomo, 1989) and the "senpai (senior)–kohai (junior)" relationship (Togashi, 2009a). As I show in Chapter 4, these relationships can be considered a type of twinship, but their essential aspect is a certain sense of connectedness organized between people who have different social statuses and roles, but who belong to the same social setup.

I believe that a key to understanding the joy and excitement in a twinship tie in Japanese culture is the concept of "placeness." In Chapter 6, I proposed that a sense of self in a Japanese patient is often organized through the way he experiences how a place experiences him, that is, through a "self–place experience" (Togashi, 2011c). In a traditional self-psychological model, this seeking for a self-place experience might be misunderstood as resistance, avoidance, or self pathology. An analyst's sensitivity to this type of experience helps him to understand and be empathic toward a sense of self in a Japanese patient.

I argue that in an intersubjective or a relational psychoanalytic model, which is proposed by a Western perspective, a struggle in a therapeutic dyad tends to be described as appearing in the context of "the subjectivity of oneself versus that of the other" (Benjamin, 1991, 1995, 2010; Orange, 2008); but in Japanese and some Asian cultures, we have to recognize that a struggle often appears in the context of "the subjectivities of oneself and the other versus place" (Togashi, 2011c). When a Japanese person is keenly aware of the subjectivities of herself and the other, the relationship is often facing collapse. In a healthy relationship, their subjectivities fit into the authenticity of the place in which they find themselves. In other words, a Japanese patient would be disappointed in the circumstances in which she dares to show and clarify her subjectivity to the other.

In this context, I hypothesize that for Japanese people—probably for anyone, regardless of their cultural background—a twinship tie is deeply related to a feeling of being in the same place with the other. I would say that a particular affective connection in a twinship tie is based on more than a sense of commonality and alikeness organized between two individuals; it is a feeling that both members of a dyad were in the same place in the past, that they are in the same place now, or, in fantasy, that they will be in the same place in the future. Indeed, as I mentioned earlier, both the "teacher–student" relationship (Taketomo, 1989) and the "senpai (senior)–kohai (junior) relationship" (Togashi, 2009a) are a particular affective connection developed by people who come together in the same place. For Japanese people, I would say, an affective connection through a sense of being in the same place often goes beyond a sense of commonality and alikeness.

In this chapter, in order to illustrate the importance of placeness in a twinship tie between Japanese people, I will first review placeness and Kohut's description of twinship. Then I will discuss *"ichiren-takushou,"* a Japanese expression that informs an understanding of placeness. For a case vignette, I will present a female patient who strongly yearns for a sense of being in the same place with her therapist. Finally, I conclude that an analyst, working through a twinship tie organized between a Japanese patient and himself, is required to be sensitive to placeness more than to sameness or alikeness.

Throughout this chapter, I will discuss placeness in twinship in Japanese culture, but I want to emphasize that this state of self can be broadly seen in any culture. It is found, in fact, in all East Asian cultures that have been classically described as "we–self" cultures.

Twinship and placeness

Kohut defines and addresses twinship in a variety of ways. In his journey of exploration of this concept, his understanding often appears contradictory and ambiguous. As Kottler and I discussed in Chapter 1, what Kohut might see in the terminology of twinship can be classified into seven categories: (1) twinship as something between merger and mirroring; (2) twinship as a process of mutual finding; (3) twinship as a sense of belonging; (4) twinship as a way of passing on talents and skills to the next generation; (5) twinship in silent communication; (6) twinship and feeling human among other human beings; (7) twinship in trauma. While, within these categories, Kohut does not put a particular emphasis on placeness, its importance can be recognized implicitly in his discussion. Especially, placeness has an essential role in (3) twinship as a sense of belonging, (4) twinship as a way of passing on talents and skills to the next generation, and (6) twinship and feeling human among other human beings.

Kohut (1984) describes a sense of belonging in twinship as follows:

> The mere presence of people in a child's surroundings—their voices and body odors, the emotions they express, the noises they produce as they engage in human activities, the specific aroma of the foods they prepare and eat—creates a security in the child, *a sense of belonging and participating*, that cannot be explained in terms of a mirroring response or a merger with ideals.
>
> (Kohut, 1984, p. 200; italics added)

A careful reading of this description leads to the conclusion that a sense of commonality or alikeness does not always have an essential role in this type of twinship experience. Kohut simply describes the sources of a feeling of security, and he attributes the feeling to our awareness that we are surrounded by human voices and body odors or noises created by human activities. He does not say in this discussion that an individual has to experience the voices, odors, or noises as alike or the same as his own. What he says here is that a person has a sense of security when she is in a place where there are human voices and body odors.

Twinship as a way of passing on talents and skills to the next generation is described by Kohut as "the little girl doing chores in the kitchen next to her mother or grandmother; the little boy working in the basement next to his father or grandfather" (Kohut, 1984, p. 204). A unique feature of Kohut's description is that he addresses a particular place to describe the illustrative images. The place in which a parent and a child find themselves in the other should be the kitchen and the basement. The persons differ in age, roles, and proficiency, but they are in the same place and feel secure there.

In the discussion of an individual's experience of being a human among human beings, Kohut uses the story of the astronauts whose space capsule lost power in outer space (Kohut, 1981, 1984). He refers to their strong yearning to return to Earth regardless of the high probability of their being burned to death during atmospheric entry. He describes their yearning as "the expression of their ultimate deepest desire [which is] the wish to be symbolically reunited with the earth: the symbol of human meaning, human warmth, human contact, human experience" (Kohut, 1984, p. 545n). Although there is a theoretical contradiction in this concept—because he uses this event as an example of both an empathic environment and a twinship experience—Kohut points here to the astronauts' strong longing to go back to a particular place in which they can experience themselves as surrounded by human experience. In this paradigm, placeness has an important role in the twinship experience.

Placeness and twinship in *ichiren-takushou*

Ichiren-takushou is a Japanese expression derived from Buddhist terminology, which means, in colloquial English, "being in the same boat." In the Kojien dictionary (6th edition, 2008), it is explained, historically, as: (1) to die a peaceful death together and be reborn on the same lotus leaf; and (2) more broadly, to share the same fate, good or bad (my translation). As I argue from a self-psychological perspective (Togashi, 2011a), it is an expression that can be used to describe a type of twinship experience. "Considering it through this definition as given by the Japanese dictionary and by the common usage of language, a subjective experience of people who yearn for *ichiren-takushou* with someone else could include a fantasy in which he shares his fate with someone as a cosmic flow and he longs to be bonded together with the other" (Togashi, 2011a, p. 138).

In this expression, the emphasis is on being in the same place (same lotus) more than it is on experiencing alikeness to another. Two people who share the experience do not necessarily have a sense of alikeness or commonality. They feel they are tightly bonded as long as they share a fantasy in which they will be reborn in the same place, even though they are currently very different.

In other words, the essential part of the experience is not the sharing of thoughts or lives, but the sharing of a place in the future. It is interesting in this expression that it would emphasize that two people are quite different, but they are strongly connected by sharing a place. This feeling is linked as well to sharing the same fate. Once they happen to be in the same place, even though coincidentally, they will be strongly connected emotionally and will organize a special type of relatedness that provides a deep joy and excitement.

As I argued (Togashi, 2011c), a conflict in a Japanese patient is often connected to a sense of placeness. It emerges through the patient's uncovering his uneasiness with place. "Place," *basho* in Japanese, has a special importance to an understanding of a Japanese patient's self-state. As I have said in Chapter 6, "place here does not mean Newtonian absolute space; it would be defined as a space subjectively bounded by and leading to the patient's roles, positions, needs, expectations, the form of relationship of the two participants, and other external factors" (Togashi, 2011c, p. 232). It is not an understanding that the place is constructed objectively and realistically; it is an ontological understanding that the place is organized or appears on its own in the intersubjective field between people. I maintain that a patient's self-experience is organized through a patient's recognizing himself in the place and in his analyst, and recognizing the place in himself and in his analyst.

Many Japanese philosophers have studied placeness in the self-state in Japanese people (Nishida, 1946; Nakamura, 1989; Ueda, 2000; Kimura, 2005). Although there are some differences in emphasis, they agree that in Japanese people a sense of their being is deeply anchored in a sense of place, or topos. As Nishida (1946) explains it, for the Japanese, "to be" means "to be within." In other words, for the Japanese, "to be with others" means "to be within the same place with others." This can be described as a form of twinship experience in their subjective experience. Isobe (1976, 1983), an anthropologist and phenomenologist, stresses that the Japanese people tend to see themselves as connected to each other through the feeling that they are within nature or are a part of a cosmic tide or flow. From this cultural perspective, Japanese people see themselves as being within the cosmos, that is, the space in which all share the same fate.

Case vignette[1]

Aiko, was a Japanese woman in her late twenties when she sought me out for psychotherapy and complained about claustrophobia, especially a fear of being in vehicles. I saw her once a week for four years in a psychiatric hospital and after she moved to another country, I continued a weekly therapeutic session by phone for four years.

Aiko is an energetic lady despite her small physique. She has many friends and tends to entertain them and others in a blithe manner. At the beginning of therapy, all she talked about were cheerful topics. She seemed to have difficulty accessing and verbalizing a deep sense of depression. When she tried to talk about the deepest sense of depression or injury, she burst out laughing. In the process of exploring her cheerful attitude in my presence, we came to understand that the measure of her laughter indicated the degree of her depression and helplessness. The more she laughed, the greater her unhappiness.

Aiko's parents disappeared immediately after she was born, and she was raised by her paternal grandparents. Her mother came back to the city in which Aiko lived a few years later, but Aiko and her mother seldom met. She had an idealized fantasy about her father who psychologically supported her. Her grandparents repeatedly talked to her only about the goodness of her father, though she had not seen her father in person ever. What occupied her mind was a deep sense of loneliness and a feeling that everything happened outside of her control.

Four years after beginning her therapy, Aiko married and moved abroad. She complained of a fear and anxiety about her separating from her friends a little bit, but she did not experience them as serious issues. She came to see her mother as more reliable than before, and she no longer had a highly idealized fantasy of her father. We determined to continue our sessions via phone while she was abroad.

A few years later, I had to move to the United States for psychoanalytic training. We agreed we would continue to have phone sessions after I moved. However, Aiko showed deep anxiety about that, although the therapeutic setting would not change at all; she was at her home abroad and called me for a session. Aiko repeatedly said, "It is okay that I moved away, but it is so scary that YOU are moving too." I interpreted her anxiety as possibly being caused by her fear of losing an important object or of being abandoned by an important object, as her parents had done, and attempted to work on the fear with her. Still, her anxiety did not decrease at all.

After I moved to the United States, Aiko began to forget her appointments regularly, about once a month. I would call her to remind her of the session. She always answered, "I completely forgot about it." I occasionally found myself wondering that something had happened to her when her phone was not answered. I felt my anxiety could particularly emerge in the relationship with Aiko: she had been waiting for the return of parents who had left her. I told her that the anxiety I had been experiencing could be similar to hers. However, despite her partial agreement with this interpretation, she kept forgetting our sessions. Our working on this anxiety in this context did not change anything.

A turning point in this stalemate was her husband's suspicion about our therapeutic work. He was totally unfamiliar with psychotherapy and questioned why Aiko kept paying money to a therapist who lived in another country. Aiko repeatedly told me that her husband mistrusted our work and wanted her to quit it as soon as possible. She said her husband wondered whether she was caught up in a scam. Although Aiko kept saying, "Don't worry about that; psychotherapeutic work with you is important to me," I found myself feeling insecure and worried that her husband, who was politically powerful, would try to ruin my career. I thought, "I can understand Aiko and maybe enable a change in her emotions since we talk to each other, but how can I change her husband's emotions when I have not seen him at all?" My shillyshallying about what to do finally led me to say to her, "You need to discuss this issue with your husband." She was very upset by this. She said, "I would not have consulted you if I had been able to do that!"

For the next three weeks, she did not call me for a session. After the third missed session, I called her. That session lasted twenty minutes. In it Aiko reported a dream:

> I and someone else are in a boat. Since I had had a phobia about vehicles, I am surprised to find myself in a boat. I cannot see the face of the person I share the boat with, and it looks like myself. We are on the ocean, and not able to see land. I wonder how I would handle it if something happened to me. Looking at the partner, I see that he or she

also looks anxious. The person and I both have two oars. I wonder if it is okay to ask him or her to row together with me.

Aiko and I did not discuss this dream at all, but hearing it changed my attitude very much. It made me realize that I had been afraid of sharing or risking my fate with her. I braced up and told myself, "What I can do for her is to pursue my own responsibility no matter what happens."

In the next session, Aiko complained about her symptoms and told me that her husband did not want her to continue therapy. Her husband was going to consult a lawyer if she did not stop seeing me. She said, "I am sorry. Maybe I am bothering you." I replied, "We have already been in the same boat. We are already *ichiren-takushou*."

After a while she said, "I fantasized that there is supposed to be a perfect world in which I do not feel anxious at all, and which provides a 100 percent peaceful life. But I might have known it is an illusion. I know I have to give up such an unrealistic daydream."

"Do you think you can give it up?"

"I am not sure. But whether or not I can do it, you and I are in the same boat."

"We are geographically in different places," I said, "but I would say we have always been in the same place so far. And I am sure we will be in the future."

Interestingly enough, soon after this session, her symptoms almost disappeared.

The basic theme Aiko and I discussed in the process of giving up what she called an illusion was her fear of being at the mercy of fate, and her mistrust of fate. She had told herself she did not believe in fate. "If this is my fate, how can I find a good meaning to my life, in which my parents disappeared immediately after my birth?" She felt nobody wanted to be with her or to share her fate. Place had special importance to her. She wanted to keep a place that she could go back to whenever she wanted. When her therapist moved away to another place, she felt he had destroyed the place she could go back to. With this understanding, she came to be able to provide help to her husband in his job, and she no longer experiences herself as being inferior to him. In her relationship with me, a mature and stable mirroring selfobject tie emerged.

Conclusion and discussion

In Aiko's sense of connectedness with me, described as *ichiren-takushou*, place has a special role. Though she moved to another country, she did not experience herself as disconnected from me. She probably experienced me as being in a place she could go back to anytime she wanted. However, she showed a strong anxiety once I, her therapist, moved to another country although her therapeutic setting did not change in any way. In this process, we could say she was afraid to recognize that we were no longer in the same place and that she could not see me in the place where she saw me before. In this context, a twinship tie between Aiko and me was organized around a sense of being in the same place more than a sense of commonality and alikeness. Throughout therapy, she has never indicated her longing to experience me as like her or to experience herself as like me. What she indicates is a longing for a confirmation that she and I are in the same place or share the same fate. In order for me to be sensitive to a particular joy and pleasure in Japanese people when they develop a twinship tie, I need to focus on essential placeness between them as well as on essential alikeness.

What is the essential function of place in a twinship experience? As we argued in Chapters 1 and 4 (see also Togashi, 2009a, 2012a; Togashi and Kottler, 2012), a sense of twinship is organized in the dialectic between sameness *and* difference, and a twinship tie is experienced by two people who have already recognized their differences consciously, unconsciously, or nonconsciously. In other words, in a twinship tie, two people are connected to each other as human beings in a way that extends beyond their inevitable differences or inequalities in life. Place functions, I would say, to connect two people emotionally and to keep them experiencing each other as the same human beings while they recognize the differences in their social roles, statuses, responsibilities, and ups and downs.

In Aiko's case vignette, place functions to connect emotionally a patient and a therapist who have different interests and anxieties based on their different roles and responsibilities. In a psychoanalytic treatment, too, the role and responsibly of a patient and an analyst are different and asymmetrical although they influence each other psychologically. It is a place in which a patient and an analyst see each other as human beings while they recognize their difference.

Nevertheless, I have to admit that this case vignette suggests that an experience of *ichiren-takushou*, of the kind that Aiko and her therapist shared in this context, cannot be fully described only by placeness, and that there is another significant aspect of this twinship tie to consider. A sense of being in the same place, which Aiko yearns for in this therapeutic process, is almost equivalent to a sense of sharing a fate. It could be that what she yearns for in this context is that she and her therapist share in a cosmic tide, which is predetermined and which stipulates all roles of people in the future. In other words, the vignette suggests a possibility that we need to pay attention to temporality as well as placeness in our consideration of the twinship tie. I believe a twinship tie needs to be considered in both dimensions.

Temporality is deeply related to a twinship tie and experience, but it has not been sufficiently explored in the context of twinship. As some analysts emphasize (Stolorow, 2007; Brothers, 2008), psychological trauma often destroys a person's sense of time. A traumatized person may lose all sense of time, or be trapped in a freeze-framed time (Stolorow, 2007; Brothers, 2008; Brandchaft, 2010). These analysts, who discuss the relationship between trauma and a sense of time, also point out a unique relationship between trauma and a sense of twinship. In short, twinship has to do with temporality; but the relationship has not been sufficiently discussed. Further discussion on twinship and temporality is necessary.

In this chapter, I have discussed placeness in a twinship tie organized between a Japanese patient and an analyst. I argue that this subjective experience is commonly formulated in Japanese culture, but do not suggest that the study is limited to Japanese culture or people. I believe it can be applied to other Asian cultures and to Western cultures. I want to emphasize here that placeness in selfobject experiences or ties has been negated in self psychology circles, and can more easily emerge in Japanese or Asian cultures than in Western culture. But as many researchers emphasize (Sober, 2000; Markus and Kitayama, 2003a, 2003b; Togashi, 2010, 2011c), a culturally and specifically focused subjective experience can always be found, more or less, in another culture or in another age. I believe this notion of placeness in the twinship experience can also be found in therapeutic dyads in other cultural settings.

Note

1 I have discussed this case vignette in my recent book as the case of Miss G (Togashi, 2011a). In that discussion, I address the mutual recognition of sameness and difference as seen in a twinship tie.

Chapter 8

"I am afraid of seeing your face"
Trauma and the dread of engaging in a twinship tie

Koichi Togashi, Ph.D., L.P.
Amanda Kottler, M.A. (Clin. Psych.)

Much has been written about individuals who have suffered trauma at the hands of others and of how their experiences challenge any possibility of transformation (Brandchaft, 1993, 2010; Beebe and Lachmann, 2002; Stolorow, 2007; Brothers, 2008). These authors have argued that trauma renders a psychological system too rigidly organized to allow itself to be perturbed by changes in the psychological milieu. As an expression of this rigidity, we believe that, while traumatized people might appear to be friendly and sociable, they are nevertheless doing all that they can to avoid being psychologically touched or "influenced" by anyone. This includes those to whom they feel drawn. Although they are inclined to seek out others who have suffered traumatic experiences similar to their own, they hold on to feelings that their traumatic experiences were different and, in an ongoing way, painfully "unique."

In the terminology of traditional self psychology, this way of relating can be described as a struggle with a twinship selfobject experience. Twinship was defined initially by Kohut (1984) as feeling vital, consistent, and secure through a sense of "essential alikeness" with another. Later, Kohut changed it to a "feeling that one is a human being among other human beings" (Kohut 1984, p. 200). Before his untimely death, Kohut (1984) had begun to explore the correlation between twinship and trauma. He argued that traumatized individuals lose the essential signposts of the human world that all humans need—although they are unaware of this need as long as such signposts are available (Kohut, 1984, p. 200).

In this chapter, our interest is in dynamic systems in which traumatized individuals like those described, seek out others with whom they can share similar traumatic experiences, but seemingly paradoxically, avoid acknowledging that these others are able to recognize similarities between them. To explore this, we draw on a therapeutic process with Hideki, an unmarried, gay Japanese patient in his thirties, whom Togashi worked with for four years once-a-week. We describe how the therapy evolved into a traumatized dyadic system, which became organized around the disruption and repair of a twinship tie between the patient and his analyst.

Hideki arrived for his first session with complaints of some dissociative symptoms and depression. He said he had felt disconnected and detached from the world for as long as he could remember. He revealed that his mother, who had been diagnosed with chronic depression, had physically abused him as a child. Almost every day she demanded that he tell her how he had behaved at school, and no matter what he told her, she would beat him. She would also regularly tie him to a pole with a rope.

Hideki told his therapist that a few years earlier he had participated in a group therapy process for patients abused by their parents. He had found that, although he liked hearing the stories told by other group members, he could not tolerate another member of the group claiming that their experiences had been similar to his, and suggesting they were in the same position as he was. As a consequence, he had decided to seek out individual therapy instead.

In this process, Hideki made two intriguing statements to his therapist. First: "I am afraid of seeing your face ... because I am scared I might see in it that you have discovered something bad or disgusting in me," and secondly: "I do not want to find evidence in your face that you have discovered similarities between us."

The first statement is easier to understand than the second. Given Hideki's abusive background it is understandable that he feared finding in his therapist's face an indication that the therapist saw him in the same way his mother had—as "bad"—and therefore in some way deserving of her random abusive behavior. But why was Hideki afraid that his therapist might discover similarities between them? We will explore this in what follows.

Twinship and trauma

Twinship is one of three selfobject experiences and transferences originally introduced by Kohut (1968, 1971). Initially, he saw twinship as an archaic form of a "mirror transference." By 1984, however, he had given it a status independent of and equal to the other two selfobject transferences and experiences, namely mirroring and idealizing. He began to consider twinship as the most significant of the three selfobject experiences contained in his theory, but, as a result of his untimely death, he wrote very little about this (Togashi and Kottler, 2012; Lichtenberg, 2012). He stated that much still "remains to be done" on the concept (Kohut, 1984, p. 194). This is still true—30 years on, the concept of twinship remains insufficiently developed in the field of self psychology.

In Chapter 1, we illustrated how Kohut represented the twinship experience in a variety of ways, some of which were quite obscure (Togashi and Kottler, 2012). We argued that, although the diversity of Kohut's descriptions may have helped broaden and deepen our perspective on the twinship selfobject experience, it has also created confusion and a number of contradictions. In spite of this lack of clarity, and although little has been written about twinship since Kohut's death, those who have focused on the concept all agree that the twinship experience is the most basic, significant, and essential of the selfobject phenomena (Basch, 1992; Ulman and Paul, 1992; Gorney, 1998; Martinez, 2003; Kottler, 2007, see also Chapter 3; Togashi, 2009a, 2012a; Togashi and Kottler, 2012).

This chapter illustrates the significance and application of a twinship experience as conceived of by Kohut, by applying his ideas to understanding a specific kind of traumatized dyadic system. It also suggests that Kohut's later ideas about twinship might be more readily understood if couched in contemporary relational terminology that we introduce in our epilogue.

The literature reveals that the idea of twinship has been linked to trauma in two ways. First, Kohut acknowledged that the disruption of a sense of "feeling that one is a human being among other human beings" is itself an essential element of psychological trauma (Kohut, 1984, p. 200). Second, as Stolorow (2007) and Brothers (2008) have shown, the experience of trauma leads to a strong need on the part of the traumatized person to look for a profound and intense sense of sameness—in Kohut's terms, an essential "alikeness" with others who have experienced similar traumatic experiences.

Disruption of a "feeling that one is a human being among other human beings"

In his discussion of a twinship experience, Kohut (1984), referring to Kafka's *The Metamorphosis*, says that "one of the most painful feelings to which man is exposed" is a loss of "the feeling that one is a human being among other human beings" (p. 200). He states that "a ... distortion in the personality stems ... from the absence of *human* humans in the environment of the small child" (p. 200, italics in original). For Kohut, the lack of this basic confirmation of being human leads to the most fundamental narcissistic injury that can be experienced in an individual's subjective world. In this environment there can be no sense of shared humanity. The signposts of the human world are lost, or worse, have become distorted. The individual will experience himself (or herself) as not "human" or, to use Kafka's story, as something to which human beings cannot and will not relate, a detestable creature—a cockroach.

When considering Kohut's emphasis on "*human* humans," we need to distinguish sharply between "a human" as a noun and "being human" as a verb. On the one hand—an individual's *recognizing of himself (or herself) as a creature understood to be human* and on the other—as *experiencing himself as being human, and as being treated as human.*

Hideki's mother did not treat him as "being human." For her, he was an object to beat, presumably to fix in some way. While this was happening, Hideki saw in her face signs that indicated and led to him experiencing himself as a bad and disgusting "being"—to be bullied, beaten, and squashed, just like a cockroach. However, in his mother's eyes, he was not a cockroach, he was a human. If he had been a cockroach, she would have killed him or let him die as did the family of Kafka's cockroach. No fixing would have been necessary, cockroaches are not human beings—they can be ignored and left to die. Instead, his mother attempted to fix him, because she knew he was human. Hideki experienced this at the hands of his mother who led him to understand that he was *a human being*—but a deficient one. In this context, the crucial feature of this type of trauma is that he was treated inhumanely by the person who saw him as a human.

By the same token, Hideki's mother, far from behaving as a *human* human being, was for Hideki an *object*—an object to be feared. As an object, she lacked the capacity to recognize his humanity and the pain she caused him by continuously beating him for no apparent or predictable reason. In such an environment, Hideki could surely never experience his mother, or indeed himself, as *human*. It makes sense, then, that he was afraid of seeing his therapist's face, for fear of finding a sign that the therapist, like his mother, had discovered the bad or disgusting thing that he had come to believe was inside him. It makes sense, too, that he was also afraid of finding a sign that his therapist, again like his mother, had become less than human—non-human. Both of these signs would, inevitably, overwhelm Hideki and fill him, like Kafka's cockroach, with a deep sense of shame, humiliation, guilt, self-loathing, and fear.

In this context, a sense of twinship can be understood as a sense of human relatedness (being human among other human beings) that enables people to experience themselves, others, and/or the environment as free from traumatization. It follows that the essential aspect of human trauma can be described as the disruption of one's sense of feeling that one is a human being among *human* humans, i.e. human beings with the capacity to relate to other *human* humans. This type of twinship goes far beyond Kohut's (1968, 1971) original description of twinship—as a sense of alikeness or sameness. It includes a deeper and more profound sense of being human in a human world—a world in which there is potential for authentic relationships with other human beings.

Trauma leads to a strong need for a profound and intense sense of sameness

In his autobiographical reflections, Stolorow (2007) considers a "longing for twinship or emotional kinship as being reactive to emotional trauma" (p. 49). To him, such a longing for twinship is often present when an individual experiences himself as shattered or destroyed by trauma. He states: "When I have been traumatized, my only hope for being deeply understood is to form a connection with a brother or sister who knows the same darkness" (p. 49).

Brothers' (2008) discussion on how psychological trauma destroys a sense of certainty in an individual reveals that traumatized individuals tend to look for an extreme sense of sameness with others and, at the same time, an extreme sense of difference from them. According to her, traumatized individuals often create dualities or dichotomies in which all people and all things are categorized into belonging either to one side or to the other. In their experiential world, complexity and multiplicity are oversimplified and lost.

Hideki's second fear—of seeing similarities between them in his therapist's face—can be partially understood using this idea. From his behavior, it is clear that he yearns to connect with other human beings. His initial willingness to enter the group therapy process suggests that he was looking for fellow human beings who knew the same darkness, and so does the fact that he liked hearing about the experience of other members in his group sessions.

From the perspective of Hideki's struggle, twinship can be understood as a selfobject longing, which emerges in the wake of trauma. However, the fact that he found the group members' suggestions of similarities with him intolerable highlights that twinship itself can be experienced as an expression of trauma. In other words, while Kohut's (1968, 1971) original description of twinship as a sense of alikeness or sameness did imply this sense of longing, this depended, inevitably, on a dissociation between a sense of alikeness and a sense of difference caused by trauma. This sense of alikeness, which Kohut originally emphasized in his concept of twinship, does not therefore necessarily include the complexity of the rich human tie.

Hideki's case draws attention to the fact that relational trauma more often than not results in intense fear on the part of traumatized individuals of recognizing the similarities between their experience and those of others. Seeking others whom they hope to experience as essentially similar to themselves does not always lead such a person to a feeling of vitality, consistency, wholeness, and security. Hideki's finding of similarities between himself and others in the group therapy process did not lead to a sense of security. Instead, this case material lends significant support to contemporary self-psychological theory, which argues that a sense of vitality, consistency, and of feeling whole and secure in the world emerges out of a much more complicated process—one which is organized through a delicate balance between sameness and differences as described elsewhere (Kottler, 2007, see also Chapter 3; Togashi, 2009a, 2012a).

The complexity of Kohut's two definitions of twinship, together with the contradictions between them, support our belief that, by the time he died, Kohut's thinking had begun to shift from a theory of "the psychology of the self" towards what we refer to as "the psychology of being human" in Chapter 1 (see also Togashi and Kottler, 2012, p. 333). This is evident in the fact that Kohut (1968, 1971) originally focused on the psychoanalytic treatment of narcissistic personality disorders and how their problems present themselves in the interpersonal field. He then classified two types of narcissistic transferences: mirroring and idealizing (Kohut, 1968, 1971), and concluded that the essential part of narcissistic pathology is not the longing for a relationship in itself, but the actual quality of the relationship longed for. This consideration led Kohut to an understanding that how human beings experience themselves depends on the way in which they are experienced by significant others. His focus was on the individual's self-experience rather than on the narcissism itself. The narcissistic transference, which Kohut renamed "the selfobject transference," and reclassified into three types (mirroring, idealizing, and twinship) can be understood as a way in which individuals experience themselves (Kohut, 1984). As we have indicated in Chapter 1 (see also Togashi and Kottler, 2012), it is our belief that by the time Kohut died his theory had expanded beyond the *self*, to the *humanized self*. Kohut's emphasis on the significance of the twinship experience marked the beginnings of his exploration of how individuals experience themselves as being human, rather than on how each individual experiences herself (or himself).

In this framework, we argue that Hideki's search for "a brother or sister who knows the same darkness" (Stolorow, 2009, p. 49) occurred in the context of what was for him a non-human environment. In the group, he was unable to experience the feeling of being a human being among other human beings (Kohut, 1984). We suggest that, even if one or more of the group members had been "essentially like" him, Hideki would not have experienced this person as providing a feeling of security—because in this environment, as a result of his relational history, he would not have been able to experience the other person as a *human* human. For Hideki could only ever experience the sister (or brother), like everyone before him, as exploiting Hideki's vulnerability or failing to validate his experience—one which was for Hideki unique, painfully distinct, and different from what any other person could ever know.

Case vignette and its discussion

In order to understand the complexities involved in this kind of dynamic system, which is well illustrated in what emerged in the dyadic system between Hideki and his therapist, we attempt to answer two questions. Firstly: How did Hideki manage his therapist's recognition of the similarities between them? And secondly: What was he protecting by doing this? To find answers we return to the therapist's work with Hideki, and examine how and through what processes his words and fears emerged.

At the beginning of therapy, Hideki kept a distant, somewhat aloof attitude towards me (Togashi). His face was stiff and formal, and his voice maintained an unfriendly tone. I felt he kept me at arm's length in spite of his being willing to clearly describe vivid and intimate details of his experience of having been abused.

In the face-to-face therapeutic setting, Hideki's way of looking at me was extreme. "Natural" eye contact with him was difficult. At times he would gaze at my face intently for a long time and at other times he would totally avoid face-to-face contact by looking down at his feet. When he looked into my face intensely, I experienced his eyes as intrusive; when he avoided seeing my face, I felt shut out.

He was extremely sensitive to how I experienced him. If I found it difficult to understand what he said, he would look into my eyes in an attempt to read what I was feeling, and ask me, anxiously, if I had any questions about what he was saying. "Maybe you don't understand what I said? Which part are you struggling to understand?" If I ventured to suggest that I understood what he felt, he responded in a way that indicated that my understanding was incorrect. An example of this was when I said, "It seems to me that you might have felt insecure most of the time at home," to which he immediately replied, "No, insecurity does not perfectly match the feeling I had. Maybe it cannot be helped, but I don't think you can understand my feeling completely." I said, "You are right. As you said, it might be difficult for me to understand perfectly the harshness of the world you have lived in. But I wonder if you could tell me more so that I may be able to have a much better sense of your feeling." I found myself feeling pressurized to find something in myself that might have been equally traumatic so as to understand his experience more accurately, but realized that even if I was able to find a similar experience of my own it could never have been as brutal as the abuse he had experienced.

After a year of meeting, Hideki asked me about my profession. He wanted to know how I had originally become interested in the mental health field, and how I became a clinical psychologist. He told me that he used to dream about working in the field, but that he had given up the dream because he recognized a fear of being emotionally close to others. I asked him if he felt my career reminded him of his former dream. He immediately denied that there was any link and emphasized that his interest had independently preceded his relationship with me. By saying "the dream was purely my own," he insisted that it was his own, unique, distinct interest to which I could lay no claim. During these discussions, although I felt that he was refusing me entry into his world, I found myself feeling closer to him by virtue of our sharing a similar interest—I could find myself in this aspect of him.

In this context, clearly, Hideki sensed a change in my attitude towards him. He suddenly and unexpectedly indicated a wish to terminate his therapy, explaining that he no longer felt secure in the relationship with me. He emphasized that, as mentioned earlier, he did not want to discover in my face that I had been able to find some similarities between us: "I hate to find your face becoming very warm and affectionate. When I see that, I know you feel that some of my experiences are similar to yours, as other people always do." Having seen this in my face, he was concerned that his "uniqueness" would disappear and with it, as he and I discovered, the safety of maintaining a psychological distance from me. In this discussion, he said he was reminded of what had happened between him and his father.

Hideki's father had witnessed the way Hideki's mother abused him as a child and had done nothing to stop her, because he was also afraid of her uncontrolled outrages, which occasionally resulted in physical attacks against him too. Because of this, Hideki's father often told him that his experience of being physically abused by his wife was the same as Hideki's experience at the hands of the same woman. Hideki never challenged this but told me tearfully that their experiences were completely different. He explained: "My father was an adult man who could have escaped the abuse, but I was a completely powerless little boy in the presence of my abusive mother." He sensed, probably through seeing his face, that his father was afraid of being alone and that this made it important for his father to see them as alike—important for his father's own twinship needs, not Hideki's. He emphasized: "My father stole the uniqueness of my experience and made it all about him."

In this discussion, I told him it had felt good to hear about his former interest in the mental health field, and asked him if he thought that this feeling of mine might have threatened him in the same way—that it would take away his sense of his own uniqueness, which he had desperately protected since his childhood—and that I, like his mother and father, was overlooking his pain and was turning the similarities between us into being all about me. This resonated with him and he agreed with this way of understanding what was happening between us. He said:

> When I talk about my traumatic experience, people either try to be empathic by finding similar experiences in my story or distance themselves by finding differences between us. But the fact is my mother did not treat me as a person. I do not think anybody can find themselves in me, or any differences between us, because they experience themselves as human and I do not. All I can do is to protect myself by holding on to myself as a person in whom nobody can find anything of himself or herself. It is the only way for me to keep my own uniqueness.

In the working through of this theme, which lasted for almost two years, Hideki and I discovered that excessive emphasis on feelings of similarities and, equally, differences between us made him feel insecure. Moment by moment in sessions, we explored an optimal balance between the similarities and the differences. In this process, I focused on what the expressions on my face might be conveying. At times, when I was deeply in touch with his subjective world, I sensed that we were making eye contact and that the knot between my brows was evident and that he could tolerate it. When his story became tragically moving, I found myself avoiding eye contact as I sensed too that a variety of silent but rapidly changing emotional expressions would be evident. In this interactive way, Hideki and I kept an optimal distance between our emotional experiences as revealed on our faces.

As a result, Hideki slowly began to bring to the sessions material in which he expected me to find myself. He was able to ask me about movies and novels that I liked, and he was increasingly comfortable with us talking about them together, while looking at each other's faces. My being able to find myself in the stories no longer frightened him, and he was less afraid of seeing my face. He was increasingly willing and able to share his feelings with others who had also been physically abused without dreading that the uniqueness of his experience would be taken away and used in the service of the needs of the other.

How does Hideki manage his therapist's recognition of similarities between them?

Hideki's case vignette supports Brothers' (2008) idea that the subjective experiences of traumatized individuals come to be ruled by dualistic thinking, and that, for the traumatized psychological system, experiential uncertainty is unbearable. This helps explain why Hideki could not allow himself to recognize the multiple and contradictory nature of the other's or his own subjectivity.

When Hideki's therapist could find aspects of his own subjectivity in Hideki while they were discussing Hideki's interest in becoming a mental health professional, his therapist was not focusing on, or even aware of the multiple aspects of his own subjectivity. The therapist was instead looking for something in his own experience that Hideki could find in himself. This meant that what his therapist recognized in the relationship with Hideki at that point was tilted more toward similarities between them than differences. In this "intersubjective conjunction" (Atwood and Stolorow, 1984, p. 47), Hideki was able only to focus on, and become preoccupied with, his experience of his therapist's having recognized similarities between them. In Hideki's experience, this ushered in the inevitability of either being rejected totally, or being used and abused solely for the needs of the other. This meant that his differences, his uniqueness—his psychological safety—were on the verge of being severely threatened in the relationship.

We could say that when Hideki and his therapist were discussing Hideki's interest in becoming a psychologist, he could probably see only his therapist's own interest or experience in the therapist's face. He could not, we guess, find his own interest or experience in the therapist's face. That would be a reason why he was afraid of seeing the therapist's face in sessions.

In Chapters 2 and 4, Togashi (see also 2009a, 2012a) has illustrated the psychological significance and complexity of a twinship experience from a perspective of contemporary self psychology. Togashi (2012a) proposes what he has termed a "mutual finding model," that is, a bidirectional perceptual-cognitive process of a twinship tie. In this model, a patient's sense of "being a human being among other human beings" is established in an analytic dyad through a delicate and empathically negotiated balance between the mutual findings of oneself and not-oneself in the other. The emphasis of this model is the multiple and contradictory nature of all that goes into a twinship experience. When an individual finds herself (or himself) in the other, she has already found in the other an aspect of her own subjectivity that is different from that of the other—one that she has hitherto not been aware of in herself.

Kottler, in Chapter 3 (see also 2007), describes struggling with a patient whom she experienced as both alike and different at the same time. While she found in her patient a path of life she herself had already gone through, she also recognized major differences between them. She states that, in this context, which accords with Togashi's (2006, 2009a) definition of twinship, the therapist's finding of herself in the patient, as well as her recognizing of his (or her) "otherness," can help to transform the patient's sense of self. In other words, the clinical process provided by Kottler reveals that a twinship experience essentially includes a simultaneous sense of sameness *and* difference.

As Brothers (2008) argues, the experience of psychological trauma makes it difficult for traumatized individuals to recognize the complex nature of human relationships. They are locked into, and limited by, dualistic thinking between sameness and difference. In an analytic relationship with such a patient, the analyst's focus is often experienced as tilted only towards the similarities between them, or only towards the differences. Thus, in such a dynamic system, although the patient seeks out a twinship tie, he (or she) cannot allow his analyst to find similarities between them because this will immediately mean that the differences between them will not be recognized. If the patient submits by acknowledging these similarities, he dreads what is, for him, the inevitability of his pain and suffering being colonized by his analyst. He fears that by doing so, he will have surrendered to his analyst the most vulnerable part of his subjectivity.

What is Hideki protecting by not allowing similarities to be found?

In Hideki's words, whenever he allowed the other to find similarities between them, he experienced a loss of the "uniqueness" of his own experience. We suggest that, in this context, this uniqueness can be understood at the experiential level as Hideki's yearning for the acknowledgment of "a pure experience of his own," one which cannot in any way be influenced by the other's experience, namely "a subject-*without*-others[1]." It is a defensive or protective state of his self-experience, an experience that he needs to protect from being contaminated, touched and/or colonized by the other. We understand his repetitive emphasis of the difference between his and the other's experiences as indicating his desperate and largely ineffectual efforts to preserve a part of his subjectivity, which he wants to believe cannot be influenced by the other's experience of him. There was an aspect of Hideki's subjectivity that had only ever been deeply influenced and used by others for their own needs. He could not avoid immediately connecting with this as soon as he saw a sign in the face of the other—that the other had found similarities between them.

We believe that, for Hideki, whose formative experiences were of being treated as not-human by his mother, the only way to survive as a human being in a human world was by rigidly maintaining and protecting a sense of being different—unique. This, by definition, has to exclude emotional ties with others. Paradoxically and tragically, Hideki's mother treated him as a *human object*. There was no recognition on her part of him as a human *subject*. By treating him as an *object*, albeit a human object, she had dehumanized him and, in the process, had destroyed his ability to trust himself as a *subject*—a subject-with-others. In the face of others, Hideki had only ever experienced himself as a human *object*—an *object*-with-others. To avoid the pain that came with this, his only option was to access, and insist on, his uniqueness. This left him able to experience himself as a human being, but alone and lonely—a subject-*without*-others. His longing for sameness between himself and others, and for the experience of himself as a human *subject,* would have been developmentally delayed and, at best, poorly negotiated in relation to others. The intense longing for sameness would remain, for the most part, dissociated.

We must emphasize here that we are not suggesting that a subject-without-others is indicative of a healthy state. Instead, we argue that it is a consequence of psychological dissociation, caused by traumatic experiences of having existed as a *subject*-without-others and, at the same time, as an *object*-with-others. We acknowledge that using the term "subject" is problematic. A long-term epistemological reflection and discussion reveals, as we mentioned earlier, that the subject is experienced or organized through her (or his) experience of being with others. In this sense, subjectivity cannot be organized or experienced without others. Yet, our clinical vignette reveals a phenomenon, which, in our opinion, is best described as exactly that—a subject-without-others.

Benjamin's (1988, 1991) mutual recognition model, in which she reflects on the development of human relationships, emphasizes the psychological meaning of experiencing him or herself in the presence of others. She states that "the other must be recognized as another subject in order for the self to fully experience his or her subjectivity in the other's presence" (Benjamin, 1990, p, 35). She argues that psychoanalysis has, historically, placed too much emphasis on the mother's psychological function for her children, namely the mother as an object. She argues that a healthy psychological relationship cannot develop from a self's experience of him or herself functioning only as an object for the other, nor from the experience of an important other functioning only as an object for the self. She stresses that meaningful psychological development occurs in the "zone of experience or theory in which the other is not merely the object of the ego's need/drive or cognition/perception, but has a separate and equivalent center of self" (Benjamin, 1990, p. 35).

We suggest that the development of human relationships grows out of a relatively systematic and ongoing oscillation between the mutual recognition of the subjectivities involved *and* the mutual experiences of the other as an object. The other must emerge as another subject *as well as* an object in the presence of the self. Too much emphasis on the individual's subjectivity or too much sensitivity towards the other's subjectivity can be as problematic as when there is too much emphasis on being an object for the other. In this sense, our discussion of a subject-without-others could be understood as a self frozen on the traumatized end of a psychological continuum reflecting the recognition of both subject and object. Hideki's self-experience is traumatically dissociated between that of experiencing himself as a subject for himself and that of functioning as an *object* for his mother. This prevented him from being able to experience his own subjectivity through the recognition of his mother's being (a subject). For him, the only way in which he could experience his own subjectivity was to erase her (and anyone else's) being in his presence or to experience himself only as an object for his mother (and others).

It is also important to emphasize that, by using the term "subject-without-others," we are not claiming that Hideki did not yearn to be connected to others. However, we argue that as a result of his trauma, his longing for a brother or sister with whom to share the same darkness had not been negotiated. Nor had his contradictory-seeming need to maintain his uniqueness or pure experience. He yearned for an other who would be able to see both her (or his) own trauma in Hideki, but who would at the same time never see her own trauma in Hideki's to the extent that the differences between them were ignored.

What we are suggesting is that Hideki's traumatization resulted in dissociation between a sense of alikeness and a sense of uniqueness. This leads us to argue that, while traumatized people yearn for "a brother or sister who knows the same darkness" (Stolorow, 2007, p. 49), it is significant that they also yearn for that same brother and sister to recognize the difference and the uniqueness of their own trauma.

Discussion

Our clinical vignette suggests that an analyst has to be exquisitely sensitive to a traumatized patient's deep and intense longing for, but equally deep dread of, an experience that allows for the mutual recognition of similarities and differences in the dyad. Furthermore, an analyst needs to be sensitive to a likely enactment in which she (or he) finds herself focusing exclusively on either the similarities or the differences in the relationship. An analyst needs to focus on the obstacles found between the patient and the world, and the balance between the dynamic system's rigidity and its openness to recognizing the multiplicity of a complex but essentially curative twinship experience.

When we, as analysts or therapists, see a traumatized patient, and use Kohut's empathic stance, we tend to try to find ourselves or our own trauma in the patient's experience and to focus on the similarities between the patient's trauma and our own. However, our discussion of Hideki's case vignette suggests that the emphasis of similarity in an analyst's subjectivity is not necessarily helpful to the patient and can destroy a twinship tie between them. The question is therefore: In what way does an analyst's focus on similarity lead to the disruption of a sense of being human among other human beings, and how can an analyst work with the disruption and repair the relatedness?

Hideki was afraid of seeing his therapist's face. Using videotaping, Beebe (2005) empirically illustrated that an analyst's face can reveal many aspects of a patient's (and the analyst's own) affective state, as well as the emotional movements that are processed in their interactive- and self-regulation. Orange (2010) and Stern (2010) beautifully describe the way in which a patient's trauma or dissociation shows up in the face of a person who is listening to their experiences. Only when a patient discovers trauma reflected in his (or her) analyst's face is he able to recognize the deep meaning and experience of his own trauma.

When Hideki saw his therapist's face, he was able to recognize aspects of his own and his therapist's affective states and the changes of their affective interaction, in the implicit dimension. He found both sharable aspects and unique aspects of his trauma in his therapist's face. However, when he was afraid of seeing his therapist's face and feared that his therapist was not validating the uniqueness of his own experiences, it is likely that this was because he could find no sign of the uniqueness of his own trauma in his therapist's face. We suggest that at that moment, the therapist's face revealed something of the similarity between him and Hideki. Hideki was able, unconsciously and non-consciously, to capture this change, and his own focus would then be tilted toward his own uniqueness. At that point, he would experience his therapist as regarding him as an object, without recognizing his distinctly different subjectivity. Such moments prompted Hideki to revert to protecting his subjectivity, thus preventing him from being able to recognize his therapist's interest in him as a *subject*. In this context, the relationship that is being organized in both Hideki and the therapist remains dissociated, with both participants failing to recognize their human subjectivities in relation to each other.

In this therapeutic impasse, an analyst needs to focus on what his (or her) own face is conveying, in order to perturb a traumatized relational system. Although an analyst is not able to see his own face during therapeutic sessions unless recorded, he can pay attention to his reactions, in order to have a sense of what facial expressions are being conveyed. In this way, the analyst can attempt to sense and capture his and his patient's emotional states and their interactive process, and find his own face reflected in his patient's face.

Conclusion

In this chapter, we have attempted to illustrate how a traumatized dyadic system is organized around a twinship tie between a patient and an analyst. This has raised an important question that has never been clearly addressed in Kohut's self psychology: Is a sense of alikeness the same as a sense of being human, or are they different?

We postulated earlier in this chapter that the two types of twinship experience are not necessarily organized in the same dimension. They are nested and mutually organized, but their functions are essentially different. A twinship experience defined as a sense of essential alikeness provides a function in which a person can experience a certain sense of self. But a twinship experience defined as a sense of being "a human being among other human beings" provides a function in which a person is able to experience himself (or herself) as being human beyond a sense of self in relation with, or to, others. A person who has a solid sense of his (or her) self may nevertheless not be able to experience himself as being human among others, or at home in the presence of others.

This raises a range of questions that we cannot address in a chapter of this brevity. Among these are: What process is involved, and what process is necessary to provide a sense of being human? How are these processes organized? How are a sense of being human and a sense of self related to each other? As we have suggested elsewhere, the key to answering these questions may lie in an examination of the psychological processing involved in the transformation from a sense of not-being-human to a sense of being human. We believe this depends on the ability to negotiate between a sense of alikeness and a sense of uniqueness. This could also be described as the transformation from an experience of being a subject-*without*-others to an experience of being a subject-*with*-others. We have discussed this using different terminology in Chapter 5, and will explore and expand on some of these questions in the chapters that follow.

Note

1 Credit for the expression "subject-without-others" is owed to Dr. Soh Agatsuma, who made this remark in his personal comments for this article presented at the 10th Anniversary Conference on the IARPP, New York, 2012.

Chapter 9

Is it a problem for us to say, "It is a coincidence that the patient does well"?

Koichi Togashi, Ph.D., L.P.

Can we say, as psychoanalysts: "It is by coincidence that a patient happens to do well as a result of psychoanalytic treatment"? Some would say, "Nothing happens by chance; there is always a cause. Otherwise, how could we make a difference to our patients?" Someone else might respond, "But chance rules the universe." We psychoanalysts know from our clinical work that the satisfactory results of our efforts come both from necessity and from contingency. Freud himself was of two minds—chance in the universe and necessary cause in the mind.

Freud (1901) stated, "I believe in external (real) chance, it is true, but not in internal (psychical) accidental events" (p. 328). From its beginnings, psychoanalytic theory has argued that a central task of treatment is to identify necessity in experience that had generally been regarded as contingent.

Yet this view stands in stark contrast to the Judeo-Christian view that our life circumstances are shaped by a divine intelligence. Along with other philosophers like Rorty (1989) and Ben-Menahem (1996), I believe that one of Freud's significant contributions was to see a human mind as an organization generated by contingencies rather than by Christian necessity. However, I maintain that his model does not sufficiently identify the clinical importance of contingency.

In the classical model of pathology, for example, neurosis is not regarded as coincidental. Rather, it is viewed as a biologically necessary outcome of psychosexual development. By addressing a patient's behavior as a manifestation of transference, a psychoanalyst attempts to identify a patient's experience that could be by necessity linked to the behavior. In this classical model, the analyst's role is to help the patient recognize that the phenomena he thought of as happening by chance are actually occurring by necessity. This model indicates that successful treatment requires the patient to acknowledge the role that his caregivers and the analyst have played in his life circumstances.

Given this perspective, therefore, a conclusion that it is a coincidence that a patient improves as a result of psychoanalytic treatment is not to be preferred over any other explanation. That would be to go against the theoretical foundations on which successful treatment relies. Accordingly, a positive treatment outcome is linked to the proper application of technique, including the analyst's correctly interpreting the patient's unconscious and the underlying dynamics.

In spite of this firm belief, Freud (1910) himself stated: "In fact everything to do with our life is chance" (p. 137). Thus, careful consideration leads us to the idea that contingency—Freud's "chance"—may play a more central role in the psychoanalytic process than was previously recognized. Contemporary models argue, for example, that trauma can shatter the human mind. But enduring trauma is not a given outcome for all people. Thus, it's not surprising that a person who is exposed to a traumatic event often asks, "Why me?" The question reveals a deep narcissistic injury. A person who relies on logic to explain why to the sufferer simply compounds the injury and confusion.

When we cannot identify what therapeutic intervention changed the patient's behavior, we often tend to attribute a patient's cure to coincidence. In such cases, we might say sarcastically or jokingly that the patient was already cured when he came to therapy. We cannot always explain a patient's change by our theories. We know that a patient can change through the effects of an event that can be described only as contingent. However, we tend not to think of it as such. Rather, we prefer to attribute the change to a therapeutic effect of our preferred theoretical perspective. So long as we are bound to a deterministic linear thinking, we are more inclined to rely on a particular theoretical prescription for treatment.

In contrast to the traditional Freudian view, contemporary self psychology, or self-psychologically oriented system theories (Lichtenberg, Lachmann and Fosshage, 1992, 1996, 2010; Fosshage, 2009; Beebe and Lachmann, 2002; Coburn, 2002, 2007; Stolorow, Atwood, and Orange, 2002; Bacal, 2006, 2011; Lachmann, 2008), are more likely to include contingency as a key factor in their model of therapeutic action. Despite theoretical differences, these theorists view the analytic dyad as a nonlinear dynamic system in which relational expectancies and experience are thought to fluctuate and transform in interaction with unpredictable contingencies. In these models, psychological organization and relational transformation are no longer seen as adequately explained within the causality model that traditional psychoanalysis has hypothesized.

Yet these models are mostly used to explain how contingencies and necessities work in a dynamic system, rather than as a means for describing the experience of the participants. How do the patient and analyst experience aspects of their process that feel random or contingent? Moreover, what effect does it have on an analytic process when an analyst and a patient allow themselves to view a therapeutic process as contingent?

Philosophical reflection on and scientific discussion of contingency and necessity have a long history (see Monod 1971; Wallace, 1986; Rorty, 1989; Mainzer, 2007; Watts, 2011). It is beyond the scope of this chapter to add a psychoanalytic perspective to that long history and to address any particular aspect of a psychoanalytic process as contingent or necessary. Rather, this chapter examines how a patient and an analyst "make sense together" (Orange, 1995) of their emotional experiences by utilizing the felt experiences of contingency and necessity.

I will first review the philosophical literature that explores the relationship between contingency and necessity, and then describe and discuss my work with a female patient who was afraid of the unpredictable. In the final discussion, I will explore the relationship between contingency and trauma with reference to dynamic systems.

Contingency and necessity

According to Merriam-Webster's Collegiate Dictionary, contingency is "1: the quality or state of being contingent 2: a contingent event or condition: as **a:** an event (as an emergency) that may but is not certain to occur <trying to provide for every ~> b: something liable to happen as an adjunct to or result of something else" (p. 250). From a colloquial perspective, we might think of an event as being contingent when two or more events that do not normally occur together according to particular causal laws have happened amid a feeling of surprise.

As simple as this definition sounds, when we seriously consider the ramifications, we immediately find ourselves challenging the implication of a cosmic order. What contingency conveys is much more complicated than we initially grasp. According to Laplace's (1812) discussion of determinism, in which the perfect intelligence recognizes a web of cause and effect in the cosmos, contingency is seen as a kind of necessity whose causality has not been discovered by human beings.

Darwin's theory on the origin of species provides an excellent example. It demonstrates that evolution, which takes place of necessity as an adaptation to environment, goes through an accumulation of contingencies. We know that, even at the genetic level, evolution by mutation takes place in purposeful ways as well as purposeless (Monod, 1971; Mainzer, 2007). Contingency and necessity are not mutually exclusive, but each occurs in the other. I believe that this premise would be applicable to psychoanalytic treatment.

Shuzo Kuki (1932, 1935, 1936) was a Japanese philosopher who was interested in exploring the relationship between contingency and necessity. After graduating from Tokyo University, where he studied neo-Kantianism, he lived and studied in Europe for eight years, from 1921 to 1929. During that time, he studied with Rickert in Heidelberg, with Bergson in Paris, and with Heidegger in Marburg.

Kuki published several papers and books on contingency, including his doctoral dissertation, between 1929 and 1939. It had been the center of his philosophical interest while he was in Europe. His understanding of contingency evolved over time. Initially, he thought of contingency as a *negation* of necessity. In his doctoral dissertation (Kuki, 1932) he delineated three kinds of judgment of necessity—categorical, hypothetical, and disjunctive, which each can be identified within the three realms: logical, empirical, and metaphysical. According to him, contingency can be delineated following the same principle.

Categorical necessity reflects, or points to, the relationship between a concept and its essential characteristics. For example, it is a necessity that the sum of the interior angles of a triangle is 180 degrees. This characteristic is contained in the concept of the triangle itself, and it's impossible to draw a triangle without meeting this necessity. The exact size of each interior angle, however, is an example of categorical contingency—one of the angles could be 40 degrees so long as the sum of the other two angles is 140 degrees. Kuki also used an individual's cultural background as an example of categorical contingency. A person is necessarily human, but where a person is born (Japan, Greece, etc.) is a contingency. Further illustrating this point in his study of Kuki, Marra states:

> [Categorical contingency] makes the individuality of race and nationality overcome the generality of being born a human being ... Contingency challenges the self-sameness (*doitsusei*) of the general category of the human being by introducing splits and conflicts into it, thus giving a specific particularity to an otherwise unmarked, anonymous generality. Categorical contingency is related to the individual (*kobutsu*) and opposes general concepts or rules.
> (Marra, 2004, p. 10)

Hypothetical necessity refers to the relationship between cause and effect; it is the phenomenon that a cause leads to an expected effect, or that an action that is taken to meet a particular purpose leads to an expected outcome. Hypothetical contingency is the reverse of hypothetical necessity; an outcome is caused by an event, which is not supposed to lead to the outcome that results; or an action that is taken in order to serve a particular purpose leads to an unexpected outcome. In Kuki's example, a tile roof caves in, resulting in injury to a person walking along the street, and a gardener digs a hole and is surprised to find a wad of money in it.

Disjunctive necessity refers to necessity within the metaphysical realm, in which the link between cause and effect would be knowable to God, even if not to a human being. For example, if one were to trip and fall over a small rock, God would have the ability to determine the series of events that led to the stone, which was chipped off a boulder, being in that particular position on that particular road at that particular moment, as well as how that person came to that same place on that same road, at that exact moment in time. Disjunctive contingency is, in this sense, the metaphysical contingency from which the causal link itself emerges.

Over the course of his philosophical reflections, Kuki's ideas evolved until he came to see contingency as a *different form* of necessity (Kuki, 1935, 1936). Although contingency means that a particular event happened by chance, it must also mean that there exists the possibility that the phenomenon might not have occurred at all. For Kuki, contingency and necessity are essentially opposite sides of the same coin. They are not mutually exclusive, but, rather, mutually interactive in the same place going hand in hand.

According to Kuki (1935, 1936), human experience is organized in the dynamic transition between necessity and contingency, that is, in "possibility." Although it is certain that necessary phenomena will occur, contingent phenomena are only possibilities among an infinite number of possibilities. Being born a human being is a necessity, but a person's being in the world at a particular place at a particular moment is contingent upon many factors. For Kuki, denying either contingency or necessity equates with disrupting the cosmic order as well as human existence. It is not until a person discovers a meaning of the only possibilities between contingency and necessity that he or she experiences him or herself as a unique human being.

Following Kuki's line of reasoning, we may conclude that when a patient (or an analyst) experiences a phenomenon as a contingent or chance occurrence, this does not necessarily constitute resistance. Moreover, the analyst (or the patient) should not be afraid to view a therapeutic phenomenon as occurring by coincidence, since dichotomizing between contingency and necessity fractures that very human experience. Psychoanalytic work is not intended to determine whether an experience is contingent or necessary, but rather to allow an analyst and a patient to see it as contingent or necessary *or both*, and to explore the meaning of such experience.

A patient who suffered from chronic depression experienced himself as having been treated by his abusive parents as non-human, a garbage can. At the beginning of therapy, our work tormented him as he himself desperately searched for the reason that his parents had treated him so badly. The inexplicability of his history left him feeling powerless, and ever more like a non-human. In other words, he viewed his traumatic childhood experience as necessary, not as contingent. Only as he came to see this experience as a coincidence, that he was the son of deficient parents who treated him poorly, was he able to experience himself as a human being, rather than a garbage can.

Case vignette

Eri, a single Japanese woman in her forties, came to see me complaining of chronic depression, physical exhaustion, and a sense of emptiness.

Approximately a year before seeking treatment, in the context of an economic recession, she was fired from the large financial company she had been employed at for many years. In spite of very quickly securing employment at another company, she found herself feeling depressed. We worked together for five years on a once-a-week basis.

At the beginning of her therapy, she came up with a question that she tended to repeat: "Why are you my therapist?" To this query, I answered that she had a right to choose anyone as her therapist; to this she responded, "What I asked is nothing of the sort. I was not saying that I do not like you as my therapist. I just felt that it is strange that you are my therapist." Some time passed before I understood her intention, but by then she had stopped asking the question.

Eri was afraid of anything unpredictable. For example, she could not live with a disruption to train services due to a typhoon or a traffic accident. When such disruptions occurred, she came to my office with a furious and despairing look even though she had been able to arrive at her appointed time. She told me, "I know this is a coincidence, but I don't like to find myself being overwhelmed by some big thing." Although she recognized that it was impossible for her to predict such events, she wished to search proactively for a way she could put herself into a safe place in advance. One day, she became excited when she found that she could cancel a session if a weather forecast told her that a typhoon was coming, but she was immediately downcast when she recognized that it was impossible for her to predict a traffic accident.

I asked, "Why do you think you cannot laugh it off by saying, 'It cannot be helped; it is a coincidence'? It is understandable to me, though, because you were fired by a large company. I guess that then you may have experienced yourself as being overwhelmed by something beyond your capability to deal with." She had tears in her eyes and said, "Still, I need to find a way of avoiding something that is unpredictable."

Eri's father tended to insist that she follow the principle of "right conduct as a human being." In many instances, the principle is trivial, as when it is applied to the way a person greets another or determines what she should wear. Eri's mother, who was severely depressed and fragile, figures here. Her father emphasized that Eri's mother would have been upset if she wandered from the principle of right conduct. Eri's father was concerned about the bad effect Eri's behavior could have on her mother's depression;

but Eri felt that there was no logical link between the propriety of her behavior and her mother's depression.

Around a year after her therapy began, I recognized an interesting aspect in Eri. She often dismissed as a coincidence events that seemed to me to be more than a coincidence. For example, she tended to draw a strict line between her responsibilities and her colleagues'. She, a very smart and successful businessperson, usually delivered almost perfect results in her assignments, but she never helped her colleagues, nor did she take care of the aspects of the job that she did not believe to be her own. Even when asked by her boss to work at a task, she often turned him down.

I believed that such an attitude had caused problems in her previous job, which could have been a reason why she was fired. I was worried that similar conduct might occur in her present job. However, she told me, "I have worked with many bosses up till now. At first, they are always very nice to me. Then they create a distance between us and hate me. I think it is a coincidence, though." I suggested that she find a reason why the pattern was repeated in her relationship with her bosses, but she did not wish to explore this.

About a year later, I happened to cancel a session with her in order to attend the funeral of a close friend. She came to her next session looking angry. She maintained that she did not hold me responsible for the cancellation and she understood that it could not be helped. "But why did it happen on the day of my session?" As she described it, that was "the ironical hand of destiny (*unmei*)." Her flowery expression surprised me, and I told her that she probably felt she was being swayed by a huge power again. She said, "I understand what you want to say. Maybe you are right." But she continued to feel depressed.

After a while, she began to come to sessions 20 minutes late. Asked for the reason, she simply told me that she was late leaving her apartment. I asked her to tell me what made her leave late, and she said that there was no particular reason. I wondered whether Eri, who is slightly dissociative, left late while she was in a depersonalized state, and I asked, "How do you feel about the loss of 20 minutes of your session?" "I don't mind … because it is a kind of destiny (*unmei*)," she said. I asked her if she could recognize the contradiction between her anger about a disruption to therapy due to a natural disaster or a funeral and her explaining her lateness as a coincidence. She maintained that she did not understand why I saw her responses as a contradiction. I saw that her necessity was my contingency, and her contingency was my necessity. Eri and I were stuck in the "intersubjective disjunction" (Stolorow and Atwood, 1992).

In the third year of her therapy, I recognized that she used the term "destiny" in a way that revealed multiple meanings. She had described the typhoon's destruction of the train service as "the ironical hand of destiny" and her being late as "a kind of destiny." But they were not the same. The emphasis in the former is on the necessity of the result of the incident, though it includes a sense of contingency as well. The emphasis in the latter is on the contingency of the incident, though it includes a sense of necessity as well. When I shared this understanding, she said:

> I believe that the world goes on based on causal laws, as my father said. Although I worked very hard in my previous company, it turned out that I was fired. Other lazy coworkers should have been fired. Why me? I did not live with that, and I was not able to consider that there was a cause for my firing in me. But "destiny" is a useful and magic word to me … As long as I see any painful events as the result of destiny, I feel easy and I am able to face my own problem without feeling any pain …

Through this discussion, I came to recognize that I had slipped into a dichotomy of contingency and necessity; so had Eri. However, our ways of thinking were opposites. We both, she and I, sought to have the other recognize the validity of our own understanding. Our explaining of how we came to reach a conclusion of contingency was, in other words, an effort to explain that our understanding was a necessity. Contingency and necessity are merely two different forms of experiencing the world. The word "destiny," however, was used in a different way. Eri used the term when she saw an event as both contingent *and* necessary.

After this recognition, I no longer felt that it was important for us to distinguish between contingency and necessity. Tension between Eri and me decreased. The relational system that had been organized between a patient who is concerned about any causal connection between herself and others and an analyst who believes his job is a search for causality had been perturbed. The emotional connection between Eri and me began to feel stronger than it had been before.

One day in the fifth year of her therapy, Eri came to see me wearing a happy expression. She had gone to a department store four days earlier and had found herself feeling good. At that time she had been thinking of me. She said, "I was thinking that you and I now know we understand each other, and we are walking down the same road together." As I listened to her, I recognized that, on that day at that time, I was walking around the same department store, although we had not met. I laughed at the coincidence and her ironic description "walking down the same road." When Eri asked me what made me laugh, I explained the reason. Then I tried to continue by saying, "We might have passed in the department store, and you may have sensed something there ..." and stopped. For I found myself seeking for causality between her feeling and our being around the same area on that day. She laughed and said, "Interesting, but I see no point in trying to find out whether we might have passed each other or not."

"Yes, I agree. But I am surprised by the coincidence, because we have been discussing for a long time your fear about an unpredictable event. You might have faced the most unpredictable event. Maybe it could be a kind of destiny whether or not we ran into each other," I said. Eri and I left open the possibility that the incident was contingent as well as necessary.

Toward the end of her therapy, Eri and I went back to her original question, "Why are you my therapist?" She revealed that she had felt something special toward me when she first met me. She came to believe that I was capable of treating her successfully, but she questioned why she had this feeling toward this particular therapist. She continued:

> However, that was not a reason why I chose you for my therapist, because I had already met you when I felt that way. The only reason I decided to come to see you is because your office is located in a convenient area for me ... Now I can tell you the other reasons. Maybe you are empathic or sincere, or you are very sensitive to my struggle; and I can explain what meaningful work we have done up till now. But even now, no one can explain "why you are my therapist," because we just happened to meet, that's all.

We shared the understanding that Eri had not been able to live with the fact that, in this world, many events occur without particular reason. She said,

"I know there is no particular reason why we met. If our encounter was a coincidence, my getting better through this therapy becomes a coincidence. That still often confuses me. How difficult it is for people to understand that we cannot find a particular reason for an incident in our lives. It is interesting, though."

Discussion and conclusion

In the psychotherapeutic work with Eri, when she or I attempted to define an event as contingent or necessary, we entered an intersubjective disjunction, and it led to our selfobject tie being fragile. In this process, I reflected on the meaning of "destiny," the term that was often used by Eri, and came to recognize that I had slipped into a dichotomy. I was aware that my claiming that an event was contingent was another side of my effort to search for necessity.

Now we could say that, an analyst's or a patient's viewing the phenomena emerging in an analytic process as merely contingent or necessary may be a sign that their relational system has become rigid and lost its openness to transformation. Allowing an analyst or a patient to view a therapeutic process as contingent may lead to the transformation of the analytic relationship; but too much emphasis on contingency is equal to viewing it as necessity. The significant thing for both participants is to leave open both possibilities.

Being tolerant of contingency does not mean seeing an event as purely contingent. Rather, it leaves open a possibility of contingency as well as necessity in a patient's and an analyst's subjective experience. Through this process, contingency comes to be found in necessity, and necessity comes to be found in contingency. The term, destiny, or *unmei* in Japanese, represents a kind of realm organized between contingency and necessity. I also could say that this is the way a patient and an analyst together make sense (Orange, 1995) of their emotional experiences through the words of contingency and necessity.

1. Dichotomy of contingency and necessity, and trauma

On what occasions do a patient and an analyst slip into a dichotomy of contingency and necessity? Both Eri and I attempted to define the stories and experiences Eri brought into my office as either contingency or necessity; but they are not categorized as one or the other. They are a contingency that is closer to necessity as well as necessity that is closer to contingency. At the beginning of therapy, Eri and I had not been able to live with uncertainty. Eri's inability to tolerate uncertainty accumulated in her developmental process with her father, and it was strengthened by the traumatic experience of being fired. For me, the uniformity of thinking accumulated in my analytic training, and it was strengthened by Eri's intolerability.

Brothers (2008) pays special attention to dichotomic thinking after the experiencing of a trauma. According to her, the human world is inherently uncertain. A trauma renders a person less tolerant of uncertainty and plunges him or her into a dichotomy. She illustrates the point through the example of people and society who experienced the events of September 11, 2001, and slipped into a dichotomy of friend or foe, same or different. In her writing, she did not refer to contingency and necessity; but we conclude here that they can be added to this type of dichotomy. In other words, a person wishes to define an event as contingent or necessary when he or she is not able to live with the uncertainties of the world.

Research has established that psychological and relational systems of traumatized people are not sufficiently open to transformation (Brandchaft, 2010; Stolorow, 2007; Brothers, 2008; Togashi, 2012c; Togashi and Kottler, 2012a). In Chapter 8, we reveal that a traumatized person tends to avoid being psychologically influenced by anyone, including those to whom they feel drawn (see also Togashi and Kottler, 2012). Such a person seeks out others who have suffered traumatic experiences similar to their own, but then they often insist that their experience was different.

We could say that Eri and I were stuck within the same kind of a traumatized relational system. We divided the human world into contingency and necessity to dispel the uncertainty of her life and my work. The longer we stayed there, the narrower our recognition became.

Eri's paternal grandfather was killed by the atomic bomb dropped on Nagasaki during the Second World War. Although she did not directly relate this fact to her inability to tolerate uncertainty or unpredictability, she, toward the end of her therapy, revealed that her father occasionally bemoaned the absurdity of random killing. We could say that Eri was raised in a family system that was traumatized by what happened at least two generations earlier. Her father's stubbornness and her mother's depression could be a part of this traumatized system. To Eri and her parents, the world is unpredictable; their relational system has been frozen as if their time has stood still.

2. Dynamic systems and contingency

What perturbed the rigid relational system organized by Eri and me and made it more open to transformation than before? One answer is given by our case vignette. A patient and an analyst who allow themselves to confront the possibility that any phenomena can be both contingent and necessary open the way to transformation. Eri's "destiny" can be understood as her effort to find contingency in necessity and necessity in contingency.

At the beginning of her therapy, Eri inquired, "Why are you my therapist?" The therapeutic process that followed from this query and that led to the answer Eri and I finally obtained describes how a rigid relational system becomes more open to transformation. Both Eri and I looked for a reasonable answer to this question, which is not supposed to have a reasonable answer. Through the therapeutic work, we finally reached the most reasonable answer—"There is no reason"—and we shared the difficulty of emotionally accepting the resulting uncertainty.

Seeing everything as necessity could lead to a pathology of obsession and compulsion, and seeing everything as contingent could lead to a pathology that negates one's sense of being. Contingency and necessity have to do with narcissism and a sense of being. Lachmann (2008) illustrates the transformation of narcissism from a dyadic system view. For him, the transformation of narcissism is a perturbation of a dyadic system, which emerges then in the empirical dimension of empathy, humor, creativity, the transcendence of mortality, and wisdom. We could say that contingency-necessity can be placed within this dimension of transformation.

3. Clinical implications

In the discussion of contingency-necessity, Kuki (1935) did not explicitly reflect on God; but as the Japanese philosopher Obama maintains (2006),

Kuki probably spent some time thinking on this theme. For God is, in a sense, the very representation of contingency and necessity within the realm of metaphysics.

Obama (2006) argues that Kuki's cosmology of contingency is the philosophy of "god at play," who plays for the sake of playing, and who descends from a Japanese cultural background. This god does not judge a person's behavior or create the fundamental rule of the world. This god does not have any purposes or ideals, and he just plays dice without particular aim except for the sake of playing, which is, to Kuki, where human anguish comes in. God at play does not provide a reason why a human being exists or why she was born.

In other words, for Kuki, a person is thrown into the world by chance. Everything in this world is beyond her capacity, knowledge, and power. It is a coincidence that a person is at a particular place, at a particular moment, and in a particular way. There is no reason why she was born of these parents, for example, who are non-empathetic and abusive, why she was born as a female, and why she was born into a middle-class family. Still, depending on a roll of the dice thrown by God, she is thrown into the world—that is the fundamental contingency in the world of human beings.

In this circumstance, how can we make sense of our being in this world? Kuki's idea suggests that we turn back to the fundamental contingency and attempt to see it as our own choice. Let us suppose that we have experienced something painful. For example, our wallet was stolen, we discovered that our classmates hate us, or we encountered a handsome boy who would never want to date us. These painful events appeared in our life by chance. If we see them purely as coincidental, our life comes to be meaningless because we have to recognize that our being is also coincidental. For the same reason, if we see them purely as necessity, our life also comes to be meaningless—because there is no space in which we can create meaning for our life on our own.

What Kuki says is this: "We need to face the fact that our being is a coincidence, and we need to make a psychological effort to transform the coincidence into a possibility, which would give meaning to our lives through a sense of agency. This process is consistent with 'a positive sense of destiny,'" as is argued by some Japanese anthropologists and ethicists (Sagara, 1984; Ishige, 1990). They emphasize that a person obtains a sense of agency in the world by believing that she can be *actively* engaged in life and death, in her destiny.

I want to emphasize here that finding a reason for a phenomenon is different from finding the meaning of it. Eri tended to draw a strict line between her responsibilities and her colleagues'. If we should ask ourselves, "Why does she do it?" we could answer: "Because her father did not want her to exert her influence on her mother"; or, "Because her mother drew a strict line between herself and Eri." These answers may or may not be true, but what is important here is that she was born of such parents without a reason. She was not able to find hope in the future until she had found a meaning in this coincidence. Through this process, Eri and I were able to acknowledge that the only way for her to find meaning in her life was to obsessively attempt to find a reason for any phenomena.

4. How contingency emerges in the process of transformation[1]

Sucharov (2013) refers to the analytic process as "a dynamic relational process (itself complex) by which we deepen our awareness of complexity, as well as a description of this qualitative shift in our experiential world" (p. 382). He recognized that moving toward complexity "entails an experiential willingness to stay in complexity, to feel and embrace the irreducible complex totality of our interconnectedness, to feel the unknowability of that totality and to bear the inevitable anxiety and disorientation when that unknowability is in the foreground of our experiential landscape" (p. 383). He continues, "When we shift our focus from complexity as explanatory discourse to complexity as lived experience, we inevitably bump up against, and perhaps blur, the boundary between psychoanalytic and transpersonal domains" (p. 393).

I believe that, as Sperry (2014) discusses, a patient's awareness of contingency emerges in the process of this "moving toward complexity." The awareness of contingency is an expression of the perturbation of a dyadic system. I will discuss the following three areas in which the theme of contingency and necessity emerges in the process of transformation.

i   From isolation to connection.
ii   From explanatory discourse to experiential discourse.
iii From search for a reason to search for a meaning.

i. From isolation to connection

When we come to the question of whether a subjective experience is contingent or necessary, we are aware that we are connected to other persons existing in this world. When Eri became upset because the train service was disrupted, or when her therapist cancelled a session to attend a funeral, she saw these events as connected to herself. When she was late for a session, she explained her lateness as a coincidence. She attempted to deny the awareness that there was a connection between her feeling and her therapist.

It was Heinz Kohut who theorized that a person's sense of self emerges in the relationship with another's subjective experience of him and the other's way of being. He maintains that a sense of being cannot be defined by itself, but can be defined by the way another person experiences him or her. Without such a selfobject milieu, a person experiences himself or herself as fragmented.

In Chapter 10, Kottler and I continue to argue that the twinship selfobject experience is especially organized around contingency. Kohut originally defined twinship as a sense of essential alikeness; but by 1984 he expanded and redefined it as a sense of "feeling that one is a human being among other human beings" (Kohut, 1984). A person's sense that he or she is a human being among other human beings is organized only around the person's finding that all human beings are connected each to the other by accident, by being at a particular moment, at a particular place, while acting in a particular way. This type of twinship cannot be organized in relation to people who lived in the past or in a different universe or as a different creature. The definition describes a way of being in this universe, organized by accidental connections between people.

Eri's question, "Why are you my therapist?", asked with a tone of astonishment, came from her struggle to find meaning in the connection between herself and her therapist in their accidental encounter. As we worked through the question, she moved from a sense of herself as alienated from the world toward a sense of herself as meaningfully connected to the other. We could say that questions about contingency and necessity emerge in the process of searching for a selfobject tie.

ii. From explanatory discourse to experiential discourse

As Kuki (1936) discussed in detail, a person's awareness of contingency or necessity derives from a feeling of surprise. A person experiences and observes a huge number of events every day, but she does not often ask herself whether an event is contingent. Only when a person has a feeling of surprise does the question come to the fore in her subjective field.

Eri came up with questions: "Why did a disruption of train services bother to take place immediately before I left for my session?" or "Why did we meet each other?" They revealed her surprise. Her surprise followed from her finding herself connected to other events in the world. A traumatized person would be unable to experience this surprise in other ways, as amusing or hopeful, but would experience it as threatening to her being, as causing fear and panic. I believe that a person reveals a feeling of surprise when he changes his language in order to capture a phenomenon. In other words, the surprise would emerge in the process of moving from explanatory discourse toward experiential discourse.

Contemporary self psychologists and intersubjective theorists often use explanatory discourses. Through their discourse, they define a psychological interplay between an analyst and a patient as a nonlinear dynamic system, and they attempt to directly depict the psychological process, often not only from explicit information-memory processing but also from implicit information-memory processing.

Experiential discourse has been used within psychoanalytic circles, including Kohut's self psychology. Traditional psychoanalytic terms, such as projective identification, selfobject experience, and internalization, are used in a discourse that describes a person's subjective experiences in a metaphorical sense. The experiences described in this discourse are experience-near and convey a powerful sense of a person's subjective experience, but they do not always indicate a concrete measurable psychological process.

Clinical psychoanalysis brings to us its theoretical history with experiential discourse, but it inherently includes in itself the sensitivity to the psychological interplay in a dyad of patient and analyst. Before contemporary psychoanalytic system theories developed, an experienced analyst practiced through his sensitivity to nonverbal and procedural regulatory process between his patient and himself, paying attention to facial expression and tone of voice. In the course of psychological transformation, an explanatory discourse, as Sucharov (2013) emphasizes, often comes to be translated into an experiential discourse, which functions to generate the meaning of a psychological experience.

The question of contingency or necessity emerges in the transformation of discourse. Eri's question, "Why are you my therapist?" could include her longing to illustrate the process by which her therapist has been chosen, but it could go beyond the longing and express surprise about her finding a significant emotional tie between herself and her therapist. We could say that the question emerged in the transitional process of the transformation.

iii. From search for a reason to search for a meaning

As I have discussed in this chapter, the question of contingency or necessity often emerges in the process of exploring the meaning of a person's life. However, questions such as "Why did this thing happen to me?" would not provide the meaning of life for this person if he attempted to search only for the reason that might have caused the event. If he wants to find the meaning of his life, he needs to see a subjective experience as both contingent and necessary at the same time. A search for the meaning of life leads to a certainty that he will be present in the future.

A patient is often obsessed with finding a reason for an unresolved traumatic experience. The search would come to be a search for meaning in the traumatic experience of his life. This is, in other words, a process of renouncing the expectation that he or she can find the meaning of trauma by searching for a reason. Indeed, Eri experienced herself as a powerless figure who was controlled by a cosmic order, and she complained about the irrationality of human life. However, in her therapeutic process, her search for a reason why she was influenced by other events in this world was transformed into a search for the meaning of her life.

The question of contingency or necessity has to do with "expectation" (Lachmann, 2008). The patient who searches for reason and the patient who discontinues the search, in other words, the patient who falls into the dichotomy between contingency and necessity, is a person who falls into the dichotomy between unpredictability and complete predictability. As Eri's words indicate, defining all phenomena in the world as coincident is to define the world as totally unpredictable. Defining all phenomena in the world as necessary is to define the world as totally predictable. The conclusion of either scenario is traumatic. For in either case, the possibility of the person's exercising meaningful power over his own future would be nullified. Neither scenario provides the meaning of life.

In the therapeutic process, Eri was able to experience herself as being in between moderate unpredictability and moderate predictability. Moderate predictability created possibilities for her future and generated a resiliency of the mind that was not overwhelmed by an event. She came to be able to attend to the uncertain world with a sense of certainty.

Psychoanalysis has paid attention to how curative it is for a patient to have a "new" experience or environment. Although the word "new" is useful in describing a patient's subjective experience, there is no "new" experience that can lead to a therapeutically meaningful transformation in an epistemological sense. The new experience, which cannot be predicted by a patient, only leads to a traumatic or threatening experience. When a patient says, for example, "It is a new experience for me, because my mother failed to provide it," this is the experience that the mother has provided to some extent on another occasion, or that the patient has seen a mother of someone who could provide the experience, or that the patient has longed for the kind of mother in his fantasy. In this sense, a new experience is always an experience that the patient had already had at some earlier time. A meaningful experience unfolds in moderate predictability and the question about contingency and necessity unfolds as the transformation moves from a search for the reason to a search for a meaning.

Note

[1] Part of this section was originally written in response to Dr. Margy Sperry's excellent discussion of an earlier version of this chapter (see Sperry, 2014; Togashi, 2014b).

Chapter 10

Being human and not being human

The evolution of a twinship experience

Koichi Togashi, Ph.D., L.P.
Amanda Kottler, M.A. (Clin. Psych.)

How is it that some people experience themselves as *being human* in relation to others? What circumstances or processes make people feel they have lost a sense of *being human*?

In our experience, traumatized patients often refer to how they do not feel human, or how they feel they have lost a sense of being human relationally. For example, a sexually abused female patient described herself as a "toilet bowl," having experienced herself as an object into which someone else's sexual impulses were disposed. In her twenties, she became involved with a caring man who related to her with warmth, as a fellow human being. She found this hard to accept; she was not used to being treated in this way and did not experience herself as a human being. When her partner treated her humanely, she felt extremely anxious and scared.

Although this patient said she did not feel like a human being, clearly she recognized herself as belonging to the human species, and therefore as "a human." However, in this relational context, because she did not experience herself as *being human* she could not recognize nor could she *feel* the experience of being treated as human. Working with this kind of patient requires a sharp distinction between the notion of "a human being" as a noun and "being human" as a verb. We suggest that it is this sense of "being human" that needs to be considered and addressed when working with these kinds of traumatized patients.

This discussion follows the challenge Kohut left the next generation of self psychologists—to explore and expand the concept of the twinship selfobject experience. In Chapter 1 (see also Togashi and Kottler, 2012b), we elaborate on Kohut's shift of emphasis in the definition of twinship from a *sense of essential alikeness* (Kohut, 1971, 1984) to a *sense of being a human among humans* (Kohut, 1984). With this shift, we argue that Kohut's self psychology made a distinct theoretical transformation from the "psychology of the self" to the "psychology of being human." This is evidenced by the fact that Kohut's main focus, before his death, was on how a person experiences a sense of being human, rather than on how they experience a sense of being a cohesive and vital self, which was how his self psychology began. Posthumously, Kohut (1984) states;

> Some of the most painful feelings to which man is exposed, unforgettably described by Kafka in *The Metamorphosis* and observable during the analyses of many people with severe narcissistic personality disorders, relate to the sense of not being human. The awareness of such a central distortion in the personality stems, I believe, from the absence of *human* humans in the environment of the small child.
>
> (Kohut, 1984, p. 200; italics in original)

Here, Kohut uses *metamorphosis* to describe pathology as a sense of not being human, experienced by people with severe narcissistic personality disorders, who we believe can be understood in contemporary terms as relationally traumatized patients. More important, for this chapter, is the meaning of this "sense of not being human" and, what Kohut meant by the absence of "*human* humans in the environment of the small child."

Twinship and a sense of being human

While Kohut (1968, 1971) defined twinship in terms of essential alikeness it makes sense that he used a word derived from "twin," which refers to a special kind of connection between two siblings understood as being alike. But, as his definition's emphasis shifted to a sense of being a human among other human beings, he continued to use the term twinship. This intrigues us. To explore this, we track Kohut's theoretical work on the twinship selfobject experience and trace the changes.

Interestingly, twinship was originally used interchangeably with the term "alter-ego" (Kohut, 1968, 1971, 1984) but Kohut never clearly distinguished them. With some exceptions (Detrick, 1985, 1986; Brothers, 1993, 1994) most post-Kohutian self psychologists use the term twinship

(Ulman and Paul, 1992; Martinez, 1993, 2003; Shapiro, 1998; Gorney, 1998; Livingston, 1998; Kottler, 2007; Togashi, 2009a, 2012a, 2012c; Brothers, 2012; Togashi and Kottler, 2012a, 2012b; Lichtenberg, 2012; VanDerHeide, 2012). For self psychologists, the word twinship, not "alter-ego," seems to have an attractive resonance with a fundamental sense of an emotional connection to the human world. But, this does not explain why Kohut retained the term "twin" after he shifted the emphasis of the definition.

The crucial difference between twins and ordinal siblings rests on the coincidence of having been in utero together for nine months and being born more or less at the same time. Whether or not twins are identical, the fact that they are in utero, the same place, together is fundamentally unique and the way they are born is uniquely significant and irreplaceable. Defined in this way, the experience of twinship differs substantially from the attachment felt by siblings, and the kind of intimacy or trust that is referred to in the substance of other kinds of intimate relationships. Likewise, it is different from a lived relational experience of idealizing or mirroring—concepts which refer to the substance of the emotional ties. We suggest therefore that twinship—a sense of being a human among humans—refers to how two people came to meet each other and have *been* together, or experienced each other, while idealizing and mirroring refer to the substance of what connects two people.

Applying this understanding to a therapeutic relationship, we suggest that an essential quality of a sense of being "a human among humans" in a twinship tie relates to the way in which the two people experience their meeting and their being together as coincidental, but also, significantly, as irreplaceable. The experience can acquire a kind of unique meaning similar to the "meeting" of siblings born as twins.

Seeing it from this perspective suggests that Kohut's original definition of twinship, a sense of essential alikeness, only refers to the substance of an emotional tie that is represented in the same theoretical dimension as that of idealizing and mirroring. This definition describes what connects one person with another or the substance of how two people are connected to each other, but not how they have been together. In other words, the original definition does not refer to the process of their being together. This could explain why contemporary self psychologists use the word "twinship" rather than the word "alter-ego." The experience has to be described as "twinship" for it to be understood, in Kohut's terms, as "the feeling that one is a human being among other human beings" (Kohut, 1984, p. 200).

People who experience this feeling describe a sense of astonishment and joy at the familiarity and comfort they experience, being with another human being, as a human being. In the discussion of the feeling that one is a human being among other human beings, Kohut (1981, 1984) uses the story of the astronauts whose space capsule lost power in outer space. They yearned to return to Earth regardless of the high probability of being burned to death during atmospheric entry, probably with their focus on their birthplace and where and how they had lived. In this context, it is the process of meeting and being together with others, and not the substance of the relationship, that becomes especially significant. This sense of astonishment and joy at the unspoken familiarity is how twins feel about their very being, their discovery, their birth, and their meeting of each other.

In the clinical context, we suggest that patients, who cannot experience themselves as being human, cannot find purpose or meaning in meeting others, let alone a unique meaning for having ever been born. Meeting others holds no significance for them; they believe they make no impact on others and that they are easily replaceable. In our psychoanalytic therapy with such patients, we believe that therapists and patients need to "make sense together" (Orange, 1995) of the meaning of the process of their meeting and being together—of the fact that they met coincidentally and that this makes their meeting and the development of their being together all the more irreplaceable and significant.

Case vignette from Togashi's work with Anna

Anna is a lesbian Japanese woman in her late forties. We have worked together for three years in once-a-week psychotherapy. She came to see me complaining of severe depression, and a sense of emptiness, which she tried to redress through sexual promiscuity with both genders.

Our "relationship" began three years before she called to officially set up a therapeutic relationship. She had been a student at a vocational school where I taught as an associate. At the time, she was studying health care and had taken a few classes of mine.

Anna was smart, cheerful, and talented. She worked hard after graduating from school, and had an excellent reputation in her professional field. She had a good sense of humor and enjoyed "making people happy." From what she said it seemed highly unlikely that any of her colleagues would believe she had been severely depressed for a long time, and that she had attempted to kill herself several times. Her wish was to fall in love with a woman on whom she could rely. Instead, she repeatedly became involved with women who were either preoccupied with suicide or who had experienced the death of someone close to them. These women used her for their own needs and she gave in to whatever was demanded of her until she was utterly exhausted.

For example, at one time, an apparently "psychologically unstable" woman, whose boyfriend had been murdered, phoned Anna at 2AM asking her to come to her. Although she lived in a city six hours away by car, Anna agreed. By the time she arrived, the woman was asleep. Anna had no key so was forced to wait some seven hours until the woman woke. In this relationship, Anna felt like an object; she did not feel human.

When Anna asked if I would become her therapist, she wondered why she had chosen me given that she had numerous other possibilities. She liked my school of thought, sensed she could trust me as a professional clinician, and liked the way I made sense of the issues discussed in my classes. But she was preoccupied with why she had chosen me, and the sense she had that I was "supposed to be her therapist."

For the first year, we worked on the devastating relationships she had experienced and her intense longing for a person who she believed would be perfectly matched with her. She described how, when she felt lonely and empty, she sought out "one-night stands." She desired women, but this did not stop her from having sex with men, after which she felt "disgusting" and far from human—she felt like a repulsive creature, alone in this world, and not connected to any human beings. It was obvious from the beginning of the therapy that she yearned for a twinship tie.

At one point, even though I had told her she could, she described how, in spite of feeling severely depressed, she had not asked for an extra session. She explained, "I am not sure what makes me feel we are a good patient–therapist couple. Our relationship feels extremely special and meaningful, but I don't know why. I felt unable to ask for an additional session until I knew why and how we came to have what feels like such a special relationship. I felt I needed to know ... why you and me ... " This led to her feeling more depressed and to engaging in sex with yet another stranger.

Our search for the origins of her deep sense of disconnection with others revealed two traumatic episodes experienced by herself and her mother. Her own involved the loss of a woman she loved deeply in her twenties. She sensed that this woman was her "soul partner." Tragically, the woman had a child and was married to an extremely abusive man. Two years into their relationship, she killed herself. Anna was shocked, quit her job, and seriously attempted suicide.

Her mother's story involved the Second World War. She was born in Manchuria, which was conquered and occupied by Japan until 1945. Six days before the Japanese government accepted the unconditional surrender of the Allied Power, the Soviet Union invaded Manchuria. Anna's mother was three years old at the time, and her family barely escaped alive. They arrived in Japan via the Korean peninsula. Anna's mother never told Anna this story in any detail, but had implied that some family members were either killed or had died during the journey.

Anna stated, "My mother is proud of being alive and having survived such trauma. Unlike me, she is certain about herself and her reason for being. I am not sure why I am alive." Anna grew up feeling curious about her mother's certainty about life, given her exposure to life-threating situations and having lost her home as a result of the war. Her mother was strong and energetic. She aggressively controlled Anna, her second daughter, and her husband. She made all the decisions, including what job her husband should have.

Anna brought many dreams to therapy, most of which had to do with the sea or ocean. Two years into her treatment, Anna described this dream:

> I was floating on the sea. It seems to be at night. I recognize that my ship had been attacked by an enemy boat, and was sinking. I was thrown overboard as a result of the attack. The sea was covered in oil. I look around at burnt heads with their eyes wide open, and some headless torsos. I am scared and feel I am going to die. I have to rescue a boy who is also floating on the sea and looks alive, but I am not sure. I wake up at this point and do not know if I have successfully rescued him.

Anna and I understood this dream identically. We immediately connected it to a fragmented sense of herself and to her mother's disavowed trauma. Further, Anna had to rescue someone even if she herself was in a life-threating situation. She was alone in the dark ocean surrounded by body parts that were no longer human beings. The boy floating on the sea probably represented the hope she had for herself, but like herself, she was not sure if he was alive.

We also both associated the dream with the Second World War. We wondered whether the ship represented one that was transporting people from Manchuria between Korea and Japan, which had been bombarded by the Allied Force. We thought that this dream replicated something of the scenes of the war which Anna's mother may have seen or heard about from others.

Discussing the dream enabled Anna to recognize a deep depression behind her mother's fiercely energetic demeanor. She reflected on how her mother emphasized the strength of her own mind and body and how this might relate to her inability to connect with the memories because of her traumatic experiences. She imagined that her mother had probably witnessed many war scenes in which people were not treated as human.

In this context, Anna began to question: Why are people born? Why was she born? How could anyone feel any certainty about their lives if there is no reason for their birth? Increasingly she reflected on the coincidence of our meeting: I was a part-time lecturer in the school, with no connection to the region. She had not planned to enroll in the program; she went without any particular plan. She asked, "What is the meaning of our meeting? Why you? These are important questions, because I cannot work out why I was born in the first place, let alone why we met." She continued, "If a bullet had hit my mother while escaping, I would not have been here." She thought she had become preoccupied with these questions because she had come to feel comfortable and secure in the relationship with me. She was aware that this was related to an experience of beginning to feel human.

I reflected on how Anna had come to feel like a special patient of mine. When I had first seen her in the school, I felt a connection to her although our encounters were infrequent. There were similarities between us. We were almost the same age and, before we verbalized anything of these feelings, there was a strong sense of an unspoken and unformulated familiarity between us. I felt her like a friend or a sibling with a deep emotional connection, which was not of a romantic nor sexual nature. "Why her?"—became a significant question for me, too. While we worked on our experiences, Anna's pattern of looking for relationships, which always ended up being abusive, stopped.

Three years into the treatment, she met Kana, a woman in the same profession. They immediately felt attracted to each other, and began living together shortly after meeting. Kana was also an isolated and closeted lesbian. It was the first experience for both of them, of being able to feel emotionally supported by another. Anna's depression lifted as a much clearer sense of what it felt like to be human in the world emerged. Anna stated, "This relationship gives me a license and a reason to be alive as a human being."

In this context, she reflected on how her mother had never spoken about Anna's birth. Anna's mother had not told her how she felt when Anna was born, or how they had celebrated her birth. From this, we understood that Anna needed to find meaning in her birth particularly given how, until then, everyone close to her had in one way or another been closely linked to death, rather than to life. At around this time she dreamt:

> I am in Europe or somewhere outside Japan, walking up a hill. There are many beautiful white houses along one side of the road, and there is a beautiful ocean on the other side. It is a wonderful fine day; the ocean is awesome. The sea is glistening with waves. I feel very comfortable and relaxed.

Anna and I understood that her mind was no longer saturated with ideas about "death." She had needed a sense of meaning in her life, especially in the fact of her birth, something her mother had not given her, but something that our therapeutic relationship had provided. We concluded that although there was no reason for our meeting and that it was only a coincidence, it was our being together that gave our encounter its special and meaningful significance and made Anna feel herself to *be* human.

Two years later, I saw Anna to ask for permission to use our work in my paper. Anna indicated her pleasure in giving me permission by saying "You gave me a meaning to our work, and my life." She said she experienced my attempt to write up her case as a license certifying the fact of her being alive in this world.

Since Anna knew that I published papers and books, she proudly told her mother that her work with me might be published in book form or in an academic journal. For the first time, she told her mother about her depression, and the lack of a sense of being human. In this conversation, her mother recalled and described the traumatic episode in which she had been evacuated from Manchuria to Japan.

Anna's mother was on the ship that carried Japanese refugees wishing to go back to Japan. The ship was overloaded, and dead people were thrown overboard into the sea. On the ship she was seriously ill and needed medication. The physician on the ship said to her parents that he needed to throw her overboard if she passed away. Fortunately, a relative obtained antibiotics for her and she recovered.

Anna's mother completely forgot about this episode and has never talked about this to anyone. Anna and I were surprised at how similar this episode was to Anna's ship dream. We were astonished by the coincidence, and came to make sense of it together by saying that her traumatized mother had denied her depression. Together, we understand that her mother's aggressive state possibly represented her effort to keep herself alive and her struggle not to pass her depression onto the next generation. But the effort was not effective and we wondered whether Anna was feeling her mother's trauma. Her mother's revelation of this story and our making sense of it in this way enabled Anna to feel that effectively, her therapy was complete.

Discussion and conclusion

Anna felt disconnected to the world and people. She felt isolated and her existence felt meaningless. Her mother had been traumatized by her life-threatening experiences during the Second World War. Her forceful behavior was a way of fiercely avoiding this reality. The consequences were traumatic for Anna who had no sense of there being any particular meaning for her birth or her being. She was looking for a person who could give her what she experienced in her therapy: "a license and a reason to be alive as a human being."

Anna's mother attempted not to pass on her depression and trauma to Anna. By not telling Anna about her birth, or about how she survived the traumatic journey, she tried to avoid creating a replica of herself. However, a traumatized person's yearning for a person in whom she could find herself was too strong and, through nonverbal interaction, Anna took over the dissociated aspect of the trauma.

In the therapeutic process, Anna questioned the meaning of the encounter and the relationship that evolved between her therapist and herself. Their shared effort to find meaning and significance in their meeting and being together enabled Anna to feel the experience of being human. Although the encounter was only coincidental, it was significantly meaningful for both of them. The essential quality of their twinship tie centered on how they had been together, more than in the substance of what connected them.

This therapeutic process indicates that the dyadic interactive process of twinship at the *experiential* level is best described in terms of a feeling that the process of being together with particular others is meaningful and irreplaceable. A twinship experience provides a profound sense of that feeling—of experiencing oneself as *being* a human among other human beings.

Our finding is consistent with Togashi's discussion on the contingency and the meaning of life in Chapter 9 (see also Togashi, 2014a). He elaborates a therapeutic process with a female patient who was afraid of anything unpredictable, and who did not like seeing any phenomenon as coincidental. Drawing on the work of Kuki (1932, 1935, 1936) a Japanese philosopher, Togashi explores how an analyst can deal with contingency, something that is seen in many aspects of our psychoanalytic work.

In Chapter 9, Togashi argues that one of the human tragedies is that we are born into this world without any particular meaning. It is pure coincidence that a person is born in any one particular place, at any one particular moment, in any one particular way. There is no personal reason why anyone is born to parents who are unempathic and abusive, or who belong to any particular culturally or socially defined group. In these circumstances, Togashi argues that the way humans make meaning of their lives is by turning back to the fundamental contingencies in their past and finding meaning in the ways in which they are born, and their way of being among other human beings.

What we discuss here is not the finitude of human life, but the contingency of human birth. Originally, all human births are coincidental and do not have meaning in themselves. Yet, human beings can and do find meaning in them, helped often by conversations with their mothers who describe how they anticipated their birth and the meaning they ascribed to this new life. These processes give meaning to life and provide an individual with a sense of being human. Twinship is the ultimate form of this. Twins are born with a unique meaning attached to the circumstances of their birth. In this chapter, we have shown how the therapeutic process can provide this essential experience—that of giving birth to, and the discovery of, the feeling of *being* human among other humans.

Epilogue

What is "being human"? – re-conceptualizing and redefining twinship

Amanda Kottler, M.A. (Clin. Psych.)
Koichi Togashi, Ph.D., L.P.

As our journey comes to an end, we find ourselves reflecting on what it is that we have achieved in this book. Overall it is clear to us that, using contemporary relational terminology, we have essentially re-conceptualized and redefined Kohut's final definition of twinship. We began the book with our own questions: What motivated Kohut to redefine twinship? What exactly did Kohut mean by a "feeling that one is a human being among other human beings" (Kohut, 1984, p. 200)? And, as the book evolved we began to ask what exactly does "being human" mean? While we have been working on this book, we have noticed that this question is being asked more and more frequently by colleagues in online webinar discussions, at conferences over the last few years, and in recent publications (see for example, Kottler, 2007; Togashi, 2006, 2009, 2012a, 2012c, 2014a; Brothers, 2012; Togashi and Kottler, 2012a, 2012b; Lichtenberg, 2012; VanDerHeide, 2012). The answers we have provided might feel a touch anticlimactic, primarily because of the incredible and deceptive complexity of the topic.

In the most general and simplistic terms, what we have in fact, discussed in the ten chapters of this book is: how and in what way do individuals come to experience a sense of belonging or, put differently, how do they come to experience themselves as "feeling at home" relationally (Kottler, 2014)? As simple as this experience and redefintion of twinship might seem at first glance, this was an incredibly difficult task. A rich human experience of feeling at home may seem to be an ordinary, commonplace feeling, but to describe the intensity in an accessible and adequate way and to give it the gravitas we believe the ideas deserve, was a struggle and a challenge. The most significant and crucial reason for this, has to do with an a priori issue, which is itself included in the experience of "feeling at home." It is an extremely fine and frail subjective experience, which, to varying degrees and depending on the relational contexts involved, every human being longs for.

Feeling at home requires individuals to be involved in a "human" world, in relationship with other humans. But, human relationships always present a risk of injury (Jaenicke, 2008). Individuals are always vulnerable in human relationships; there is always the risk of discovering unexpected, unbearable, and seemingly irreconcilable differences in the intimate other (Togashi, 2014d). There will always be an aspect of the other's subjectivity, which is not experienced as connected to us (Benjamin, 1991, 1995), and which could possibly prevent that "feeling at home" experience. As we have demonstrated in this book, it is not unusual for individuals to have experienced others who have, instead of relating to them as human beings, used them as "things," objects, or as mental representations of themselves.

In order to feel at home, individuals need emotional relationships with others, but, in these relationships, there is always a risk of being wounded by the discovery that this other who was initially trusted, and appeared to be connected in the way the individual has yearned for, is a lie.

This human dilemma is described in Martin Buber's reflection, *Ich und Du* (Buber, 1923). Buber describes:

> The actual other who meets me meets me in such a way that my soul comes in contact with his as with something that it is not and that it cannot become. My soul does not and cannot include the other, and yet can approach the other in this most real contact.
>
> (Buber, 1999, p. 56)

For him, *Ich-Du* ("I–Thou") is an intimate dialogue organized in the mutual and authentic existence of two beings (Frie, 2011). Our whole being is involved in the whole universe, which is seen in the subjectivity of Thou—a Thou who has his own freedom and his own initiative, but who is nevertheless, emotionally connected. For Buber, a sense of alienation and fear is the result of an environment in which a human being cannot find this kind of dialogue. This is, for Buber, an Ich–Es ("I–It") relationship. As Orange (2010) discusses, Buber's language meets the idea of intersubjective systems theory (Orange, Atwood, and Stolorow, 1997;

Stolorow et al., 1987), in which "persons are always already embedded in relational contexts" (Orange, 2010, p. 19). As psychoanalysts and psychoanalytic psychotherapists, we need to ask ourselves if we are maintaining this dialogue in our work. We have to recognize that, as human beings, we always run the risk of treating a patient as Es (it), not Thou; and as we have demonstrated in this book, this kind of enactment is likely when as clinicians, we are unable to risk and tolerate that "feeling at home" feeling with our patients. Our patients and ourselves long for the experience of "feeling at home"; but the feeling is organized on a knife's-edge balance between I and Thou, between the similarities and the differences, the connectedness and the disconnectedness, and between the necessity and the contingency of our meeting.

From what we have said above, and throughout this book, the reader will not be surprised to read that another major reason for our struggle to make our ideas accessible, relates to the language available for us to use to describe this deceptively simple aspect of human subjectivity and human experience. It was impossible to satisfactorily describe the experience of not "feeling at home" using traditional psychoanalytic terms such as "functional deficit," "disruption of ego structure," "fragmentation of the self," or "splitting of self- and object representation."

This is not surprising given that "feeling at home" was not a focus for Freud who survived two world wars, and for whom the world was a place in which individuals were required to adjust themselves to a slow and painful process of civilization—not humanization. Freud's theory, and much that has followed, was aimed at describing how human beings can adjust themselves to make use of their developing psychological abilities to fulfill their wishes. "Feeling at home" would have seemed, to the psychoanalyst in that historical context, and to many psychoanalysts today, too naïve and simplistic to be considered a goal for psychoanalytic treatment. So, our dilemma was and is, what language would give the experience the gravitas it deserves? What language would describe this sense of feeling at home or not feeling at home—a feeling which goes way beyond a function or malfunction of the internal psychic structure? What language could we use to describe the depths of a feeling of profound confidence about being human in this world, or, in contrast, a total collapse of being human?

In spite of its inadequacy, we did reluctantly draw on some psychoanalytic buzzwords when we found it impossible to discuss this seemingly very simple feeling in any other way. Dissatisfied, we stretched concepts and language in ways that might seem awkward to the reader, as it did to us, but it is our hope that readers will find a way to stretch themselves into the words and concepts we ultimately chose.

In closing, we wish to comment on a twinship experience that has emerged between us in spite of our having come from such utterly different contexts. Our two voices have developed a rich and intense series of dialogues relating to the detailed content and the choice of vocabulary used in each of the chapters we wrote together and the overall format of the book. The similarities and the differences, the coincidence and necessity of our meeting have enabled us, at the conclusion of the journey to more easily articulate our similar, different, mutual, and authentic relationship with the topic and contents of this book and with each other. We both look forward to this also being the beginning of many more shared journeys.

References

Abramowitz, S. (2001). Adult homosexual development and the self. Paper presented in workshop entitled "The self and orientation: the next step" at The 24th Annual International Conference on the Psychology of the Self, San Francisco.

Agger, E. (1988). Sibling relationships. *Psychoanalytic inquiry*, 8, 1–134.

Aron, L. (1996). *A meeting of minds: mutuality in psychoanalysis*. Hillsdale, NJ: The Analytic Press.

Atwood, G. E. and Stolorow, R. D. (1979). *Faces in a cloud: intersubjectivity in personality theory*. Northvale, NJ: Jason Aronson.

Atwood, G. E. and Stolorow, R. D. (1984). *Structure of subjectivity: explorations in psychoanalytic phenomenology*. Hillsdale, NJ: The Analytic Press.

Atwood, G. E. and Stolorow, R. D. (1997). Defects in the self: liberating concept or imprisoning metaphor. *Psychoanalytic dialogues*, 7: 517–522.

Bacal, H. A. (1981). Notes on some therapeutic challenges in the analysis of severely regressed patients. *Psychoanalytic inquiry*, 1 (1), 29–56.

Bacal, H. (1985). Optimal responsiveness and the therapeutic process. H. A. Bacal (Ed.), *Optimal responsiveness: how therapists heal their patients* (pp. 3–34). Northvale, NJ: Jason Aronson.

Bacal, H. A. (1990). Does an object relations theory exist in self psychology? *Psychoanalytic inquiry*, 10, 197–220.

Bacal, H. A. (1998). Optimal responsiveness and the specificity of selfobject experience. In H. A. Bacal (Ed.), *Optimal responsiveness: how therapists heal their patients* (pp. 141–170). Northvale, NJ: Jason Aronson.

Bacal, H. A. (2006). Specificity theory: conceptualizing a personal and professional quest for therapeutic possibility. *International journal of psychoanalytic self psychology*, 1(2), 133–155.

Bacal, H. A. (2007). Discussion of Judy Pickles's case presentation from the perspective of psychoanalytic specificity theory. *Psychoanalytic inquiry*, 27, 125–138.

Bacal, H. A. (2011). *The power of specificity in psychotherapy: when therapy works and when it doesn't*. New York: Jason Aronson.

Basch, M. F. (1986). Can this be psychoanalysis? In A. Goldberg (Ed.), *Progress in self psychology* (Vol. 2, pp. 18–30). New York: Guilford Press.

Basch, M. F. (1992). *Practicing psychotherapy: a casebook*. New York: Basic Books.

Basch, M. F. (1994). The selfobject concept: clinical implications. In A. Goldberg (Ed.), *Progress in self psychology*, (Vol. 10, pp. 1–7). New York: The Analytic Press.

Beebe, B. (2005). Faces-in-relation: forms of intersubjectivity in an adult treatment of early trauma. In B. Beebe, S. Knoblauch, J. Rustin, and D. Sorter. *Forms of intersubjectivity in infant research and adult treatment* (pp. 89–144). New York: Other Press.

Beebe, B. and Lachmann, F. M. (2002). *Infant research and adult treatment: co-constructing interactions.* Hillsdale, NJ: The Analytic Press.

Benjamin, J. (1988). *The bonds of love: psychoanalysis, feminism, and the problem of domination.* New York: Pantheon.

Benjamin, J. (1990). An outline of intersubjectivity: the development of recognition. *Psychoanalytic psychology,* 7S, 33–46.

Benjamin, J. (1991). Fathers and daughters: identification with difference. *Psychoanalytic dialogues,* 1, 277–300.

Benjamin, J. (1995). *Like subjects, love objects: essays on recognition and sexual difference.* New Haven, CT: Yale University Press.

Benjamin, J. (2010). Can we recognize each other? Response to Donna Orange. *International journal of psychoanalytic self psychology,* 5 (3), 244–256.

Ben-Menahem, Y. (1996). Michel Foucault: history as therapy. *Psychoanalysis and contemporary thought,* 19, 579–610.

Bertelsen, P. (1996). General psychological principle in Kohut's self psychology reconsidered from a phenomenological perspective. *Journal of phenomenological psychology,* 27 (2), 146–173.

Blechner, M. J. (1996). Psychoanalysis in and out of the closet. In: B. Gerson (Ed.), *The therapist as a person* (pp. 223–239). Hillsdale, NJ: The Analytic Press.

Boss, M. (1963). *Psychoanalysis and daseinanalysis.* L. B. Lefebre (Trans.). New York: Basic Books.

Brandchaft, B. (1993). To free the spirit from its cell. In A. Goldberg (Ed.), *Progress in self psychology* (Vol. 9, pp. 209–230). Hillsdale, NJ: The Analytic Press.

Brandchaft, B. (1995). Resistance and defence: an intersubjective view. In A. Goldberg (Ed.), *Progress in self psychology* (pp. 88–96). Hillsdale, NJ: The Analytic Press.

Brandchaft, B. (2001). Obsessional disorders: a developmental systems perspective. *Psychoanalytic inquiry,* 21 (2), 253–288.

Brandchaft, B. (2010). Reflections on the unconscious. In B. Brandchaft, S. Doctors, and D. Sorter, *Toward an emancipatory psychoanalysis* (pp. 221–242). New York: Routledge.

Bromberg, P. M. (1989). Interpersonal psychoanalysis and self psychology: a clinical comparison. In D. Detrick, S. Detrick, and A. Goldberg (Eds.), *Self psychology: comparison and contrasts* (pp. 399–423). Hillsdale, NJ: The Analytic Press.

Brothers, D. (1993). The search for the hidden self: a fresh look at alter-ego transferences. In A. Goldberg (Ed.), *Progress in self psychology,* (Vol. 9, pp. 170–191). Hillsdale, NJ: The Analytic Press.

Brothers, D. (1994). Dr. Kohut and Mr. Z: is this a case of alter-ego countertransference? In A. Goldberg (Ed.), *Progress in self psychology,* (Vol. 10, pp. 99–114). Hillsdale, NJ: The Analytic Press.

Brothers, D. (1995). *Falling backwards: an exploration of trust and self-experience.* New York: W. W. Norton.

Brothers, D. (2008). *Toward a psychology of uncertainty: trauma-centered psychoanalysis.* New York: The Analytic Press.

Brothers, D. (2012). Trauma, gender, and the dark side of twinship. *International journal of psychoanalytic self psychology,* 7 (3), 391–405.

Buber, M. (1923). *I and thou*. R. J. Smith (Trans), New York: Scribner Classics.

Buber, M. (1999). *Martin Buber on psychology and psychotherapy: essays, letters, and dialogue*. Syracuse, NY: Syracuse University Press.

Bucci, W. (2002). The referential process, consciousness, and the sense of self. *Psychoanalytic inquiry*, 22, 766–793.

Buirski, P. (2005). *Practicing intersubjectively*. New York: Jason Aronson

Buirski, P. and Haglund, P. (2001). *Making sense together: the intersubjective approach to psychotherapy*. Northvale, NJ: Jason Aronson.

Clark, D. (1987). *Loving someone gay*. Berkeley, CA: Celestial Arts.

Coburn, W. J. (2002). A world of systems: the role of systematic patterns of experience in the therapeutic process. *Psychoanalytic inquiry*, 22 (5), 655–677.

Coburn, W. J. (2007a). Complexity made simple: exploring a nonlinear dynamic systems perspective. Paper presented at the 30th International Conference on the Psychology of the Self, Los Angeles, California.

Coburn, W. J. (2007b). Psychoanalytic complexity: pouring new wine directly into one's mouth. In P. Buirski and W. J. Coburn (Eds.), *New developments in self psychology practice* (pp. 3–22), New York: Jason Aronson.

Coburn, W. J. (2007c). What is a weeble anyway, and what is a wobble, too? *International journal of psychoanalytic self psychology*, 2(4): 463–473.

Detrick, D. (1985). Alterego phenomenon and alterego transference. In A. Goldberg (Ed.), *Progress in self psychology* (Vol. 1, pp. 240–256). New York: Guilford Press.

Detrick, D. (1986). Alterego phenomenon and alterego transference: some further considerations. In A. Goldberg (Ed.), *Progress in self psychology*, (Vol. 2, pp. 299–304). New York: Guilford Press.

Doi, T. (1962). Amae: a key concept for understanding Japanese personality structure. In R. J. Smith and R. K. Beardsley (Eds.), *Japanese culture: its development and characteristics* (pp. 132–139). Chicago: Aldine.

Doi, T. (1981). *The anatomy of dependence* (Revised paperback ed.). Tokyo: Kodansha International.

Doi, T. (1986). *The anatomy of self: the individual versus society*. M. A. Harbison (trans.), Tokyo: Kodansha International.

Fosshage, J. (2004). The explicit and implicit dance in psychoanalytic change. *The journal of analytical psychology*, 49, 49–65.

Fosshage, J. (2005). The explicit and implicit domains in psychoanalytic change. *Psychoanalytic inquiry*, 25 (4), 516–539.

Fosshage, J. L. (2009). Some key features in the evolution of self psychology and psychoanalysis. In N. VanDerHeide and W. J. Coburn (Eds.), *Self and systems: exploration in contemporary self psychology, Annual of the New York Academy of Science*, 1159, 1–18.

Freud, S. (1901). The Psychopathology of everyday life. *The standard edition of the complete psychological works of Sigmund Freud* (Vol. 6). London: Hogarth Press.

Freud, S. (1910). Leonardo da Vinci and a memory of his childhood. *The standard edition of the complete psychological works of Sigmund Freud* (Vol. 11, 59–137). London: Hogarth Press.

Freud, S. (1930). Civilization and its discontents. *The standard edition of the complete psychological works of Sigmund Freud* (Vol. 21, pp. 57–146). London: Hogarth Press.

References

Frie, R. (2010). Culture and context: from individualism to situated experience. In R. Frie and W. J. Coburn (Eds.), *Persons in context: the challenge of individuality in theory and practice* (pp. 3–19). New York: Routledge.

Frie, R. (2011). Psychoanalysis, religion, philosophy, and the possibility for dialogue: Freud, Binswanger, and Pfister. *International forum of psychoanalysis*, 21, 106–116.

Frie, R. (2013). The self in context and culture. *International journal of psychoanalytic self psychology*, 8, 505–513.

Frie, R. (2014). What is cultural psychoanalysis? Psychoanalytic anthropology and the interpersonal tradition. *Contemporary Psychoanalysis*, 50(3), 371–394.

Gehrie, M. J. (2002). Heinz Kohut memorial lecture: reflective relativism and Kohut's self psychology. In: A. Goldberg (Ed.), *Progress in self psychology* (Vol. 18, pp. 15–30), Hillsdale, NJ: The Analytic Press.

Gorney, J. E. (1998). Twinship, vitality, pleasure. In A. Goldberg (Ed.), *Progress in self psychology* (Vol. 14, pp. 85–106). New York: The Analytic Press.

Hagman, G. (1996). Flight from the subjectivity of the other. In A. Goldberg (Ed.), *Progress in self psychology* (Vol. 12, pp. 207–219). New York: The Analytic Press.

Heidegger, M. (1927). *Sein und Zeit*. J. Macquarrie & E. Robinson (Trans.) New York: Harper, 1962.

Hershberg, N. (2011). Narcissus revisited: a link between mirroring and twinship selfobject experiences—A discussion of Nancy VanDerHeide's, "A dynamic systems view of the transformational process of mirroring." *International journal of psychoanalytic self psychology*, 6 (1), 58–66.

Hoffman, I. (1983). The patient as interpreter of the analyst's experience. *Contemporary psychoanalysis*, 19, 389–422.

Hollway, W. (1984). Gender difference and the production of subjectivity. In: J. Henriques, W. Hollway, C. Urwin, C. Venn, and V. Walkerdine (Eds.), *Changing the subject*. London: Metheun.

Ishige, T. (1990). *Sekkyokuteki unmeikan no taito* [in Japanese]. Kikan Nihon Shisoshi, 35, 37–66.

Isobe, T. (1976). *Mujo no Kozo*. Tokyo: Kodansha [in Japanese].

Isobe, T. (1983). *Nihonzin no sinkoshin*. Tokyo: Kodansha [in Japanese].

Iwanami Shoten (2000). *Kojien* (6th Ed). Tokyo: Author.

Jaenicke, C. (2008). *The risk of relatedness: intersubjectivity theory in clinical practice*. New York: Jason Aronson.

Kieffer, C. C. (2004). Selfobjects, oedipal objects, and mutual recognition. *The annual of psychoanalysis*, 32, 69–80.

Kimura, B. (2005). *Kankei to shiteno jiko*. Tokyo: Misuzu Shobo [in Japanese].

Kohut, H. (1959). Introspection, empathy, and psychoanalysis. In P. H. Ornstein (Ed.), *The search for the self* (Vol. 1, pp. 205–232). New York: International Universities Press.

Kohut, H. (1968). The psychoanalytic treatment of narcissistic personality disorders: outline of a systematic approach. In P. H. Ornstein (Ed.), *The search for the self* (Vol. 1, pp. 477–509). New York: International Universities Press.

Kohut, H. (1971). *The analysis of the self*. Connecticut: International University Press.

Kohut, H. (1977). *The restoration of the self*. Connecticut: International University Press.

Kohut, H. (1981). Introspection, empathy, and the semicircle of mental health. In P. H. Ornstein (Ed.), *The search for the self,* (Vol. 4, pp. 537–567). Madison, CT: International Universities Press.

Kohut, H. (1984). *How does analysis cure?* Chicago: University of Chicago Press.

Kohut, H. (1996). *The Chicago Institute Lectures.* P. Tolpin and M. Tolpin (Eds.), Hillsdale, NJ: The Analytic Press.

Kottler, A. (2007). Twinship and "otherness": a self-psychological, intersubjective approach to "difference". In P. Buirski and A. Kottler (Eds.), *New developments in self psychology practice* (pp. 207–222). New York: Jason Aronson.

Kottler, A. (2014). Feeling at home, belonging, and being human: Kohut and self psychology. Paper presented at 37th Annual International Conference of the Psychology of the Self, Jerusalem, Israel.

Kottler, A. and Swartz, S. (1995). Talking about wolf-whistles: negotiating gender positions in conversation. *South African journal of psychology,* 25 (3), 184–190.

Kuki, S. (1932). Guzensei (Doctoral Dissertation). *The complete works of Kuki Shuzo* (Vol. 2, 267–322). Tokyo: Iwanami Shoten [in Japanese].

Kuki, S. (1935). Guzensei no mondai. *The complete works of Kuki Shuzo* (Vol. 2, 1–264). Tokyo: Iwanami Shoten [in Japanese].

Kuki, S. (1936). Modalities of contingency. *Philosophy of contingency and astonishment* [in Japanese], 25–45. Tokyo: Shoritsu-Shinsui.

Lachmann, F. M. (1993). A self-psychological perspective on Shabad's "Resentment, indignation, entitlement." *Psychoanalytic dialogue,* 3: 509–514.

Lachmann, F. M. (2000). *Transforming aggression: psychotherapy with the difficult-to-treat patient.* Northvale, NJ: Jason Aronson.

Lachmann, F. M. (2008). *Transforming narcissism: reflections on empathy, humor, and expectations.* New York: The Analytic Press.

Lachmann, F. M. and Beebe, B. (1993). Interpretation in a developmental perspective. In A. Goldberg (Ed.), *Progress in Self Psychology* (Vol. 9, pp. 45–52). New York: The Analytic Press.

Lachmann, F. M. and Beebe, B. (1995). Self psychology: later, the same day response to editors' follow-up questions. *Psychoanalytic dialogues,* 5, 415–419.

Laplace, P. S. (1812). *Théorie analytique des probabilités.* A. I. Dale (Ed., Trans.) *Philosophical essay on probabilities.* New York: Springer, 1994.

Lee, R. R. and Martin, J. C. (1991). *Psychotherapy after Kohut: a textbook of self psychology.* Hillsdale, NJ: The Analytic Press.

Lichtenberg, J. (1985). Humanism and the science of psychoanalysis. *Psychoanalytic inquiry,* 5, 343–365.

Lichtenberg, J. D. (2003). Communication in infancy. *Psychoanalytic inquiry,* 23 (3), 498–520.

Lichtenberg, J. D. (2012). Twinship: an appreciative discussion. *International journal of psychoanalytic self psychology,* 7 (3), 406–413.

Lichtenberg, J. D., Lachmann, F. M., and Fosshage, J. L. (1996). *The clinical exchange.* Hillsdale, NJ: The Analytic Press.

Lichtenberg, J. D., Lachmann, F. M., and Fosshage, J. L. (2010) *Psychoanalysis and motivational systems: a new look.* New York: Routledge.

Livingston, M. (1998). Harvest of fire: archaic twinship and fundamental conflict within a community and in group therapy. In I. N. H. Harwood and M. Pine (Eds.), *Self experience in group: intersubjective and self- psychological pathways to human understanding* (pp. 58–69). New York: Taylor & Francis.

Löwith, K. (1928). *Das individuum in der rolle des mitmenschen.* Darmstadt: Wissenschaftliche Buchgesellshaft (1969) [Japanese translation].

Mainzer, K. (2007). *Der kreative zufall: wie das neue in die welt kommt.* Munich: C. H. Beck [Japanese translation].
Markus, H. R. and Kitayama, S. (2003a). Culture, self, and the reality of the social. *Psychological inquiry*, 14, 283–288.
Markus, H. R. and Kitayama, S. (2003b). Models of agency: sociocultural diversity in the construction of action. In V. Murphy-Berman and J. J. Berman (eds.), *Cross-cultural differences in perspectives on the self* (pp. 1–57). Lincoln: University of Nebraska Press.
Marra, M. F. (2004). *Kuki Shuzo: a philosopher's poetry and poetics.* Honolulu, HI: University Of Hawaii Press.
Martinez, D. L. (1993). The bad girl, the good girl, their mothers, and the analyst: the role of the twinship selfobject in female oedipal development. In A. Goldberg (Ed.), *Progress in self psychology* (Vol. 9, pp. 87–107). New York: The Analytic Press.
Martinez, D. L. (2003). Twinship selfobject experience and homosexuality. In M. J. Gehrie (Ed.), *Progress in self psychology* (Vol. 19, pp. 41–56). New York: The Analytic Press.
Martinez, D. L. (2006). Discussion—A new definition of twinship selfobject experience and transference by Koichi Togashi. Presented at 29th International Conference on the Psychology of the Self, Chicago, Illinois.
Meltzoff, A. (1985). The roots of social and cognitive development: models of man's original nature. In T. Field and N. Fox (Eds.), *Social perception in infants* (pp. 1–30). Norwood, NJ: Ablex.
Meltzoff, A. (1990). Foundations for developing a concept of self: the role of imitation in relating self to other and the value of social mirroring, social modeling, and self practice in infancy. In D. Cicchetti and M. Beeghly (Eds.), *The self in transition: infancy to childhood* (pp. 139–164). Chicago: University of Chicago Press.
Mitchell, S. A. (1993). *Hope and dread in psychoanalysis.* New York: Basic Books.
Mollon, P. (2001). *Releasing the self: the healing legacy of Heinz Kohut.* London: Whurr Publishers.
Monod, J. (1971). *Chance and necessity: an essay on the natural philosophy of modern biology.* New York: Knopf.
Nakamura, Y. (1989). *Basho—topos.* Tokyo: Kobundo [in Japanese].
Nakane, C. (1972). *Japanese society.* Los Angeles: University of California Press.
Nishida, K. (1946). Bashoteki ronri to shukyoteki sekaikan. In S. Ueda (ed.), *Nishida Kitaro testugaku ronshu III.* Tokyo: Iwanami Shoten [in Japanese].
Obama, Y. (2006). *Kuki Shuzo no tetsugaku* [in Japanese]. Kyoto: Showado.
Oliver, N. (2007). *Lars and the real girl* drama film directed by Craig Gillespie.
Orange, D. M. (1995). *Emotional understanding: studies in psychoanalytic epistemology.* New York: Guilford Press.
Orange, D. M. (2008). Recognition as: intersubjective vulnerability in the psychoanalytic dialogue. *International journal of psychoanalytic self psychology*, 3 (2), 178–194.
Orange, D. M. (2010a). Beyond individualism: philosophical contributions of Buber, Gadamer, and Levinas. In R. Frie and W. J. Coburn (eds.), *Persons in context: The challenge of individuality in theory and practice* (pp. 43–58). New York: Routledge.
Orange, D. M. (2010b). *Thinking for clinicians: philosophical resources for contemporary psychoanalysis and the humanistic psychotherapies.* New York: Routledge.
Orange, D. M., Atwood, G., and Stolorow, R. D. (1997). *Working intersubjectively: contextualism in psychoanalytic practice.* Hillsdale, NJ: The Analytic Press.
Philipson, I. (2010). Pathologizing twinship: an exploration of Robert Stolorow's traumatocentrism. *International journal of psychoanalytic self psychology*, 5(1), 19–33.

Pickles, J. and Shane, E. (2007). Mutual recognition and mutual regulation: windows between relational and self-psychological worlds. Paper presented at 30th Annual International Conference of the Psychology of the Self, Los Angeles.

Roland, A. (1994). Identity, self, and individualism in a multicultural perspective. In E. P. Salett and D. R. Koslow (eds.), *Race, ethnicity, and self: identity in multicultural perspective* (pp. 3–16). Washington, DC: NMCI Publication.

Roland, A. (1996). *Cultural pluralism and psychoanalysis: an Asian and North American experience*. New York: Routledge.

Rorty, R. (1989). *Contingency, irony, and solidarity*. Cambridge, UK: Cambridge University Press.

Sagara, T. (1984). *Nihonjin no shiseikan*. Tokyo: Pelican Books [in Japanese].

Sakabe, M. (2010). Subject of the absence and absence of the critique. In K. Sasaki (Ed.), *Asian aesthetics* (pp. 13–18). Kyoto: Kyoto University Press.

Sander, L. W. (1983). Polarity paradox, and the organizing process in development. In J. D. Call, E. Galenson, and R. Tyson (Eds.), *Frontiers of infant psychiatry* (pp. 315–327). New York: Basic Books.

Sander, L. W. (1985). Toward a logic of organization in psycho-biological development. In K. Klar and L. Siever (Eds.), *Biologic response styles: clinical implications* (pp. 20–36). Washington, DC: Monograph Series American Psychiatric Press.

Sander, L. W. (2002). Thinking differently: principles of process in living systems and the specificity of being known. *Psychoanalytic dialogues*, 12 (1), 11–42.

Shane, E. (1992). The latest word: a discussion of three major contributions to self psychology by Ernst Wolf, Howard Bacal, Kenneth Newman and Joseph Lichtenberg. In: A. Goldberg (Ed.), *Progress in self psychology*, (Vol. 8, pp. 215–228), Hillsdale, NJ: The Analytic Press.

Shane, E. and Shane, M. (1993). The role of fantasy in shaping and tracking female gender choice and sexual experience: to make love or to make believe? That is the question! *Canadian journal of psychoanalysis*, 1: 127–143.

Shapiro, E. (1998). Intersubjectivity in archaic and mature twinship in group therapy. In I. N. H. Harwood and M. Pine (Eds.), *Self-experience in group: intersubjective and self-psychological pathways to human understanding* (pp. 47–57). New York: Taylor & Francis.

Sober, M. (2000). *Teach me dreams: the search for self in the revolutionary era*. Princeton, NJ: Princeton University Press.

Sperry, M. (2014). Complex contingencies: discussion of "Is it a problem for us to say, 'It is a coincidence that the patient does well'?" by Koichi Togashi. *International journal of psychoanalytic self psychology*, 9 (2), 101–107.

Stern, D. N. (2004). *Present moment in psychotherapy and everyday life*. New York: International Universities Press.

Stern, D. B. (2010). *Partners in thought: working with unformulated experience, dissociation, and enactment*. New York: Routledge.

Stolorow, R. D. (1988). Integrating self psychology and classical psychoanalysis: An experience-near approach. In A. Goldberg (Ed.), *Progress in self psychology* (Vol. 4, pp. 63–70). New York: The Analytic Press.

Stolorow, R. D. (1997). Dynamic, dyadic, intersubjective systems: an evolving paradigm for psychoanalysis. *Psychoanalytic psychology,* 14 (3), 337–363.

Stolorow, R. D. (2007). *Trauma and human existence: autobiographical, psychoanalytic, and philosophical reflections*. New York: The Analytic Press.

Stolorow, R. D. (2010). Individuality in context: the relationality of finitude. In R. Frie and W. J. Coburn (Eds.), *Persons in context: the challenge of individuality in theory and practice* (pp. 59–68). New York: Routledge.

Stolorow, R. D. and Atwood, G. E. (1992). *Context of being: the intersubjective foundations of psychological life.* Hillsdale, NJ: The Analytic Press.

Stolorow, R. D. and Atwood, G. E. (1994). The myth of the isolated mind. In A. Goldberg (Ed.), *Progress in self psychology* (Vol. 10, pp. 233–250). New York: The Analytic Press.

Stolorow, R. D., Atwood, G. E., and Orange, D. M. (2002). *Worlds of experience: interweaving philosophical and clinical dimensions in psychoanalysis.* New York: Basic Books.

Stolorow, R. D., Brandchaft, B., and Atwood, G. E. (1987). *Psychoanalytic treatment: an intersubjective approach.* Hillsdale, NJ: The Analytic Press.

Strozier, C. B. (2001). *Heinz Kohut: the making of a psychoanalyst.* New York: Farrar, Straus and Giroux.

Stuss, D. (1992). Biological and physiological development of executive function. *Brain and Cognition,* 20, 8–23.

Taketomo, Y. (1989). An American-Japanese transcultural psychoanalysis and the issue of teacher transference. *Journal of the American academy of psychoanalysis,* 17, 427–450.

Teicholz, J. G. (1999). *Kohut, Loewald, and the postmoderns: a comparative study of self and relationship.* New York: Routledge.

The Boston Change Process Study Group (2002). Expliciting the implicit: the local level and the microprocess of change in the analytic situation. *International journal of psychoanalysis,* 83, 1051–1062.

Togashi, K. (2006). A new definition of twinship selfobject experience and transference. Paper presented at the 29th International Conference on the Psychology of the Self, Chicago, IL, October.

Togashi, K. (2009a). A new dimension of twinship selfobject experience and transference. *International journal of psychoanalytic self psychology,* 4 (1), 21–39.

Togashi, K. (2009b). A self-psychological consideration on kakugo: disillusionment of an archaic narcissistic fantasy. *Journal of Japanese clinical psychology,* 27 (4), 432–443 [in Japanese].

Togashi, K. (2010). An effort to find self-psychological concepts in an Asian culture. *International journal of psychoanalytic self psychology,* 5 (1), 113–115.

Togashi, K. (2011a). *Sokoteki jikoai kuso karano datsusakkaku purosesu.* Kazama Shobo [in Japanese].

Togashi, K. (2011b). Sisutemu riron tono chigai. In *Introduction to relational psychoanalysis* (pp. 133–153). Tokyo: Iwasaki Gakujutsu Shuppansha [in Japanese].

Togashi, K. (2011c). Contemporary self psychology and cultural issues: "self-place experience" in an Asian culture. In *Psychoanalytic lecture series: self psychology,* (Vol. 9, pp. 225–246). Taipei: Pro-Ed Publishing Company.

Togashi, K. (2012a). Mutual finding of oneself and not-oneself in the other as a twinship experience. *International journal of psychoanalytic self psychology,* 7 (3), 352–368.

Togashi, K. (2012b). Placeness in the twinship experience. In *Psychoanalytic lecture series, self psychology,* (Vol. 10, pp. 253–270). Taipei: Pro-Ed Publishing Company.

Togashi, K. (2012c). Developmental trauma and the analyst's face. Paper presented at the 2012 Self Psychology Conference, December 17th, Taipei, Taiwan.

Togashi, K. (2014a). Is it a problem for us to say, "It is a coincidence that the patient does well"? *International journal of psychoanalytic self psychology*, 9 (2), 87–100.
Togashi, K. (2014b). From search for a reason to search for a meaning: response to Margy Sperry. *International journal of psychoanalytic self psychology*, 9 (2), 108–114.
Togashi, K. (2014c). A sense of "being human" and twinship experience. *International journal of psychoanalytic self psychology*, 9(4), 265–281.
Togashi, K. (2014d). Certain and uncertain aspects of a trauma: response to Doris brothers. *International journal of psychoanalytic self psychology*, 9(4), 289–296.
Togashi, K. and Kottler, A. (2012a). "I am afraid of seeing your face": trauma and the dread of engaging in a twinship tie. Paper presented at the 10th Anniversary Conference on the IARPP, New York, March.
Togashi, K. and Kottler, A. (2012b). The many faces of twinship: from the psychology of the self to the psychology of being human. *International journal of psychoanalytic self psychology,* 7 (3), 331–352.
Togashi, K. and Kottler, A. (2013). Being human and not being human: the evolution of a twinship experience. Paper presented at the 36th Annual International Conference on the Psychology of the Self. Chicago, IL, October.
Tolpin, M. and Lachman, F. (2006). "Forward and leading edge transference: application to doing psychotherapy" Paper presented at the 29th International Conference on the psychology of the self, Chicago, Illinois, October, 26–29.
Tonnesvang, J. (2002). Selfobject and selfsubject relationship. In A. Goldberg (Ed.), *Progress in self psychology* (Vol. 18, pp. 149–166). New York: The Analytic Press.
Ueda, S. (2000). *Watashi towa nanika*. Tokyo: Iwanami Shoten [in Japanese].
Ulman, R. B. and Paul, H. (1992). Dissociative anesthesia and the transitional selfobject transference in the intersubjective treatment of the addictive personality. In A. Goldberg (Ed.), *Progress in self psychology* (Vol. 8, pp. 109–140). Hillsdale, NJ: The Analytic Press.
Ulman, R. B. and Paul, H. (2006). *The self psychology of addiction and its treatment: Narcissus in Wonderland*. New York: Routledge.
VanDerHeide, N. (2009). A dynamic systems view of the transformational process of mirroring. *International journal of psychoanalytic self psychology*, 4 (4), 432–444.
VanDerHeide, N. (2012). Can you hear me now? Twinship failure and chronic loneliness. *International journal of psychoanalytic self psychology*, 7 (3), 369–390.
Wada, H. (1998). Loss and restoration of sense of self. In A. Goldberg (Ed.), *Progress in self psychology,* (Vol. 14, pp. 107–124). Hillsdale, NJ: The Analytic Press.
Wallace, E. R. (1986). Determinism, possibility, and ethics. *Journal of the American psychoanalytic association* 34, 933–974.
Watts, D. J. (2011). *Everything is obvious: once you know the answer*. New York: Crown Business.
White, M. and Weiner, M. (1986). *The theory and practice of self psychology*. New York: Brunner and Mazel.
Wolin, R. (2001). *Heidegger's children*. Princeton, NJ: Princeton University Press.

Index

'n' refers to end of chapter notes.

"Aakifa" case 85–9, 92–4
abusive backgrounds 120, 126–7, 142
addicts 19
affective experiences 107–9, 134
Agatsuma, S. 135n
agency and coincidence 150–1
"Aiko" case 113–17
alter-ego 1, 6, 158–9
Amae 29–30
American psychoanalysis 12
analysts: contingency/necessity 139; dread of seeing face 119–35; fantasy co-creation 77–8; patients being like 25, 27, 30, 37, 59–60; placeness 112
"Anna" case 160–7
anxiety 60, 114
archaic mirror experience 120–1
archaic selfobject experiences 83–4, 88
artistic sense 66–7
Asian culture 95–106, *see also* Japanese culture
astronaut story 18, 20, 71, 111, 160
authenticity 64–5, 75, 87, 100

Bacal, H. A. 74, 77
"being human" 157–67; meaning 169–72; psychology of 2–3, 7–23, 125, 158; trauma and 122
"being-with-others" 64–5
"being" in the world 87
belief systems 50

belonging, sense of xviii, 3, 12–14, 19, 110, 169
Benjamin, J. 40, 63–4, 99, 108, 132, 170
"Bianca" character 79–85
"bibliotherapy" 52
bipolar self 14
birth, finding meaning in 164, 166–7
"blow-up doll" story 79–85
Brandchaft, B. 43
Brothers, D. 21, 62, 123–4, 130, 148
Buber, Martin 170

cancelled session effects 103, 104, 144
Can-you-find-yourself-in-me 25–7, 37, 40
categorical necessity/contingency 140
causality model 139, 145–6
chance 138, 142
children: amae 29–30; contingency/necessity 142; countertransference 33; "feeling human among others" 38; mutual finding 63–4; self psychology 97; talents/skills passed on to 14–15, 110–11; trauma and 127–8, *see also* infant research
Christian view 137
classical models 137
claustrophobia 113
clinical psychoanalysis 153
Coburn, W. J. xxii, 63, 75, 95, 97, 106, 138, 175, 176, 178, 180
co-creation: fantisized experience 77–8, 83–4; self–state sustenance 91

cohesive self 56
coincidence 137–55, 163–4
collective selfobject support 55
communication: "Franco" case 46; silent communication 16–17, 26, 63
community involvement 81, 84–5
complexity theory 95, 106, 151
connection: "Eri" case 145; isolation to 152–3; twinship and 159, 163–4
contingency 137–42, 145–9, 150–5, 166
countertransference 33, 41

Darwin, Charles 140
death 164
dependency 102–3
depression 51, 66–7, 81, 113, 120, 142–4, 149, 160–2, 165
destiny 144, 147, 149–50, *see also* fate
determinism 140
developmental levels, self 39–40
developmental models, mutual finding 63–4
diaries 86–7
dichotomic thinking 148
dichotomy, contingency/necessity 145, 147–9
difference: fantasies and 89; sameness and xvi–xix, 2–4, 9, 11, 16, 40–2, 56, 61–4, 68–9, 107, 116; self psychological/ intersubjective approach 41–57; trauma and 123–4, 128, 130, *see also* "otherness"
discourses: coincidence 153–4; difference 42–3, 47, 50, 56, 57n; not-oneself 60–1; self psychology 96–9, 106
discursive practices 43, 47, 49–50
disjunctive necessity/contingency 141
dissociation and trauma 133–4
diversity *see* difference
"doing" in the world 87
Doi, T. 29
dominant discourses 50, 57n
dualistic thinking 129–30
dyadic interactive process 166
dyadic system theory 98–9, 121, 126, 135, 149, 151
dynamic relational process 151
dynamic systems 119, 126, 130, 133, 139, 149

Eastern culture *see* Asian culture; Japanese culture
ego psychologists 12, 98
emotional connection 145, *see also* connection
empathic resonance 49–50, 55–6
empathy 18–19, 35, 71
"Eri" case 142–55
expectation 154
experiential discourse 96, 97–8, 99, 106, 153–4
experiential level, dyadic process 166
explanatory discourse 96, 98–9, 106, 153–4
eye contact 46, 126, 128

face of analyst, dread of seeing 119–35
faces of twinship 8–22
fantasies 26, 29–30, 32, 37, 73–94, 113, 115
fantasy selfobject: function of 75–7; relatedness 82; trailing edge dimension 86, 90, 92–3
fate 104–5, 111–12, 115, *see also* destiny
"feeling at home" 169–71
"feeling human among others" 18–20, 27, 38, 45, 50, 53, 59–71, 73–4, 121–3, 160, 167
feminist theory 50
finding *see* mutual finding
first-order self 39
forward edge concept 52–3
forward edge dimension: fantasy selfobject 76, 92–3; transitional selfobject 78, 84
"Franco" case 45–56
Freud, Sigmund 3, 98, 137–8, 171
Frie, R. i, xxii, 3, 95, 100, 170, 176

gay male patients 42–3, 45–56, 120
"genie" fantasy case 74
Germany 20
gods at play 150
group therapy 120, 124
"Gus" character 79–81, 84

Heidegger, M. 64–5
heterosexuality 44, 47

Index

"Hideki" case 120, 122–4, 125–35
homophobia 57n
homosexuality 42–4, *see also* gay male patients
"*human* humans" 122–3
humanistic trend, psychoanalysis 3
humanization: primal source 38; self 125; trauma/recovery 73–94
hypothetical necessity/contingency 141

ichiren-takushou 109, 111–12, 115–17
idealized fantasies 113
idealizing 121, 125; relatedness 70–1; transference 34
implicit dimension, infant research 17
infant research 17, 65–6, *see also* children
interactive processes: analyst/patient 60; experiential level 166
interactive regulatory processing 17, 65–6
intersubjective conjunction 129
intersubjective disjunction 145, 147
intersubjectivity theories 2, 41–57, 95, 96, 98, 170
intimacy 80–1
I-self structure 100
Isobe, T. 102
isolation 152–3, 165
"I–Thou" 170–1

Japanese culture 60; case vignettes 66–8, 113–17, 142–7, 160, 162–3, 165; clinical illustrations 30–7; clinical implications 149–50; placeness 108–9, 111–12; "self–place experience" 96–8, 99–106; trauma and 120; vertical relationship 27–30
Judaism 13, 20, 137

Kafka, Franz 122–3
"Karin" character 79–80
"Ken" illustration 30–4, 40
"kinship transference" 108
kohai–sempai relationship 32–3, 108–9
Kohut, Heinz: early childhood 9; own trauma 19–20
Kottler, A. 61–2, 85–91, 130
Kuki, Shuzo 140–2, 149–50, 153

language 13, 171
Lars and the Real Girl film 75, 79–85, 90, 92
lesbian patients 160–2, 164
lesbian therapists 42, 48–9
Lichtenberg iv–vii, xv, xxii, 3, 17, 121, 138, 159, 169, 177
Like-to-feel-we-are-alike 25–6
loneliness 83
Löwith, Karl 64–5

marginalization 41–2, 57n
"Margo" character 81–2
Martinez, D. L. 38–9
meaning: "being human" 160, 164, 166–7, 169–72; searching for 154–5
meaninglessness: coincidence and 150; isolation 165
meeting others 160
merger, twinship as 8–10
The Metamorphosis (Kafka) 122
metamorphosis, "not being human" 158
"Midori" case 66–8
mirroring: experience 51, 70–1; mutual finding 10–12; transference 8–10, 26, 120–1, 125
moderate predictability 155
Morawetz, Ernst 9–10, 17
Muslim culture 85–9
mutual dimension, selfobject 27, 37
mutual finding: selfobject fantasy 85, 94; "self–place experience" 106; similarities 130; twinship as 10–12, 59–71, 107
mutual recognition 2, 10, 40, 63, 75, 132–3

Nakamura, Y. 101
Nakane, C. 28
narcissism, transformation of 149
narcissistic personality disorders 125
narcissistic transference 1, 125
nature, Japanese culture 102
Nazi Germany 20
necessity 137–42, 145–9, 153–4
needs: fantasies 30; trauma and 123–5
neurosis 137
"new" experiences 155
Nishida, K. 101
non-human things, examples 22–3

"not being human" 157–67
not-oneself, finding in the other 59–71

Obama, Y. 149–50
objectification 90
"object oriented" experience 78
Object Relations and Kleinian theory 44
"objects": "Anna" case 161; fantasies 73, 76, 82; "Hideki" case 122–3, 131
"object-with-others" 132
Oedipus complex 10–11, 15
oneself, finding in the other 59–71
Orange, D. M. 70, 108, 134, 138, 139, 147, 160, 170–1
"otherness" 41–57, 78, 93, 99, 130, *see also* difference; "feeling human among others"

paranoia 31
pathology model 137–8, 158
patients: being like analysts 25, 27, 30, 37, 59–60; coincidence patient does well 137–55; fantasy co-creation 77–8; placeness 112
personality disorders 125
phone sessions 35, 113–14
placeness 107–17
"place–self experience" 95–106, 108
"possibility", contingency/necessity 142
postmodernist theories 50
predictability 155
Proust, Marcel 14
psychoanalysis: American 12; coincidence patient does well 137; discourses 153–4; humanistic trend 3; "new" experiences 155; Object Relations and Kleinian theory 44; self psychology 2; trauma centered 8
psychological development 64
psychological trauma *see* trauma
psychology: "being human" 2–3, 7–23, 125, 158; self 7–23, 125, 158

reason, searching for 154–5
reciprocity, transference 26–7
recognition 103, 104, 112, 129–30
recovery, trauma 73–94
regulatory processing 17, 65–6

relatedness: fantasy selfobject 82; placeness 112; selfobject 70–1
relational dynamic processes 151
relational psychoanalysts 98–9
relational system, "Eri" case 147, 148
relational trauma 124, 134
relationships: fantasized objects 73, 76; "feeling at home" 170; Japanese culture 108–9
"right conduct" 143
rigidity and trauma 119
Roland, A. 100
"Ryoko" illustration 34–7, 40

sameness: difference and 61–4, 68–9, 107, 116; trauma and 21, 121, 123–5, 130–1, *see also* similarities
"Satoshi" case 96, 102–6
second-order self 39
Second World War 162–3
security 38, 55, 110, 124–5
self: cohesive 56; developmental levels 39–40; "Franco" case 52; humanization 125; mutual finding 65; psychology of 7–23, 125, 158; "subject-with-others" 135
self-awareness 101
selfobject: concept of 7; experience 25–40, 48, 54, 59, 120; fantasy 85, 94; "feeling human among others" 19; place and 99–100; relatedness 70–1; support 47, 49, 51, 55; transference 1, 25–40, 120–1; transitional 73–94; vertical relationship 28
"self–place experience" 95–106, 108
self psychology 2; "being human" 157–8; case vignette 102–5; coincidence 138; contemporary 95–106; cultural issues 95–106; difference 41–57; twinship definition 59
self–state sustenance 82–3, 91, 112
self-structure, cultural differences 100–1
selfsubject relationship 39
sempai–kohai relationship 32–3, 108–9
sexuality *see* gay male patients; heterosexuality; homosexuality; lesbian...
siblings 158–9

"signposts of human world" 119, 122
silent communication 16–17, 26, 63
similarities: not allowing to be found 131–3; recognition 129–30, *see also* sameness
skills, passing down 14–16, 110–11
social ranks, vertical relationship 28
social systems, *sempai–kohai* relationship 32
South African culture 41–57
specificity theory 98
stereotypical images 31
Stolorow, R. D. 8, 21, 62, 93, 105, 121, 123, 125, 129, 133, 138, 145
subjectivity: destroying twinship tie 134; discursive practices 43; fantasies and 83–5, 87–9, 93; mutual finding 11; placeness 108–9; sameness/difference 64, 68–9; self developmental levels 39–40; self psychology and 96, 98; similarities 129–33; twinship definition 25
"subject oriented" experience 78
"subject-with-others" 135
"subject-without-others" 131–3, 135n
Sucharov, M. S. 151
surprise and necessity 153
system theories: "being human" 170; dyadic 98–9, 121, 126, 135, 149, 151; self psychology 95–6, 98–9, 105, 138

Taketomo, Y. 28–9
talents, passing down 14–16, 110–11
"Taurik" case 89–94
"teacher–student" relationship 108–9
"teacher transference" 28–9
temporality and placeness 117
therapeutic dyad, difference and 56
things *see* non-human things
"Thou" 170–1
Togashi, K. 11, 48, 51, 130, 160–5, 166
trailing edge dimension: fantasy selfobject 76, 86, 90, 92–3; self–state sustenance 82–3
transference: "kinship transference" 108; mirroring 8–10, 120–1, 125; selfobject 1, 25–40, 120–1

transformation: contingency emerging 151–5; narcissism 149
transitional selfobject 73–94
trauma: "being human" 157, 162, 165–6; case vignette 126–35; chance and 138; contingency/necessity 147–9; dread of engaging in twinship tie 119–35; Kohut's own 19–20; recovery/humanization 73–94; sameness/difference 62; search for reason/meaning 154–5; temporality and 117; twinship in 21–2
trauma centered psychoanalysis 8
twins 158–9
twinship: choice of term 6; as concept 1; definitions 2, 7–8, 12–13, 25, 59, 62, 107; evolution of experience 157–67; historical overview 26–7; many faces of 8–22; new dimension of 25–40; re-conceptualized 169; re-defined 169
twinship ties: dread of engaging in 119–35; fantasy to transitional selfobject 73–94; place's function within 116

uncertainty 148
"uniqueness" 127–8, 129, 131, 134
unmei see destiny
unpredictability 139, 143, 148, 155

VanDerHeide, N. 11
vertical relationship, Japanese culture 27–30

Wada, H. 13
Wadsworth, Robert 17
we-self structure 100–1
Western culture: placeness 117; self structure 100; subjectivity 108–9; system theories 105
Winnicott, Donald 78
women, dominant discourses 57n

zero-order self 39

eBooks
from Taylor & Francis

Helping you to choose the right eBooks for your Library

Add to your library's digital collection today with Taylor & Francis eBooks. We have over 50,000 eBooks in the Humanities, Social Sciences, Behavioural Sciences, Built Environment and Law, from leading imprints, including Routledge, Focal Press and Psychology Press.

Choose from a range of subject packages or create your own!

Benefits for you
- Free MARC records
- COUNTER-compliant usage statistics
- Flexible purchase and pricing options
- All titles DRM-free.

Benefits for your user
- Off-site, anytime access via Athens or referring URL
- Print or copy pages or chapters
- Full content search
- Bookmark, highlight and annotate text
- Access to thousands of pages of quality research at the click of a button.

Free Trials Available
We offer free trials to qualifying academic, corporate and government customers.

eCollections

Choose from over 30 subject eCollections, including:

Archaeology	Language Learning
Architecture	Law
Asian Studies	Literature
Business & Management	Media & Communication
Classical Studies	Middle East Studies
Construction	Music
Creative & Media Arts	Philosophy
Criminology & Criminal Justice	Planning
Economics	Politics
Education	Psychology & Mental Health
Energy	Religion
Engineering	Security
English Language & Linguistics	Social Work
Environment & Sustainability	Sociology
Geography	Sport
Health Studies	Theatre & Performance
History	Tourism, Hospitality & Events

For more information, pricing enquiries or to order a free trial, please contact your local sales team:
www.tandfebooks.com/page/sales

www.tandfebooks.com